NAZISM:

AN ASSAULT ON
CIVILIZATION

NAZISM:

AN ASSAULT ON CIVILIZATION

BY

ALFRED E. SMITH	DOROTHY THOMPSON
LUDWIG LORE	MAX WINKLER
JOHN HAYNES HOLMES	BERNARD S. DEUTSCH
ALBERT BRANDT	WILLIAM GREEN
LUDWIG LEWISOHN	WERNER HEGEMANN
EMIL LENGYEL	STANLEY HIGH
STEPHEN S. WISE	ALICE HAMILTON
MIRIAM BEARD	I. A. HIRSCHMANN
SAMUEL GUY INMAN	CHARLES H. TUTTLE

With a Preface by ROBERT F. WAGNER

Edited by

PIERRE VAN PAASSEN *and* JAMES WATERMAN WISE

HARRISON SMITH AND ROBERT HAAS
NEW YORK . 1934

CONTENTS

A PREFACE

BY ROBERT F. WAGNER

*T*wo decades ago the spark at Sarajevo set the world aflame with hate. It was a tragic experience for thousands of German-Americans to witness from afar the immediate transformation in the land of their childhood. The energy and genius that had produced a nation of poets and thinkers were perverted to serve the evil ends of war. Four years later the guns were silenced, and the friends of the German people watched with gladdened hearts the founding of a great republic on the ruins of a great empire.

Now there has come the sad realization that hate cannot be extinguished overnight by the signing of compacts of peace. The bitterness of war and the hardships of the post-war period have produced in Germany an ingrowing distemper gnawing at her own vitals. Even if this were manifested only by the vilification of the five hundred thousand Jews who have loved and served the Fatherland, it should provoke the active resentment of mankind. Nor can Feuchtwanger and Walter, Einstein and Wassermann, Kahn and Helferding, be driven into exile without robbing all civilization of treasures incomparably precious.

But persecution is never confined by arbitrary bounds, and it is impossible to suppress a race without suppressing the ideals for which it stands. The rationalized campaign against Jewry threatens some of *the highest aspirations that Israel has bestowed upon the world—the love of personal liberty, the reverence for learning, the desire for international co-operation, the extension of social justice to working people. A régime whose philosophy and practices are antithetical to these aspirations throws down a challenge to enlightened opinion everywhere.*

It seems to me that as Americans we have three clear duties. We must marshal the conscience of mankind against the brutal treatment of minority groups. Secondly, we must strive to awaken the German people to a consciousness of their splendid traditions in order that they may regain their love of liberty and justice and exert again their ennobling influence upon literature and science and the arts. Most important of all, we must take the lead in perfecting instrumentalities and inaugurating policies for the establishment of permanent world peace. For it is war that brings in its wake the most horrible manifestations of man's inhumanity to man.

INTRODUCTION

BY JAMES WATERMAN WISE

L ITTLE more than a year ago, the Nazi movement
in Germany represented but one of a number of conflicting parties, struggling for power in a country which
—owing in part to a heritage of post-war injustice and
in part to the world-wide economic crisis—had lost faith
in itself and hope as to its future. Today that movement and Germany are interchangeable terms. The
Swastika has not alone replaced the flag of the Republic as the official emblem of Germany's reversion from
democracy to dictatorship under the Third Reich; it
has come to symbolize a phenomenon—political, economic, social, cultural, human—of profound and far-
reaching implications which may be summed up in the
single word: Nazism.

Nazism is not limited to Germany alone. Apart from
the obvious effect which so fundamental a change in
national structure and international policy as took
place in Germany, must have upon all nations in our
intimately interdependent world, the German Government is today energetically engaged in Nazi propaganda
beyond its own borders. Movements employing all the
methods, symbols, and ideologies of Hitlerism are being
fostered throughout Europe, Central and South America, and in the United States. Thus it becomes doubly
imperative that Americans should know exactly what
Hitler and his party have done in and to Germany,
and what they are attempting in other lands.

It is the conviction of those who have written the various chapters in this book that the advent of Nazism is calamitous alike to Germany and to the world. Yet they represent no single political philosophy, economic stratum, racial group, or religious fellowship. Their judgment has been made neither hastily nor in the spirit of enmity to the German people. Some among them have been pre-eminent as friends and furtherers of that people, not only during recent years but when the World War made friendship for Germany difficult, even dangerous, in English-speaking countries. Like the author of the Preface, Senator Robert F. Wagner, who is himself an American of German birth, they are not open to the charge of being anti-German. Moreover, they are profoundly informed as to the case at issue. The distinguished roster of their names is not so much a matter of choice as of chance, for the editors invited their contributions upon the sole basis of their interest in and knowledge of the problem with which each was to deal. Thus the majority among them are trained observers in socio-political fields; they bring to their subjects a detached mood and an impartial mind; they have had the opportunity in the course of the last year to record and analyze at first hand the events and impressions here set down. They have not based their judgments on rumor or propaganda for or against the Nazi Government. They have scrupulously sifted the evidence, and their conclusions are founded not on what Hitler and his associates deny and repudiate but on what they freely admit and proudly boast.

It is not necessary here to state in detail the nature of the indictment—no weaker word is adequate—against the Third Reich, of which the chapters that follow form the separate counts. It is necessary, however, to present the basic viewpoint of the editors in planning and preparing this volume. Namely, that Nazism, whatever its relations to other current political and social trends, must be considered *sui generis* if its meaning and implications are to be correctly appraised and its challenge met.

Hence, it is impossible to label it either as a revolutionary or reactionary movement and thus to pigeonhole its aims and acts. Nazism may be technically classified as a revolution since, with its coming, the republican form of government was overthrown in Germany, but it is a clear misuse of terms to describe as revolutionary a movement which enslaves rather than liberates the masses, which throws the gears of political, social, and economic progress into violent reverse. Again, it would be an absurd over-simplification to consider Hitlerism merely as a Fascist development. It is patent that the economic motivation of both phenomena is identical, that each is a last-ditch stratagem of an obsolescent capitalism to maintain the economic and social *status quo*. But to dismiss Nazism as a German variant of Fascism and nothing more is to confuse, not clarify the issue. Differences in degree, if they are great enough, become differences in kind.

Thus, whatever its economic motivation, Nazism is in essence the regression of an entire nation to a sub-civilizational level. The extent of this regression may be gauged from its insistence on race as the determinant of the state, and its sequent expulsion or extermination of all who do not belong to the racial majority; from its attitude toward women and the inferior status it assigns them; from its scarcely veiled glorification of war as the goal of national life and as the norm of international relations; from its intellectual regimentation and its ruthless suppression of political, religious, and even scientific freedom—in sum, from the totalitarian state envisaged by Hitler and executed by his government.

It is on this basic regression that attention must be riveted. To comprehend its full significance, no single aspect must be over-stressed; not the incredibly but incontrovertibly brutal persecution of Jews, of liberals, of radicals, of Communists; not the truculent chauvinism of the Third Reich's foreign policy; not the propaganda of Aryan superiority and the cult of race-hatred disseminated abroad; not the destruction of labor movements or of workers' rights; not the cynical contempt for liberal, for democratic, for moral values. Each of these is but one phase of that tragic relapse of Germany to barbarism which, viewed in its entirety, is a threat to the peace of the world, an assault on civilization itself.

That threat must be understood, that assault withstood. The easy evasion that the fate of Germany is its own concern and not the business of other nations, is inadmissible. Hitler has made clear by word and deed that what he has enforced at home he will seek to impose abroad. Nor may refuge be taken in the facile assumption that what has been perpetrated in Germany is inconceivable in the United States. Nazism appeals to the worst in men and peoples, to the latent bigotries, to the suppressed hatreds, to the primitive fears which still burn beneath the surface of modern life. Against that appeal—never so insidious and sinister as when it is ignored—this volume warns the American people.

PART ONE

IN THE THIRD REICH

THE RECORD OF

PERSECUTION

BY DOROTHY THOMPSON

"THE quotation which you asked for is from Hamlet, and reads, 'Denmark is a prison'."

These words are in a letter, received in January, 1934, from an acquaintance in Germany. Needless to say no one had asked him for a quotation. By way of Hamlet he hoped to escape the censor. He is not a Jew, nor a communist, socialist, or even liberal. He is a nationalist and conservative.

"As you may guess, the death of Jacob Wassermann has depressed me utterly," writes another friend, who was an intimate of the great writer who died in January. "His end was more tragic than his life. Constantly at war with himself, always searching for truth, exploited by everyone, overburdened with work—thus

1

he lived. And then he died—of the fact that he was a German and a Jew. The doctors talk of angina pectoris because it is thought sentimental to say that men die of broken hearts. But Wassermann's heart survived just one year of the Hitler régime. He could not deny that he was a Jew. He could not live without being a German."

From another letter: "It is only eight months since I saw you last, but it seems that as many years lie between. Everything possible has happened, and what the future will bring only the Gods know—or perhaps only the demons. Individual fates are tragic. Among my own friends, not the Jews are hardest hit, but the nationalists and the Center-people (Catholics) and, worst of all, the pacifists. One of my acquaintances, a municipal physician, lost his job because he wrote in a medical review, an article entitled 'The Doctor and Peace'. A young actor friend of mine was murdered because he dared to be against national socialism."

Denmark is a prison! Thus cried Hamlet in his desperation over the state of his country. Rosenkrantz and Guildenstern took issue with him. "We think not so, my Lord," said Rosenkrantz. To which Hamlet replied bitterly, "Why, then, 'tis none to you; for there is nothing either good or bad but thinking makes it so."

Perhaps a majority of the people of Germany belong to the breed of Rosenkrantz and Guildenstern. The chorus of those who are happy in the Third Reich is a vast one. Perhaps, even, the great majority, feeling that their fates and the fate of the nation are synonymous, rejoice in the conviction that a new era, free from class hatred, enjoying an inner community and solidarity of blood, and based upon leadership, self-confidence, and pride, has dawned for Germany.

But there are many thousands of Hamlets in Germany whose thinking cannot be directed into making Nazism good. They are the *conscious* victims of the Third Reich. I say *conscious* because every man, woman, and child in Germany is a victim if his thinking makes him so. It is essential for students of Nazi Germany to turn their major attention away from exclusive observation of the more obvious persecutions of specific groups, and note that there is *general* persecution in Germany of *all* individualism. Every man, woman, and child in Germany has been *deprived* of something, and of something which, until March, 1933, the beliefs and experience of the civilized world had taught to be good. The things of which every German has been deprived are objects for which mankind has fought during centuries, and which have been regarded as a *sine qua non* of a cultured and peaceful western state. In modern commonwealths the right to enjoy them has been suspended—if at all—only in time of war, under siege from the outside, and their restoration has been hailed as one of the major blessings of peace. Equipped with them, the individual has felt himself enhanced in his personal dignity and honor, and protected, not only against the outside, as one member of a threatened community, but protected, on the inside, against the hysterias of mass movements of his fellows, the tyrannies of mobs, and the potential oppression of the state itself. I refer to the so-called rights, enjoyed under the sovereignty of a written law, before courts, responsible not to the temporary administration of the political state, but to the law itself. It is an essential

of these rights that they should be based upon a law
which one can know, that the individual should be in
a position to defend himself under that law; and so
majestic has been the conception of law, that it has
presumed the right of the individual to proceed against
the state itself, and even to collect damages.

The individual who lives under such a reign of law,
has his rights clearly defined. The individual who does
not, lives, no matter how outwardly orderly his sur-
roundings may be, in a prison—or in a jungle.

Law, in Germany today, like law in ancient Sparta, is
improvised. Not a soul living in Germany has real legal
security, because law emanates from ukases issued by
the Leaders. One cannot "switch oneself" as the Nazi
expression (*Gleichschaltung*) has it, to a position, once
and for all in conformity with the Nazi state, but one
must switch oneself anew every morning. What was
legal today may be established as illegal tomorrow, and
the law is no more stable than a stock market report.
One can be punished in Germany for crimes and misdemeanors which belonged in neither category at the
time they were committed. One can be punished for
crimes which it is presumed one may commit in the
future. One can be punished for crimes which someone else may conceivably commit against one (this is
the only sense of the so-called "protective arrest" by
which thousands of Germans have been deprived of
their physical freedom). One can be punished for
past, present, or future crimes and misdemeanors which
may exist wholly in the mind of someone else.

Marinus van der Lubbe, for instance, was beheaded
in December, for the crime of arson for which there

was no death penalty at the time it was committed, and his fellow co-defendants, although acquitted by a Nazi court, are retained in prison with no specific charges preferred. Thousands of pacifists are incarcerated for activities which are not, even now, defined in law as illegal. Protestant pastors and Catholic priests are imprisoned for expressing religious beliefs although even the present state is constitutionally sworn to protect them. The Weimar constitution has not been legally abrogated and the present Chancellor, indeed, took his oath to it, but it is violated in essence and in detail by the ruling oligarchy and there is no possibility of testing the legality of their actions. In April for instance, I personally raised the question with the Prussian Ministry for Justice, as to how Jews could be deprived of civil rights guaranteed to them under the still existing constitution, and was informed that the measures taken against them, such as the Civil Servants Law, were passed *in anticipation* of forthcoming constitutional changes. It must be emphasized that such constitutional changes can only—inside the framework of the law—be made by the Reichstag, therefore the decrees in force violate the constitution on the presumption that the government, having an absolute majority can, at any time so change the constitution as to make the laws retroactively legal.

Law does not govern Nazi Germany. Force and the arbitrary and unchallengeable decisions of a small oligarchy, made from day to day, govern. Their decrees *are* the law, and one of them, *Reichsjustiz Minister* Frank, succinctly defined law (Right) as "whatever is good for Germany." One must amend it to read "Whatever is good for Germany"—in the eyes of the ruling oligarchy—for to challenge or protest the validity of official actions is itself a punishable crime.

It is a crime in Germany to observe crime. The official name for the offense, is the "spreading of atrocity legends," but it is not imperative upon the prosecutor to prove that what is spread is a legend. Thus, on April 1, 1933, a young Jew in Kiel who attempted to prevent, by force, Nazi Storm Troopers from entering the premises of his father, wounded a Nazi and was subsequently lynched by the crowd. The incident was officially reported by the Nazi press. But a few weeks later a woman was sent to prison for months accused of stating that a young Jew had been lynched in Kiel. To defend oneself is an offense. Nazi storm Troopers have no legal authority to make arrests, but resistance to arrest by Nazi Storm Troopers is a misdemeanor.

The theory of equality is abrogated. The Nazi "world outlook" disdains the whole principle of equality as a heritage of the outlived French Revolution and as false to biological fact which discerns vast inequalities between men. Thus the theory of liberal democracy is wilfully distorted, because the "equality" of the French Revolution, the equality which Lincoln referred to in the immortal phrase in the Gettysburg Address, has nothing to do with biological equality, but presumes only equality *before the law.* There is no longer equality before the law in Germany. In the early days of the Nazi so-called revolution, Wilhelm Göring, as Prussian Minister of the Interior issued a judgment which remains the basis of action: That given an open encounter between uniformed Nazis and civilians, it is the duty of the police to support the uniformed Nazis.

There is, in other words, definitely one law for Nazis and one law for other Germans.

The entire German people are subjected to espionage such as is only parallelled by the system which one nation uses against another in time of war, or such as that exercised in Communist Russia by the OGPU, and formerly in Imperial Tsarist Russia by the Okrana. This espionage is carried on by Wilhelm Göring's Secret Political Police, which enjoys executive powers as well, and can make arrests and pass sentences without recourse to the courts. It operates without warrants, it is governed by no rules except such as are self-imposed. It can break into any private dwelling; it can employ torture and third degree methods; there is no appeal from its actions or its decisions. It can and does make arrests "on suspicion" and hundreds of its victims are never informed and never know why they have been taken up. Noel Panter, for instance, a British subject, correspondent of the *London Telegraph*, was arrested without any warrant, no charges were preferred against him, he was released finally, on the intervention of his government, and was deported from the country, presumably for making a report concerning the arms carried by publicly parading storm troopers—a report which was later and on another occasion confirmed by Frederick Birchall, correspondent of the *New York Times*, *without* incurring similar action. The case is used to illustrate the *improvised* character of the action taken by the self-governing police against German residents.

The presumption that independent bodies with police powers, such as the Nazi auxiliary police, the Nazi Storm Troopers—whose powers are not confirmed be-

fore but often are officially justified after the act,—and
the secret political police may operate in their own interests and be motivated by reasons of personal revenge
or cupidity is hotly denied by Nazi officials who call
upon the self-sacrificing loyalty and discipline of the
Nazis as witness that this is out of the question. And
yet there are scores of bonafide instances of Nazis who
have robbed their victims, of arrests which have been
engineered by personal enemies, of denunciations
which have been made by commercial or professional
rivals. More important than the individual facts is
the incontrovertible reality that the individual citizen
has no recourse in law against the actions of these
bodies. He is delivered over to them, is utterly dependent upon them—upon their justice, impartiality, and
incorruptibility.

In such a condition of things the only recourse of the
people is to say yes; yes, on every occasion, to every
new whimsy of the nation's dictators. To be in a minority in any realm of thought or action is to lay oneself
open to the suspicion of plotting action against the
state, and to endanger one's own personal safety. And
—not only to endanger one's own personal safety, but
to jeopardize totally innocent relatives. For the Nazis
have put into practice a particular refinement of persecution,—a practice which even in war time has awakened civilized protest: the taking of hostages. Thus, if
a German living abroad expresses himself adversely to
the Nazi régime, but cannot be apprehended by the
German authorities, his relatives may be imprisoned
in his place. This policy has been made perfectly clear
to German socialists, to German Jews, and to all dis-
senters, and has proved one of the most effective ways

of depriving all citizens of any tendency to protest. It is not necessary to point out, that this is precisely the technique of kidnappers, who prevent their victims from using the protective forces normally at their command by threatening the life of some loved one.

It is this condition of suspension of law which we describe as terror. The statement that order prevails does not dismiss the accusation. Men can live under a terror which is accompanied by complete order, if all men can be brought to complete acquiescence. Fortunately for one's view of the human race, this state has never yet, so far as I know, been achieved. It is not particularly apropos whether a hundred men are beaten up, or a thousand, whether ten thousand people are put into concentration camps, or a hundred thousand, whether people are assassinated or commit suicide. There are many ways in which terror can operate. The economic weapon, used ruthlessly against the Jews, is no less a terroristic weapon than are brass knuckles and strong-arm tactics. A terror can operate merely by a consistent propagandizing to the effect that opposition will be met by ruthless force—if everyone knows that the force is there and that there are no legal means to combat it. Civilization regards as a state of terror any condition under which people are not protected against assaults on their persons or liberties by an impartial law which circumscribes not only what the individual citizen may do to society but what society— organized in the state—may do to the individual. No individual and no group of individuals have any protection against the decisions or vagaries of the autocratic state in Germany.

The argument which is used to justify the wholesale

arrests in Germany, of persons against whom no specific charges are preferred, is that "After all this is a revolution." At the same time, however, the leaders have declared on several occasions that the revolution is over. In the summer of 1933, Hitler threatened to take the most ruthless action against National Socialists, members of his own party, who held another view, namely that the revolution was only beginning, and who pointed out to him that the socialist part of the National Socialist program—the confiscation of war profits, the nationalization of monopolies, and the breaking up of department stores for the benefit of the little man—had not been carried out. Not only is the revolution over, but the Nazis make no claim that it is menaced from any internal source. On the contrary, Hitler made a statement some months ago to the United Press that no head of a government in the whole world had so large a proportion of the people with him. The vote on the government's policy, after leaving the League of Nations, showed the population to be almost unanimously behind the Chancellor. The outside world may question the sincerity of the voters or the value of the plebiscite as any test of real public opinion, considering the conditions under which it was taken, but the Nazis supposedly do not so question it. We are therefore confronted with the phenomenon of a government which declares itself to be absolutely entrenched by popular will for at least a decade to come, which at the same time finds it impossible to tolerate the expression of opinion of even the smallest dissenting minority, which considers it necessary to conduct universal espionage amongst its own people, and which continues to make purely political arrests. Clearly there is some discrepancy here, unless we are to believe that the new German suppression of all minorities, like German re-armament, is not directed toward any purpose or policy, but represents a desirable world outlook, is considered a superior form of life.

"Common good must take precedence over individual good." It is under this slogan of noble sound that the individual is persecuted in Nazi Germany. Specfically, what groups are being persecuted?

Roughly they may be divided into three classes.

(1) All individuals and groups of individuals who occupied a position of leadership in the former German Republic.

(2) All individuals or groups whose expressed or implied attitude of mind threatens, differs from, or seeks to reform the existing system of the National Socialist state.

(3) All individuals or groups whom the National Socialist state has decided not to assimilate into the new Social Order.

It must always be borne in mind that the National Socialist state is a totalitarian organization, resting upon a theoretical tribal union of racial blood-brothers, governed by a party, which in turn, is completely responsible to and the instrument of, one man. The entire system, in party and state, is appointive, and it all emanates, without any check whatsoever, from the single Leader. This system recognizes no field in human activity as outside its province. Its aim is to achieve a social system embracing every department of life, including art, religion, science, and education, and com-

pletely subservient to the National Socialist World Outlook.

Since a fundamental tenet of this World Outlook is
the theory that all virtue is biological, and inheres in
racial characteristics and racial inheritances, that the
German people are Aryans, and that no non-Aryan can,
or should, be included in the brotherhood of the new
order, the persecution of the Jews is directed at removing them altogether from Germany. In this it differs
from the other forms of persecution, in that it regards
the victim as—and for no fault of his own—incorrig-
ible. Actually the *physical terror* exercised against the
Jews as such has been less active than that exercised
against other groups, and for a very good reason: from
the other groups what is wanted is submission. But it
is the aim to *eliminate* the Jews. Obviously it is impossible to assassinate half a million Jews in cold blood,
and therefore the "cold pogrom" is undertaken which
forces them to leave Germany by closing down one by
one opportunities to earn a living or educate their children beyond the elementary grades, and by social os-
tracism.

This campaign of persecution has been eminently
successful. Sixty thousand Jews have already left Germany, in spite of the extraordinary difficulties of finding other homes in a world where nearly every country discourages immigration. Those whom circumstances force to remain, live as undesirable aliens with
all the disadvantages of that condition. With very limited exceptions, which do not extend beyond this generation, they have been shut out, by legal decrees, of
every public position, which is economic catastrophe in
a state as highly bureaucratized as Germany, out of all

of the Higher Professions—medicine, teaching, law, and journalism—in which their traditional love of learning has made them eminent. Persistent social pressure has driven them from the stage, the concert platform, the conductor's podium, and made their continued industrial and mercantile activity precarious in the extreme.

By defining as a Jew, anyone with one-quarter Jewish blood their number has been vastly increased and a class of people has been created whose spiritual homelessness has no parallel, for they have never felt any community with Jews, and now are not Germans. The inner struggles of thousands of these people cannot be described, it can only be encompassed by the sympathetic imagination. For many remain undiscovered, at war with themselves, uncertain whether to affirm their origins and take the consequences or to continue to sail under a false banner, and for many the struggle has been too much, and they have taken their own lives. They and all Jews belong to class three of the persecuted, the pariahs, the unassimilable.

In the other two classes of the persecuted are Jews and Germans, conservatives and radicals, monarchists and communists.

It must continually be recalled that the Weimar Republic during the fifteen years of its existence, was only for very brief periods governed by the socialists, or by any single party, but was for the most part in the hands of coalitions, ranging all the way from the majority socialists (Social Democrats) to the German Nationalists. The Nazi state waged war against this whole system and has held all the former leaders responsible for it, although not equally. Thus, although the party of the German Nationalists has been dissolved, and the former leaders demoted and made innocuous, the fact that the Nazis themselves came into power through their instrumentality, has softened the treatment which they have received, and an effort has been made to absorb them, including some of their leadership. Nevertheless, many German Nationalists have been the objects of Nazi persecution. They were the leaders of the *Stahlhelm*, the association of former officers, and this organization was not switched into line, as the phrase has it, without opposition, and for this opposition its leaders paid. Most of the leadership in the German Protestant revolt against the Nazifying of the church is German Nationalist, and the Nazi party has proceeded against these courageous Christians, arresting many of them, inflaming their congregations against them, insisting that they are traitors to the new Germany. Where the state has not desired to intervene— for reasons of foreign or domestic policy—the party which is, in reality, the state, has been ready to do so, for in Germany, as in Communist Russia, party and state are identical but one cannot be held responsible for the other.

The persecution of former leaders has been directed with particular virulence against Socialists, former trade union officials—those who did not come over to the new state—and, with lessened hatred, against leaders of the Catholic center, particularly those of the left wing and former democrats. Of course, Communists, who were themselves a revolutionary party, and engaged in active physical combat with the Nazis before the latter came into power are especial victims. Many of these leaders, particularly Socialists and Communists, were arrested without more ado, and are still in prisons and concentration camps. Against Catholics and against all bourgeois groups, the persecution has been somewhat more cautious. But no opportunity was lost to effect arrests on trumped up charges of former corruption, or to make it perfectly clear that continued liberty could be bought only at the price of absolute silence.

With the leaders of the Weimar Republic totally eliminated from the scene, the Nazi terror is now, and will in the future be, concentrated on suppressing those individuals or groups whose intellectual or spiritual attitude seem to threaten the hundred per cent success of the Nazi World Outlook.

The Nazi World Outlook asserts that the welfare of Nazi Germany must be the sole ethical criterion for every German. There is no law and no good which transcends or can transcend national law and national good. The Nazi state is a fighting brotherhood in which the warrior virtues are to be cultivated at the expense, if necessary, of all others. They are hardiness, fortitude, endurance, and blind obedience. Humanitarianism is a weakly offshoot of a sickly and degenerate liberal era. There is no such thing as abstract truth, nor is it desirable that science or philosophical thought should search for it. There is only truth which is good or bad for Germany. There is no individual art but only art as the expression of a folk. Tolerance, like humanitarianism, is not a virtue but a vice of weaklings. There is no loyalty except loyalty to Nazi Germany. The World Outlook is embodied in the Leader, who must be regarded, as long as he is leader, as infallible.

Menacing this World Outlook are considered to be all organizations or groups which have alliances in other countries, and which have any sort of world outlook of their own. Thus, all international pacifist organizations, of whatever nature, are broken up, and their leaders and active members persecuted. Both the Protestant and Catholic religions are under suspicion, and rightly so. The Nazi World Outlook is not in harmony with the idea of a Universal Savior. The Party would like to see a National Church established, based upon a National Creed, whose teachings would assist in the making of a heroic Germanic type. Actually much progress has been made by the German Christians toward the establishing of such a church and only the sudden and unexpected consolidation of conservative forces inside both churches has prevented the *Gleichschaltung* of the church along with all the political parties. Although in persecuting the churches the Nazis are running up against a strong public opinion, they have not desisted; the state, to be sure, keeps clear of the fracas but its other hand, the party, continues, and if any priest or pastor allows himself to extend his criticism beyond the actual church struggle, to the fundamental issues, he is liable to go to prison—and some of them have.

Almost all artists who attained any eminence under the Republic, whether as writers, painters, or architects, are either banned or discouraged in the Third Reich. All writers who depicted the horrors of war; painters whose art reflected the revolutionary chaos of the post-war period; architects whose concepts of modern urban housing were influenced by the ideals of the socialist state—these men have no place in the Third Reich, and scores of them are destitute at home or in exile. The art academies and associations have been stampeded into servile submission and those few artists who have insisted that art could not be made a state servant and remain art, have been forced out of them, have no chance to exhibit, and are drifting abroad, hoping to re-establish themselves elsewhere. The distribution of the works of such eminent Germans as Thomas Mann, Alfred Doeblin, Rene Schickele, Stefan Zweig, whose books have not actually been banned, is permitted only under conditions intensely humiliating to the personal dignity of these men. They are forced to give written declarations that they will not contribute to publications which criticize the National Socialist régime. They can serve their art only by withdrawing entirely from public activity.

In the schools and universities some of the finest Aryan teachers have been removed from their positions because they insisted on retaining the belief that the cultivation of the critical function, rather than blind obedience, is an object of education.

It is impossible even to guess how many of the thousands who have been clapped into prisons and concentration camps, or subjected to gruelling torture at the hands of Storm Troopers, have merely been guilty of doubting the infallibility of the Leader. It is, for instance, dangerous to say in Germany today: "What, the price of beef has gone up five pfennigs!" Such a remark may be interpreted by a patriotic bystander as defeatism. A youngster who got himself photographed in a false moustache in hilarious caricature of the Chancellor went to prison for it.

For there is no criticism so small that it may not, in the minds of the authorities, constitute a menace to this powerful state. The craftsman-owner of a small Bavarian cabinet-maker's shop, employing only half a dozen workmen, who remarked when his men came in one morning, giving the Nazi salute: "Why can't we say Good Morning as we always have," was taken off to concentration camp the next day.

In the first year of the National Socialist régime, the campaign of persecution has gone through several stages. There was, in the early weeks of the régime, a campaign of active terror, carried on by the Storm Troopers, and seemingly directed chiefly against individuals toward whom individual Nazi troopers had a grudge. Men and women were taken from their homes, usually in the dead of night, and beaten, dosed with castor oil, forced through humiliating rites, and threatened with death. Some of them died. There are in existence hundreds of affidavits of such attacks, of unquestionable authenticity. This activity which despite German counter-propaganda reached the outside world was suspended as the better organized, less obviously brutal, but more consistent persecution took its place. The weapons which the Nazi state now exercises against its critics are (1) the economic weapon, and (2) prison or concentration camp. The first weapon leads to exile, for the blacklisted worker can find no second job.

The concentration camp is an institution established because the regular penal institutions offered insufficient room. Supposedly they correspond to war-time prisoners' camps. According to German officials prisoners are well-fed and well-treated.

On a very few occasions foreign correspondents have been allowed to visit some of the concentration camps and report what they saw. They were never, however, allowed to interview prisoners without the presence of a guard. The few prisoners who have been released and have gone abroad have usually shown no disposition to describe conditions, probably in consideration of friends or fellow prisoners in Germany. There have been some exceptions. One such wrote his experiences for the *Chicago Daily News* after the German Consul in Chicago had accused the *Daily News* Berlin correspondent, Edgar Mowrer, of exaggerating atrocity reports. He gave his name to the *News* which was able to establish his identity, but he asked that it be withheld from publication. This is what he wrote:

The writer is a German, neither a Socialist, nor a Communist, not a Nazi, nor anything else, not a Hebrew, just a plain everyday German, whose ancestors have lived in the City of Magdeburg since the year 1208. During these seven centuries my family on maternal and paternal sides, were soldiers, professors, tradesmen, bishops and priests, with farmers and bankers, with good citizens in every walk of life, and I am the grandson of a professor of agriculture, and the son of a Lutheran minister. All we have ever been to Germany, was just Germans. My father, a preacher, fell in battle before Brest-Litowsk, as did sixteen more members of my immediate family.

I arrived in the United States in 1931, to study dentistry, having decided to become a Medical Missionary in the former German colonies in Africa. I returned to Germany late in 1932, and made my home with a distant relative in Augsburg. This relative had married about twenty years ago the daughter of a Jewish manufacturer in Cleveland, whom he met in Germany. Having himself had reverses in business, his American father-in-law being very wealthy, sent him every month enough money to live a comfortable life, and my relative was considered a rich man in Germany.

During the month of May, every good German was expected to contribute to the Nazi cause. My relative, being considered rich, was naturally approached, and when he explained that all his money is being sent to him from America, and that he has very little to give, he was denounced as "against Hitler." During the end of May, he received from Cleveland his usual check, or draft, which was duly confiscated, as money coming from Jews, and to be used in anti-Hitler propaganda. My cousin, therefore, wrote to Cleveland, not to send him any more money, but to send same to me, in care of another address. On July second, I received a draft from Cleveland for 800 marks, which I cashed, turning the money over to my cousin. The following night, about 2 o'clock in the morning, the police arrested me. The following morning I was accused of having received money under a fictitious address, from anti-German sources, to be used for anti-Nazi purposes, etc. I was accused of sabotage, and all other crimes. My trial was a farce. I had no chance to explain. Two days later I found myself in the Concentration Camp in Dachau, where I also found my cousin, badly beaten up, a complete wreck.

And now permit me to relate what I have seen during my ten weeks incarceration:

The guards are either young rowdies of the worst type, or young university students out of employment. The "prisoners" are representatives of all walks of life. Hardly any one of them knows exactly why they have been interned. It seems that the Nazi authorities take a delight in interning the sons of wealthy fathers for, as long as families of the prisoners bribe the guards with goodly sums of money, they are not mistreated. As soon as the tribute is not forthcoming, or in too small sum, the prisoner is immediately subjected to very bad treatment, his food allowance is reduced, he is put to very hard labor, etc. One of the guards had in his charge a young man, about twenty-two years old, the son of a very wealthy Jewish publisher. The young man seemed very ill and weak, and was confined to a so-called hospital. The father sent money regularly to the guard, to provide some comfort for the son. It was one of my duties to scrub the floor in the hospital, and I had several occasions to talk to this young man. He informed me that he was not sick at all when brought to the camp, but bad treatment, beatings and under-nourishment made him ill, and he was being kept ill on purpose for fear that his father's contributions to the guard might stop.

During the first week of July a new batch of prisoners was received, about thirty, ranging in age from eighteen to sixty-five years. All of them, as they were lined up for registrations, showed that they were badly treated on the way to camp. Some had their faces beaten to a pulp, others had their teeth knocked

out, their clothes torn from their bodies, all were
covered with filth.   One elderly man walked on a
crutch, which one of the guards kicked away from
him, and the old man fell down, bleeding.   The
guards let him lie, where he fell.   These prisoners
had to stand in a row, in a very hot sun, for about
three hours.   Every time one of them moved, he received a beating.   One of them, a very short, stout
man, asked for water, as he seemed about to faint.
The guard, a very smart, educated young man, judg-
ing from his appearance, reached for a tin cup, in
which he urinated; one other guard forced open the
prisoner's mouth, and they poured the urine in his
mouth.

Five prisoners, all beyond the age of fifty, were
engaged in hauling very heavy wooden boards, during a very hot day. These five men, alleged to be very
dangerous communists, were apparently weakened by
lack of food and physical punishment. Two of them,
seemingly utterly exhausted, stopped in their labor,
to catch their breath.   Immediately at least ten
guards jumped on them and belaboured them with
their fists and sticks, until all these five elderly men
sunk to the ground unconscious.   The guards then
dragged them by their feet to a barrack.   Two of
these men were never seen again.   It is presumed
that they, as so many others, *died of pneumonia.*
It is quite peculiar how many, many die in Dachau
of pneumonia.   It is a new expression of being either
beaten, tortured or starved to death.   It is peculiar,
how many prisoners utterly disappear without a trace.

During my first week in Dachau, I was completely
ignored by the guards.   My daily work was assigned

to me, mostly sweeping and scrubbing. No one visited me, and I received no mail. If some one from my family did write me, I did not get their letters. I never spoke to my cousin, although I saw him. He, being in another part of the camp, I had no way of communicating with him. But, on July 16 or 17, I was called to the office of the Camp commandant, and there I saw my cousin. The commandant, assisted by several other officials, examined me, asking questions rapidly,—why I was interned, why I left America, why I returned to Germany, who my friends were in America and in Germany, etc. I was finally asked if I, or my family had any money, how much, and where it was kept or hidden. Upon my informing them that neither I, nor my family had money I was taken away, and placed in another than my former barrack. From this day on I was very badly treated, my food allowance was cut down to an almost starvation point, and I was assigned very hard labor. About a week later, I was called again and once more "examined," this time by four guards. I was told in very plain language that, unless I make arrangements to get money, I shall be transferred to "the other side" of the camp, which means where refractory prisoners are kept, and brutally treated. I was handed paper and pencil and ordered to write to my family for money, which I did. A few days later I received a letter from my mother (the first one since my incarceration), telling me that there was no money in the house, but that she had written to Cleveland, the relatives of my cousin, for funds, to be sent by cable. On August 11, I was informed that my mother had received permission to visit me. On

August 12 I was led to the office of the Commandant
and there I met my mother. She had received a
cable from my cousin's Jewish relatives in Cleveland, with instructions to draw any amount of money
from a business friend living in Rotterdam. This
business friend was with my mother. I do not know
how much money changed hands, but a few days
later I was transferred again to better quarters, better food, and again a few days later I was released,
together with my cousin, with strict instructions not
to talk, under penalty of being returned to the concentration camp. My cousin went to Denmark, while
I returned to America.

The terror has not stopped in Germany. Its actual
extent is not known. A few months ago, several reliable
foreign correspondents agreed together that this could
be made as a conservative statement: "Scores have
died, and perhaps hundreds; hundreds and perhaps
thousands have been physically tortured; tens of thousands have been imprisoned; sixty thousand have been
exiled."

There remains all the rest of the sixty million Germans who must accept the imprisonment of their minds
and souls.

THE WAR ON RELIGIOUS

FREEDOM

BY STANLEY HIGH

Hermann GÖRING, lover of uniforms, once arrayed himself in the robes of *Summus Episcopus* of the Prussian State Church. This little known incident occurred in June, 1933, when a group of church leaders attempted to elect Dr. von Bodelschwingh as Germany's first national bishop—without asking state permission. Göring seized a telegraph blank and laid some pretty plain words before Prussia's Minister of Cultural Affairs. Prussia's kings had been literal heads of the church, stated the Prime Minister, and since the present head of the Prussian Government, himself, was the direct successor of these earlier kings, the church could not act without his participation. Göring at that time insisted that this historical tradition made it impossible for the church to create an office of national bishop, much less fill it, without his approval.

This interpretation of General Göring's is supported by a powerful faction within the Nazi party. They point to the fact that the church did not sever its relationship to the state after the Kaiser, its head, abdicated, and after the Republic was established. The church chose to demand legal recognition for its financial claims upon the state. These claims date back to the Napoleonic wars, when the state borrowed from the church and promised to pay interest forever after. The church has accepted these subsidies annually since. According to the London *Times* the state pays 100,-000,000 marks each year out of the overburdened taxpayers' pockets. And this in a land that found it "inferior" to continue reparation payments to a devastated country! Furthermore, the Nazis point to the fact that the state collects the taxes levied by the church, and this entire machinery of collection is an expense borne by the state. It is only natural, say the Nazis, that if we are expected to support the church we have certain claims in return.

A second line of Nazi argument is this: We saved the church from Communism. It owes its very existence to us. A practical way of showing gratitude is to follow Hitler's leadership unquestioningly. This argument strikes home, for a German pastor's fear of Communism is infinitely greater than an American or British pastor's fear. Germany has as an intimate neighbor a giant power which in a frenzy swept out its national religion as an unsocial opiate. These Lutheran pastors know the religious fate of the 2,000,000 German settlers in Russia. The pastors do not feel so sure that the masses of Germany evaluate German Lutheranism as a socially progressive element. They fear it is looked on as "other-worldly" and economically conservative—in a land which was and is seventy-five per cent socialistic. Every churchman in Germany knows that the workers have no love for the evangelical church. During the Republic the two most powerful labor parties, the Social Democrats and the Communists, blocked ecclesiasticism in every way. The

Nazis are also largely a workers' movement. In spite of Hitler's twenty-fourth point, may not an unmanageable tide of bolshevistic anti-clericalism arise within Nazi ranks, which will seize on some pretext or other to cripple Christianity in Germany for generations to come? This is the reason why hundreds of National Socialist pastors, who have voted for Hitler for years, find themselves in the ranks of the League of Opposition Pastors. They are against Communism in all forms, even in its manifestations within their own party's membership.

The third reason why the Nazis feel that they have a right to "take over" the church is that they have a superior *Weltanschauung*. Many Nazis know so little of Christianity that they feel their world view is superior to that of Christianity. Others, more versed in the teachings of Jesus, only claim that the Nazis have a more purified interpretation of Jesus than the traditional evangelical church in Germany. The church, say the Nazis, is other-worldly—Jesus and we are this-worldly. National Socialism has given birth to several theologians whose writings are furnishing theoretical bases for human activity. The church must be shaken out of this other-worldly daze, and be made to serve the daily needs of the German nation.

To understand the Nazi's attitude to the church, then, the three points given above must be kept in mind. First, a church which receives financial assistance from the state must retain unswerving allegiance to the state. Second, the Nazi thesis, accepted widely in church circles, that Hitler saved Germany from Communism. Third, that National Socialism thinks it represents a practical attitude toward human endeavor much more in the spirit of Jesus of Nazareth than the transcendental abstractionism of the existing German church.

We may not pass from this examination of underlying motives without first mentioning a very human element which has possibly played a larger rôle than any of the above three. It is the insatiable thirst for power on the part of many young Nazis in the church. When Hitler came to power there was a rush for rewards from all sides. Men in law, medicine, journalism, politics, labor organizations, and the like, displayed their scars of battle and claimed the fruits of victory. The Nazis within the church had been especially persecuted because of the obvious un-Christian racial teachings of National Socialism, and because of the Nazi doctrine of force. Hence, when Hitler came to power these time-tried henchmen felt themselves especially deserving of substantial ecclesiastical advancement.

That was the rub. Among the responsible church leaders themselves there was only suspicion and distrust for these fanatical and inexperienced youths. The laymen were Nazi by the score, but very few of even the party-members of longest standing desired politics to intrude into the church. They wanted no opposition to Hitler from the clergy, to be sure, but they wanted something above nationalism preached from the pulpit on Sunday. Deep within the German conception of religion lies a cleavage between things temporal and things eternal. The good Nazi, who at the same time was a good Christian, wanted Hitler to rule supreme in the temporal. This was a large enough sphere for the Leader. The eternal could be left for Christ. In other words the young Nazis who engineered the *Putsch* on the evangelical church in June, 1933, were men of personal ambition but scant religion. They set out to render unto Caesar the things that are God's.

Even before the terrorized March election by which Hitler squeezed out a legal authorization for his four-years' dictatorship, the church had sensed its danger. On March 8 General Superintendent D. Dibelius sent a letter to all pastors in his area defining the relations of church and state, and warning against allowing politics to enter into church government. The job-hunting Nazis greeted this as high treason against Hitler, to whom every knee must bow—and set about to originate their most subtly dangerous method of attack: to brand all opponents as political reactionaries.

This method of calling the church leaders reactionary was destined to prove amazingly opportune. It is well known that many founders of the German Nationalist (Monarchist) party after the war were pastors and leading Protestant laymen. Doehring, preacher at Berlin's massive *Dom*, sat in the Reichstag as a German Nationalist delegate until the Nazis came in. The church always felt homeless in the Republic. It condemned the democracy as an expression of Catholic-Jewish-Marxist elements, not the true Germany. Under the Kaiser they had known state protection. Under the Kaiser their annual grants had not been in danger. Under the Kaiser there was royal patronage, pageantry and pomp. *Hoch der Kaiser!*

Monarchism has always been feared like the plague by the Nazis—for it represents the intellectual and traditional administrative genius of Germany. It is the representative of the only successful government Germany has known—the era from Frederick the Great to 1914.

For centuries the German people have heard these Monarchists barking commands. For centuries the Germans have moved swiftly and unquestioningly to obey. Naturally the Nazis fear this element, as recent suppressions indicate.

April, 1933, found the young Nazi church leaders in full swing. Together with a large group of sincere Christian National Socialists they constituted a party calling themselves German Christians. Their fellow members were moved by the same racial discrimination and gratitude for Hitler's salvation from Communism, but they differed greatly from these ecclesiastically ambitious youths in their attitudes to fellow Christians and in gentlemanliness in general. It is difficult to write impartially of the German Christian movement, for the leadership has consistently been more radical than the main body. Many groups have even withdrawn from the Reich leadership, though maintaining the name "German Christian." The movement suffers constantly, as in this present chapter, by the necessity of identifying it with its leaders and its publication, "The Gospel in the Third Reich."

The German Christians took up a slogan: "We must have new elections!" There had been elections in November, 1932, but the Nazis were convinced that Hitler's coming to power had so changed the structure of the parishes that the officials elected six months before no longer represented public opinion. Many who know the feelings of the real evangelicals of Germany certify that this demand for a new election was not desired by the vast majority of the church members

who actually did something with their religion. It was
instigated by these same adventurers who hoped to gain
something for themselves out of the frenzy of revolution which their own merits never could secure. It is
of utmost significance that just at this juncture the
National Socialist party made a gesture toward these
ambitious youths by appointing their leader, Pastor
Joachim Hossenfelder, as advisory assistant (*Hilfsref-
erent*) in the Prussian Ministry for Cultural Affairs.
This appointment occurred on April 21. One day later
a daring move was made by the German Christians in
Mecklenburg. They planted a commissioner in the
church, with state approval. It was the attempt of
militant National Socialists to see how this strong-arm
procedure was taken by the German People.

A commissioner in the Mecklenburg church! It was
a signal for an outburst of protest all over Germany.
Telegrams, protests, appeals flooded in on Hindenburg
and Hitler. Within four days the commissioner was
sent back to Hamburg whence he had come.

By this time the forces which opposed the *"Gleichschaltung"* (co-ordination) of the church realized that
they must stand together if this Nazi tornado were to
be kept out of religion. May 9 is the date on which
the Young Reform Movement was founded. This
later found its most active expression in six thousand
pastors who banded together into an Emergency Opposition League. A laymen's group also has cast in
its lot with the pastors. This Opposition League did
not originate to defend any radical economic or social
principles. German Christianity has never expressed
itself progressively in these directions as has American and British Protestantism. The German pastors

were trying to keep two things: first, the theoretical
right to free speech and free activity in church politics;
second, the right to keep the church offices free from
inexperienced opportunists not expressing the true
church. From April on, the warfare between German
Christians and the Opposition League has been the
most persistent unsolved problem within the oncoming
totalitarian state of Hitler.

It became clear to the older church leaders that they
must rid Germany of her twenty-eight separate provincial churches. Reluctantly they met together to devise
some way in which this might be done artificially, while
retaining the older status in reality. The German
Christians may have detected this lack of real appreciation of the new unity in Germany. At any rate they
seriously considered a *Putsch* by which they would
elevate Hitler's confidence man, Army-chaplain Ludwig
Mueller, to be the first Bishop of a united German
church. The church leaders, sitting in grave council,
suddenly were confronted by this disturbing rumor
that the younger Nazis were planning to seize the German church just as they had once seized Mecklenburg.
Only now the issue was much more serious because
Mueller was involved. An attack against Mueller would
certainly lend itself to interpretation as an affront
against the revered Chancellor himself. In desperation they determined to elect the saintly and respected
Dr. Frederick von Bodelschwingh as Reichsbishop of
the new united German church.

Bodelschwingh's election was a signal for an outburst of fury on the part of the German Christians un-
paralleled at that time. On May 27, two days after
the announcement of the new primate, the German

Christians countered by a bombastic rejection of Bodelschwingh and said they would only be content with Mueller. That worthy himself appeared before the microphone and informed all Germany that Bodelschwingh would never do; the new *Reichsbischof* must be a man incorporating in himself the new spirit. He must be a German Christian, demanded Mueller. There was little doubt in anyone's mind whom Mueller would like to see elevated to this supreme honor.

Between the dates of June 22 and 26 the most stupendous interference of a state in church affairs in modern times occurred. State officials peremptorily released duly elected church officials and replaced them by "commissioners" of doubtful qualifications for church office. From the head of Prussia's church cabinet down to parish councils the Nazi turnover took place. By June 24 Bodelschwingh saw his authority assumed by others, at governmental behest, so he withdrew. His dignified statement was forbidden in the press. Only a few harmless sentences were reproduced.

The German Christians everywhere called for a special day of thanksgiving. The day was dampened, however, by the publishing beforehand of a protest letter from Hindenburg. It was an open rebuke, the first of its kind directed at Hitler since January 30. But it worked. Hitler, on the same day ordered the Commissioners withdrawn and a new election called to determine the mind of the church population.

Hitler sent a special letter to Frick, Minister of the Interior, charging him with supervising an impartial election. The letter was published in the entire press. But the Nazis had tasted blood. A little thing like a sincere wish of the Leader was not to be stopped for.

They got up an election on typical Nazi principles, allowing their opponents no election material, accusing them of being traitors, ordering out to vote thousands of S.A. men who hardly knew a German church existed. Then they turned out to count the votes and tell the world about it. The church-going people also ran, but their effort was feeble compared to the landslide. Hitler had urged an impartial election, but so much Nazi enthusiasm swept over Germany that the Leader himself was swept away, and consented, though a Roman Catholic, to give an election speech before a Protestant election in which he told all loyal Germans to go and place an "X" before the German Christian party. Who could blame the rest of the Nazis for being impartial too?

With this terrorized election in their pockets the German Christians went out to blot opposing Christians from the memory of all good Germans.

They called a Prussian Synod. A law was adopted which said that if the wife of a pastor had even one-eighth Jewish blood the pastor was to be suspended. It was a stirring moment when a pastor arose to read a protest against the recent election methods. He was greeted by such jeering that he and his comrades were forced to leave the assembly. Cries of "Traitor" and threats filled the air. A like atmosphere prevailed at the National Synod held in Wittenberg on September 27. The Associated Press reported the curious spectacle of 200 theological students from Saxony who marched into the august gathering and stood rigidly at attention, not even removing their packs, as all good soldiers should have done. After having elected Mueller the "first" *Reichsbischof* and having likened

Hitler to Luther many times the enthusiasts returned home proud and content.

Just as everyone was consigning the opposition to the dump-heap of lost causes the German Christians forgot propriety and made a speech in public which they always intended to make only around the intimacy of beer-mugs. Dr. Reinbold Krause arose before some 9,000 German Christians of Berlin, whose district leader he was, and opened fire against the Jewish Old Testament. The applause encouraged him so he fired a few rounds at superstition in the New Testament. He ridiculed Palestine as a land to attract German pilgrims, and suggested their own Fatherland. The meeting adopted his sentiments with no opposing voices. But next day all Germany was shocked. Mueller felt the whole German Christian structure toppling down about his ears. The other German Christian leaders were shocked that so many Germans still had sentiments about the Bible, but decided expediency to be the better part of valor, so they got together with Mueller and decided to pretend they were filled with dismay at the views of Krause and therewith dismissed him. So he was cruelly sacrificed. When Krause recovered from his shock at this betrayal by his old comrades he made some revelations which were embarrassing. He mentioned that Werner and Freytag, two leading German Christians, had expressed heartiest approval of the speech immediately afterwards.

This Krause incident started an exodus of the best leaders out of the German Christians. The wave of resentment so shook the movement that Hossenfelder, its leader, was removed and an unknown lawyer named

Kinder elected to succeed him. It was a triumph for
the Emergency Opposition League.

Just before Christmas, 1933, Mueller committed an
act which brought the church *en masse* against him as
they had been against Hossenfelder a few weeks earlier.
Without warning Mueller signed away the 700,000
Protestant youth to von Schirach's Hitler Youth. So
far as is known the initiative of this came from Mueller
himself, to prove to the Nazis that he still was an important personage. Mueller had come into bad repute
among Nazi leaders because his section of the German people were the only ones not meekly submitting
to Nazification. As Vice-Chancellor Papen was later
to remark, "A church without its youth is a church
without a future." Under pressure Mueller had re-
pealed the Aryan paragraph which substituted race for
faith as the test of salvation. This had turned the
German Christians against him. Now the opposition
were even more against him because he had crippled
the Y.M.C.A. and the Y.W.C.A., the two most powerful Protestant organizations in the Reich.

Opposition church leaders assembled at Halle on
January 4, prepared to appoint a successor for the
unqualified, indecisive Ludwig Mueller. A clever rumor turned up, supposedly from sources near Hitler,
that the Leader would be most offended if his confidence man were disgraced in that way. From this
moment on a sinister form appears over the German
church struggle—the apparition of the June state interference come back to life. This time Minister of Air
Göring, Prussian *Summus Episcopus* self-styled, was
determined to crush the opposition so that it could
never rear its head again.

Arrests of Protestants and Catholics started in January and have continued at a daily pace. Prof. Karl Adam, distinguished Catholic theologian of *Tübingen*, was dismissed for stating that for Christians, Jewish history must always remain unique since it gave Jesus Christ to the world.

Non-uniformed rowdies broke into the home of Gerhard Jakobi, second in command of the opposition pastors, and beat him up with brass knuckles. Göring commanded his inspector of secret police, Dr. Diehls, to gather data on the opposition pastors. The band of 6,000 pastors recalled the testimony of the fiery Göring at the Reichstag trial that it was evidences gained from telephone-tapping which had caused Dr. Oberfohren to commit suicide, since they revealed his Monarchistic anti-Fascistic plotting.

It was General Göring who marched into a meeting of church leaders with Hitler, and produced evidence from wax-records proving that Pastor Martin Niemöller, League leader and submarine hero of the World War, was treasonable. It was Göring who induced Mueller to decree dictatorial power over the church, setting aside the need of consultation with the church cabinet. Unless someone within the National Socialist Party realizes the historical consequences of this terrorization of the Christian Church in Germany one of the darkest chapters in modern religious history will be written. A hundred pastors have been suspended at this writing. Other hundreds await momentarily the price of their loyalty to conscience.

The *Christian Century* has twice commented editorially on the greatest danger of the totalitarian state to modern civilization. This danger is seen in the demand for conformity on the part of all human institutions to one narrow standard. To surrender that condition of society in which education and religion, science and the arts contribute unfettered toward the rich development of a nation's genius is to lose the finest flower of human progress.

THE DISFRANCHISEMENT OF

THE JEW

BY BERNARD S. DEUTSCH

A YEAR ago Adolf Hitler was returned to power as Chancellor of Germany by a huge elective majority and astounded the world with the method chosen by him to celebrate the victory of his party. Simultaneous with the installation of the Nazis as the governing power in Germany, there was initiated a series of premeditated brutalities against the Jews with the sanction and the connivance of the government.

"The Night of the Long Knife," once a threat to the Jews and an invitation to new Nazi adherents, became a reality. After the first few weeks it came to connote torture, arrest, incarceration in concentration camps as well. How many persons were killed, how many tortured, how many "lost" in protective arrest remains a mystery even today. The period of open terrorization has passed, although there are unmistakable signs that it still exists. For the Jews, physical attack has yielded to a subtler, more machiavellian torture—the noose of the Aryan paragraph.

For thirteen years the leaders of the National Socialist Party created in speech, in writing, in caricature, a picture of the *deus ex machina* responsible for the suffering of the country in the image of the Jew.

Indeed, seven of the twenty-five Articles of the Constitution of the National Socialist Party deal with the elimination of the Jews from the life of the country on the grounds that their racial heritage renders them inimical to the welfare of the State. During the entire period of the rise to supremacy of the Nazi party, this image of an inimical race was indelibly imprinted on the consciousness of a people impoverished by war and unable to recuperate its possessions in a post-war world in the grip of depression. Within three weeks of Hitler's election, it became obvious that the threats of Nazi haranguers were to be codified into the law of the land; that the Weimar Constitution based upon our own Constitution, was to be scrapped for the Nazi version of law, order and national economy, based on the theory of a scapegoat.

In the year which has passed, it has become obvious from the records of Nazi Germany itself that Hitler cannot fulfill his promises of bread and work, and that an impatient and hungry population is to be deflected from its justified demands by sadistic acts and the creation of a national scapegoat in the form of the 600,000 Jews of Germany. Despite the pronouncements of the Minister of Propaganda and Public Enlightenment, faithfully recorded by an intimidated and controlled press, unemployment in Germany shows no appreciable drop. According to the reliable correspondent of the *Manchester Guardian* writing as recently as January 12, conditions in Hitler's Reich are today as bad, if not worse, than in 1932 in the year of the scrapped Weimar Republic. "One of the principal claims made in behalf of the Hitler régime is that it has been successful in reducing the number of unemployed in Ger-

many," he writes. "There was a reduction of 2,300,-
000 in the number of registered unemployed between
the end of January, when it was 6,047,000, and the
end of November, when it was 3,714,000. The last figure was 1,641,000 less than twelve months before. Some
part of the reduction in the unemployed is obviously
due to the recent increase in industrial activity, which
has taken place in Germany, as in Great Britain, the
United States, Italy, and other industrial States. The
increase in the volume of production for the year is put
at twelve percent. The increase in the output of consumption goods was, however, only about eight percent,
and as the *Economist* has pointed out, the total wages
and salaries bill did not begin to increase until the
third quarter of 1933. 'This means that fresh employment was only found at the expense of those already occupied, by cutting down their hours of work and reducing their wages correspondingly.' Moreover, the unemployment statistics themselves are open to question.
. . . The actual number of unemployed is admitted to
be considerably larger than the number registered. The
'invisible unemployed' are now reckoned at about 1,-
500,000, as against 2,000,000 at the beginning of last
year, when an authoritative estimate put Germany's unemployment total, visible and invisible, at about
8,000,000."

Nazi political and social economy are today predi-
cated on the following articles of the Party program
adopted on February 25, 1920:

Article 4—None but members of the nation may
be citizens of the State. None but those of German
blood, whatever their creed, may be members of the

nation.   No Jew, therefore, may be a member of the nation.

Article 5—Any one who is not a member of the nation may live in Germany only as a guest and must be regarded as being subject to laws pertaining to foreigners.

Article 6—The right to determine how the State shall be governed and its laws made is to be a prerogative of the members of the nation alone.   We demand, therefore, that all public offices, of whatever kind, whether in the Reich, in the States, or in the smaller political sub-divisions shall be held by members of the nation alone.

Article 7—We demand the State obligate itself first of all to provide earnings and living possibilities for the members of the nation. If it is not possible to feed the entire population of the State, people who are not members of the nation must be expelled from the Reich.

Article 8—All further immigration of non-Germans is to be prohibited.   We demand that all non-Germans who have immigrated to Germany since August 2, 1914, shall be forced to leave the Reich.

Article 23—We demand a legislative battle against deliberate political lies and their propagation in the press.   In order to make possible the creation of a German press we demand that:

a.   All editors of and contributors to newspapers which appear in the German language must be members of the nation.

b.   Non-German newspapers require the specific permission of the State for publication.   They may not be printed in the German language.

c. Any financial participation or influence in a German newspaper by a non-German is to be forbidden by law and punished by suppressing the paper as well as by the immediate expulsion from the Reich of the non-German in question.

Article 24—We demand freedom for all religious sections in the State so far as they do not endanger the State or work against the customs and morals of the German race. The party as such represents the view of a positive Christianity without binding itself to any particular confession. It fights the spirit of Jewish materialism in us and outside us and is convinced that a lasting convalescence of our people can take place only from the inner conviction of common usefulness or individual usefulness.

In effect the Hitler régime within a twelve-month has succeeded in rendering the 600,000 Jews of Germany outcasts in their native land, pariahs in a country in which their ancestors have lived for more than thirteen centuries, and to whose world repute in the arts, the sciences, the professions, they have made outstanding contributions.

The inviolable right of citizenship by birth has been wrested from them; avenues of economic livelihood are closed to them. They are denied the right to practice the liberal professions. They are barred from membership in the labor unions. They may not be employed in the retail and mercantile fields. Livelihood through the land is closed to them. Their property is being confiscated. Their movements, their mail, their families, are subjected to espionage. Their children are denied an education. 65,000 Jews are refugees abroad, in flight from Hitler oppression, separated from family, friends, and economic livelihood. Thousands of Jews are confined in concentration camps. Many thousands are maimed for life as the result of Nazi torture. And hundreds are in fresh-made graves.

It is true, of course, that the Jews are no longer the sole victims of Hitler oppression. Catholics, Protestants, liberals, and all dissidents are today being regimented. What has happened to the Jews, however, is the index of the folly and the fury of the Hitler régime. Their heinous crime is the crime of race, and for that, a whole people is to be exterminated!

The first three weeks of Hitler's rule gave free rein to the dammed up thirst for vengeance of the Nazi rank and file. Brutalities, indescribable in their horror, were permitted by a sympathetic government and carried out by the Nazi army. It was only when the civilized world was moved to spontaneous protest which in New York expressed itself in the great Madison Square Garden meeting, on March 27, 1933, initiated by the American Jewish Congress, with which 20,000,000 Americans were identified through their accredited representatives that the Nazi government was given pause. It was then that it entered on the second and subtler phase of its avowed program of exterminating the Jews.

On March 29 the Government of the Third Reich officially ordered a boycott to be instituted against all Jewish places of business, April 1. When this noble act, too, aroused the protest of an astonished world, the Government of Adolf Hitler invented the Aryan paragraph. It created a mythical Aryan race based on a spurious scientific theory repudiated by all scientists of repute. To this Aryan race the Jews were an alien and contaminating influence, and hence must be destroyed. Further, it was decreed that any person having one Jewish grandparent was a non-Aryan, and a member of the contaminating race. Aryanism became overnight the index to civic, social, business, political, cultural, economic rights. It became, too, the foundation of the new code of the German Reich.

Thus, sereatim, the following important decrees were incorporated into the law of the land.

On April 1, Minister of Justice Kerrl issued a decree barring Jews from practising as notaries, which expressed itself in the following terms:

Maintenance of public order and security will be exposed to serious danger if Germans are still liable to be served with documents in legal proceedings which have been drawn up or certified by Jewish notaries. I accordingly ask that Jewish notaries be urgently advised in their own interests to refrain until further notice from exercising their calling.

In this connection the attention of notaries should be drawn to the fact that should they refuse to comply with this recommendation they will expose themselves to serious dangers in view of the excited state of public opinion. Notaries should be recommended to inform the competent presidents of provincial courts that they will refrain from exercising their calling pending the issue of further regulations regarding conditions applying to notaries.

On April 4, the new Hitler law for the restoration of the civil service in line with the new Aryan paragraph was adopted, thus giving legal sanction to the wholesale ouster of Jews from public positions. The text of this law declares:

Par. 1 (1) For the restoration of a nationally minded Regular Civil Service—there may be dismissed those who come under the following rules, even if, according to the general laws valid at present there is no basis for such action.

Par. 3 (1) Civil servants of non-Aryan origin must retire; as regards the honorary officials they must be dismissed.

(2) The above section does not apply to officials who were already employed as officers of the civil service on the first day of August, 1914, or who during the Great War fought at the front for Germany or her allies, or who lost their fathers or sons in the War. Further exceptions may be granted by the Minister of Interior, in cooperation with the competent heads of specific Ministries or by States' authorities, regarding civil servants working abroad.

Par. 1 (4) The Federal Railways Company and the Reichsbank are authorized to make arrangements in conformity with these rules.

Three days later, on April 7, a new decree defining the meaning of Par. 3 of the law for the restoration of the regular civil service was issued, declaring:

1. Non-Aryan descent means descent from non-Aryan and especially Jewish, parents or grandparents, even though only one of the parents or grandparents was of the Jewish religion.

2. If a civil servant was not already a civil servant on the first of August, 1914, he must prove that he is of Aryan descent, or that he fought at the front in the War, or that he is the son or the father of a man killed during the War.

3. If the Aryan descent is doubtful, an opinion must be requested from the authority on race ques-

tions (*Sachverstaendiger für Rasseforschung*) of the
Ministry of the Interior.

An addition to this law, issued on April 7, 1933,
states:

Officers within the scope of this law also include
judges and teachers in the public school system,
teachers at scientific universities, and also the full
and assistant professors who have been relieved of
their official duties. In addition, honorary professors,
non-official assistant professors and privatdozenten
at universities are to be considered officers within
the scope of this law. Likewise the former court
(royal) officials and the notaries, even when they
only draw fees, have the status of public officers.
Officials of the old and new military forces and the
members of the protective police of the states are
public officers, but military officers, health officers,
veterinary officers, subaltern officers and enlisted
men of the old and new military forces do not have
the status of officer. . . .

By the terms of this decree, the same regulations are
also "to be applied to the civil service regulations of
the states, local communities, and of the other bodies,
institutions, and foundations of public law. . . .

Further, The German State Railways, the Reichsbank, the public-legal religious societies, and the
confederations are empowered to decree similar regulations.

Proof of the Aryan descent of national officials and
their wives is required by this decree which says:

(1) One who is to be appointed a national official
has to prove that he and his wife are of Aryan descent. Every national official, who wishes to marry,

has to prove that the person whom he desires to marry is of Aryan descent.

(2) The proof is to be made by the submission of documents (birth certificate, marriage certificate of the parents).

(3) If Aryan descent is doubtful, an opinion is to be obtained from the expert for racial investigation accredited to the Minister of the Interior.

On April 10, following the wholesale eviction of Jews from the practice of the legal profession, the following law was enacted to regulate their admission to practice:

Par. 1.   The admission of lawyers, who are non-Aryans within the meaning of the law for the restoration of Regular Civil Service may be cancelled until the thirtieth of September of 1933.   This rule may not be applied to lawyers already admitted before the first of August, 1914, or who, during the Great War fought at the Front for Germany or her allies or who lost their fathers or sons in the War.

Par. 2.   Admission to the Lawyers' Corporation may be refused to lawyers who are not of Aryan descent in the sense of the law for the Restoration of the Regular Civil Service—even if there exists none of the reasons enumerated in the Regulations for Lawyers.

The same rule must be observed in cases where a lawyer wishes to be admitted to another court.

On April 10, a law was issued ordering "new elections of grand and petit jurors to take place immediately.   New commercial judges to be appointed before July 1, 1933."

Three days later, on April 13, the Bavarian Minister of Justice issued the following decree:

Grand and petit jurors who are of Jewish descent shall no longer be permitted to attend sessions of the grand juries and criminal courts. They shall be replaced by assistant jurors who are not disqualified on these grounds.

Until the appointment of new commercial judges, the following shall apply: Commercial judges who are of Jewish descent shall no longer be permitted to serve. The President of the State Court shall appoint in their place another commercial judge of the same or another chamber.

On April 24, the decree concerning the admission to Patent Lawyers' Association was issued:

Par. 1   Patent lawyers who are within the meaning of the Law for the Restoration of the Regular Civil Service (non-Aryans) may be struck off the roll of the patent lawyers on file with the Patent Office.

This does not apply to patent lawyers whose names were on the roll on the first of August, 1914, or to those who fought during the War at the Front for Germany or her Allies, or who have lost fathers or sons in the War.

Par. 2. The admission to the examinations referred to in par. 4 of the law referring to patent lawyers and their inscription on the roll of patent lawyers may be refused to individuals who are non-Aryans in the sense of the law for the Restoration of the Civil Service.

On April 25, after all the schools had been closed to permit the Hitlerization of teachers, curriculum and books, the legal Aryanization of the schools was authorized creating a *numerus clausus* for Jews in schools, colleges, and universities. This law stipulates:

The number of non-Aryan Germans, within the meaning of the Law for the Restoration of the Regular Civil Service, who may be admitted to Schools, Colleges and Universities, must not exceed the number proportionate to the Aryan students in each school, college or university as the total number of non-Aryans in Germany is to the total population of Germany. This proportion is fixed uniformly for the whole of the German empire at 1.5. If in certain schools the number of non-Aryan students has, in accordance with law, to be reduced, the proportion of non-Aryans may be five percent.

These rules do not apply in cases of non-Aryans whose fathers have fought during the War at the Front for Germany or her Allies or to children whose parents were married before the adoption of this law if the father or mother or two of the grandparents are of Aryan origin. The number of these students may not be included when calculating the quota of the non-Aryans.

Children of East European Jews who entered the Country after August 1, 1914, are to be entirely barred.

On April 25, a law was enacted eliminating Jewish physicians from employment in the Government Health Insurance Service from which a large proportion of physicians derive a major portion of their incomes. The laws says:

Article 1. The work of panel doctors of non-Aryan descent must cease. Further admission of such physicians as panel doctors in the national health insurance service is forbidden.

Article 2. The registration is permitted only if the physician is of German nationality and is of Aryan descent. Non-Aryan descent does not cancel a doctor's registration if that doctor has done military service during the War on the side of Germany or her allies, or if his father or sons have fallen in the War.

Par. 8 of the law stipulates that to the petition for registration as a panel doctor there must be attached:

a. Birth certificate and certificate proving that the petitioner as well as his parents and grandparents are of Aryan descent.

b. For physicians of non-Aryan descent the father or sons of whom have fallen in the War, authenticated proof of the fact.

c. For physicians of non-Aryan descent who have taken part in the War, proof that they fought at the Front or rendered medical service at the Front or in an isolation hospital.

Par. 27. The associations of panel doctors on the first of July, 1933, must proclaim as cancelled the admission of all physicians who are not capable of being admitted in conformity with the new rules. This need not be applied to physicians who practiced before the first of August, 1914, providing they have not shown any Communist sympathies.

On May 4, an addition to the decree for the Restoration of the Regular Civil Service orders:

Par. 3. Service contracts of persons of non-Aryan

descent must be annulled within one month effective at the end of the following month.

On May 4, a decree was enacted forbidding any firm to have more than three percent of Jews in its employ.

On May 5, the famous Jewish publishing firm of Mosse, publishers of the *Berliner Tageblatt*, were compelled by the Government to give up control of the paper to the Nazis and to turn over its earnings for the past fifteen years to establish a fund for war veterans.

On May 6, the retirement was ordered of all officials of non-Aryan descent to whom exceptions in the Civil Service law do not apply.

On May 12, a law was enacted forbidding the establishment of new retail stores or the enlargement of existing retail stores, specifically aimed at Jews thrown out of professional life and seeking new avenues of livelihood in this manner.

On May 15, the law prohibiting Jews from inheriting land was issued. According to Article 2 of the Law:

Only a German citizen of German blood can inherit land as a farmer.

German-blooded is he who has neither Jewish nor colored blood within four generations.

Future marriages with persons of non-German blood deprive an heir-apparent of his legacy.

On June 27, the Jews were barred from the German labor front of wage earners created by the government to replace the trade unions.

On June 30, under the decree regulating the Newspaper Profession, all those of non-Aryan descent or Aryans married to non-Aryans were debarred from holding positions as editors.

On July 13, the Jews were excluded from all mercantile and retail fronts under the terms of a new decree ordering employees to make declarations of their non-Jewish descent. This decree was enacted preliminary to the creation of a huge Government Labor Front, membership within which is necessary in order to secure employment.

On July 17, it was decreed that only Germans, i. e., Aryans, may make movies and Jews were ordered ousted from all phases of the motion-picture industry.

On July 18, a new citizenship law was enacted declaring citizenship by birth nullified and rendering citizenship open only to Nazis and members of the Government Labor Front.

The same day, the Reich Minister of Finance decreed that the marriage subsidies of 1,000 marks created by the government may not be spent in shops of Jewish merchants, despite the fact that the Jews are taxed in order to create this subsidy.

On July 26, an official order of the Ministry of Education announced that all Jewish lecturers throughout the Reich will automatically be dismissed for the term of 1933-4.

On July 26, the sale of grain and cattle to Jewish dealers was prohibited.

On July 29, the naturalization rights of East European Jews were withdrawn.

On August 1, such Jewish physicians as were permitted to practice under the Civil Service Law were forbidden to consult with non-Jewish physicians or to make recommendations to them.

On August 8, a new ordinance amending the Civil Service Law decreed that only such Jewish physicians would be permitted to retain practice in sick benefit posts as actually served at the front during the World War.

On August 9, Jewish dentists were prohibited from treating patients under the government's health insurance plan.

On August 16, it was established that Jews may not plead in courts or serve as executors.

On August 17, the Berlin Court ruled that Jews doing business in Germany do so at their own risk.

On September 13, the Department of Commerce advised Christian firms to obtain special Aryan signs, and the Jews were to be regarded henceforth as "guests" of the nation.

On September 23, the Minister of Education, Bernard Rust, ordered the liquidation of concessions granted to Jewish schools.

On September 23, it was decreed that henceforth only Aryan photographers are to be permitted to take press photos.

On October 2, the Minister of Justice of Prussia decreed that:

Jews, Negroes, and other colored races are prohibited from legal or civil intermarriages. Existing civil intermarriages to be considered void.

On October 2, the government decreed that all non-Aryans without exception are to be cleared out of, all institutions not later than April 1, 1934.

On October 6, the Berlin Labor Court decreed that being Jewish was sufficient cause for dismissal.

On October 7, it was announced that not a single Jewish physician was left in the Berlin Ambulance Service.

On October 17, it was made known that there are forty-seven German cities without a single Jewish attorney.

On November 14, publishers were informed that contracts with Jewish writers were to be considered void.

On November 18, a new Federal decree stipulated that:

Marriages transferring name and nobility to Jewish brides be dissolved; no judicial ratification of adoptions if parents and child differ racially.

On November 23, the Minister of Labor prohibited the practice of Jewish physicians and dentists from sick fund lists in cities with populations of 100,000 or more.

On December 13, radio stations and the press were ordered to reject advertisements of Jewish establishments.

On December 13, it was announced that the Prussian schools were completely purged of Jewish employees.

On December 20, by a joint decree the Ministries of Popular Enlightenment and Propaganda, of the Interior, and of Justice, ruled that beginning with January 1, 1934, the practice of the journalistic profession is barred to Jews, with the exception of front-line war veterans.

On December 26, the Prussian Ministry of Education ruled that no free scholarships in the future would be awarded to Jewish students. A similar ruling was announced by the Minister of Education of the State of Hesse.

On December 27, the Prussian Minister of Economics ordered the expulsion of all Jewish instructors in industrial and artisan schools.

On December 28, the Minister of Education announced that only students who are "physically and spiritually mature and of strict nationalistic reliability" will be enrolled in Reich universities—thus barring Jewish students.

On January 5, 1934, compulsory registration of the racial descent of all German families was ordered.

On January 9, the Prussian Minister of Education announced that non-Aryan students are barred from taking their final examinations.

On January 17, Dr. Robert Ley announced that the German Labor Law which becomes effective May 1, creating a united labor front of both workers and employers, will completely exclude the Jews.

On January 31, Minister Göring issued instructions to police stations throughout the country to compile lists of emigrants for the purpose of punishing those who fled the country since the advent of the Hitler government should they ever return to Germany.

On February 6, it was decreed that Jewish banks in Germany are prohibited from carrying the title of *Volksbank*.

These are the principal laws enacted by the German Government to bring about the elimination of the Jews from every phase of the country's life and to rear the walls of a spiritual ghetto in the Third Reich.

There are today towns throughout the Reich to which admission is closed to the Jews. The sign "No Jews Allowed" is proudly flaunted by the municipalities of Oberrosbach, Unterrossbach, Limbach, Norderney,

Gross Groebach, Marburg, Herolsberg, Bubenfurth, Mittelfranken, Boedelsee, Glasbeck, Westphalia Giessen, Ansbach, Neidenberg, Nordseebad.

Already 17,200 East European Jews in Prussia and in Southern Westphalia have had their naturalization papers revoked.

The yellow passport system has been introduced for Jewish students in German universities, many of which have established a *numerus nullus* against Jews.

The practice of *Schechita,* the Jewish ritual method of slaughtering animals for food, has since May 1 been a legal offence in Germany.

Jewish children are compelled to attend classes where racial science in the terms of pure Aryanism is taught.

A whole chapter might be devoted to the record of Germany in connection with the discrimination practised against Jews in sports. Despite the repeated assurances given by representatives of the German Government in an effort to mollify public opinion and to retain Berlin as the seat of the 1936 International Olympic Games, there is no possibility for the Jews to participate in sports.

Jewish architects, Jewish chemists, Jewish druggists, Jewish milk dealers, Jewish veterans, Jewish brokers, are expelled from professional and trade associations. Jewish department store owners are compelled to dismiss their Jewish employees. The citizenship is revoked and the property confiscated of such outstanding personalities as Professor Einstein, the world-famous scientist, Lion Feuchtwanger, distinguished novelist, Dr. Georg Bernhard, noted journalist, Emil Ludwig, the renowned biographer, and others.

These are the facts. This is the record of the disfranchisement and degradation of a once affluent and
important section of a great nation. Here is the self-
indictment of the Nazi government—cumulative evidence of the sadistic fury of a world power which has no
parallel in modern history.

It is a challenge to the civilized nations of the world.

THE DEBASEMENT OF

THE PROFESSIONS

BY WERNER HEGEMANN

THE new plight of the learned professions in Germany is without parallel, at least in modern history. Mussolini, fighting liberalism, did not prevent his opponent Benedetto Croce from publishing a "History of Europe" which is a frank glorification of liberalism and of the superior wisdom of Cavour. This greatest of Italian statesmen said: "There is no great man who is not a liberal; the degree of love of liberty is proportionate in every man to the moral education attained by him."

In France the dictatorship of Napoleon III (not less than the equally short-lived caesarism of Napoleon I) has been justly blamed for interfering with the freedom of public opinion. But while Victor Hugo had to flee from France, Lanfrey could stay and publish there the most complete and scourging criticism of Napoleon I and of the destructive short-comings of caesarism. In England criticism was possible even during the nationalistic excitement of the World War, and a few years after the War a conscientious objector was made Prime Minister. In these "Western countries" the professions preserve at least some of their freedom and dignity even during the catastrophies of war, caesarism, or Fascism.

The utter debasement of the German professions, as
it was recently achieved by Nazism, can be understood
only by looking at its historical background with its
never-ending precedent of intellectuals abused, tortured, killed, exiled, or driven to suicide. "A German
writer—a German martyr! You won't find it otherwise," said Goethe shortly before he died.

To the true friend of Germany there could be no
more heartrending tragedy than this German tradition.
To the unconcerned observer it offers many tragi-com-
ical features. From every corner of Germany's learned professionalism, old or new, pops a scurrilous humor. Its peculiar brand was suggested by a warm admirer of German philosophy, Benedetto Croce, in the
following terms: "Hegel, the supreme philosopher of
his age, defined spirit in terms of liberty and liberty
in terms of spirit. Yet because of certain of his politi-
ical tendencies and theories he deserved to be called
servile rather than liberal."

Indeed, in former times, the German intelligentsia
developed a transcendental faculty for talking in one
sense and acting in the opposite direction. Nowadays,
of course, the German professions bow under the dictatorial mustachio of Chancellor Hitler, for the sole
reason that Hitler has dubbed the action of his party
a "liberty-movement." "Practical reason" taught them
that slavery is freedom if one submits to it of one's
own "free will."

The learned professions in Germany always liked to
be called "free professions." Even those of their members, who actually fought against their enslavement,
preferred to obscure the fact that they never had been
free. "All written history," said Goethe, "is euphem-

ism." A more realistic and equally sublime version was given to this Goethean idea by the professor of philosophy, Theodor Lessing, before he fled to Czechoslovakia and was shot—in 1933, by one of Hitler's "comrades." Before this professor was thus "displaced," he upheld in a subtle book the thesis, that the business of the historian is to give sense to the ever senseless achievements of history and success. What a task for those historians who have not left Hitlerland!

The desire for pleasant euphemism found its expression in the name of the highly meritorious "Emergency Committee in Aid of Displaced German Scholars." Unfortunately this committee can deal only with such "displaced" German scholars for whom the cruel wisdom of God's German governors has not, as for Theodor Lessing, found place in another world or in Nazi prisons, as it did for the fine novelist Renn von Golssenau, and the editor of the excellent weekly *Weltbühne,* Carl von Ossietzsky. The Emergency Committee reported (end of January, 1934) that "the number of German scholars placed in new posts (outside of Germany) is estimated at 275. Many of these are temporary. At least 1,200 scholars are still unplaced . . . At least twenty per cent of these displaced scholars are not Jews." Nor are these scholars all university professors. They belong to many professions and to widely varying creeds.

The problem to be solved is neither a Jewish nor a new problem. Hitler claims to have "saved western civilization from Bolshevism." But he also and more justly claims to sustain old Germanic traditions "against an unsympathetic western world." In fact, the debasement of the professions began with the migration of the Teutons and the conquest of the Roman Empire by these barbarians. Hans Delbrück (of the University of Berlin), one of the best modern historians of Prussia, and an ardent idealizer of that country, established the fact: "Before the great migration of nations, Europe was ruled by Roman aristocrats imbued with Greek culture. As a result of this migration, the Roman aristocracy was replaced by the Germanic aristocracy of warriors who were analphabets and did not want literary culture." After this mighty replacement, posts for free scholars got scarce in this world.

The period of Renaissance and Humanism hardly brought a real "reformation" to Germany. Luther was successful there only because he made a bad situation worse. The clergy of the Lutheran "State Churches" explicitly subjected themselves to the ruling princes, whom Luther had submissively made supreme bishops and spiritual dictators within their respective countries. The recent fight against a rebellious clergy showed the Catholic Hitler in a faithful effort to restore Luther's authentic, though narrow, conceptions. They preclude a worthy interpretation of professional duties.

Delbrück tells (*Weltgeschichte* II, 143) that even in the nineteenth century prominent members of the Prussian aristocracy could neither write nor talk German (or any other language) correctly. The same was especially true of the "greatest" Prussian king, Frederick II. Again and again Hitler thunders against bookishness. His own writings are full of turns worthy of the ruling aristocracy of Prussia.

The famous archaeologist Winckelmann fled from the "great" Frederick's Prussia with the words: "I am utterly aghast when I think of Prussian despotism and the slavery of the people. Better a circumcised Turk than a Prussian!" About the same time another classic writer of Germany, E. G. Lessing, left Prussia with similar maledictions against "the most slavish of all countries."

Only once in his lifetime of eighty-two years did Goethe pay a visit, of a hurried five days, to nearby Berlin; upon his return he asserted: "In Prussia I have not uttered a single loud word that could not have been printed." Soon afterwards, Goethe's sudden flight to Italy was caused—this was proven only a century later—to a large extent by the detection of his having taken part in a "conspiracy" (Goethe's own word) against the despotism of Frederick II, who fortunately died during Goethe's Italian trip. Schiller having written *"In Tyrannos"* could flee to the asylum of Weimar. In that good old time the rivalry of a hundred small states made fleeing inside of German territory possible. There was safety in numbers. Today Hitler wants the unitarian state with *Anschluss* of all German-speaking territories, so that no oasis of liberty shall be possible in the new and greater Germany.

Examples of great German writers having to flee could be multiplied. They prove that the fight against the debasement of the German professions is old and that the best Germans took part in it. Therefore Nazism could not be satisfied with subjecting only the contemporary members of Germany's "free professions," the teachers, priests, lawyers, physicians, scientists, artists, writers, etc., to gag-rule and semi-military control. The dead are more dangerous than the living. The ostracizing of the deceased, yet not quite powerless inspirers of German thought was more important than hound-

ing their living, but powerless, disciples into prison or
out of the country.

Nine years before Hitler took Bismarck's chair, the
war-hungry university students of Königsberg, future
supporters of Hitler, consented to attend the ceremony
in honor of Kant's two hundredth anniversary only on
the condition that this dangerous philosopher's treatise
on Eternal Peace should not be mentioned by the professional orators at the celebration. In 1933 the Nazis
"cleansed" the Prussian "Academy of Poets." They
cleansed it of poets, chased the distinguished novelist
and critic, Heinrich Mann, from its presidency and
delivered the institution to his obsequious admirer,
Benn (and to similar drolls like the *Kulturminister*
Rust). But this was of little avail as long as old Lessing, Heinrich Mann's great predecessor in the fight
against Prussian gag-rule, was permitted to pass as a
German classic. Not only had Lessing, in 1768, raged
against the oppressive dictatorship of the "great" Frederick (after trying to heroize him), whom the Nazis
today glorify as "the first National Socialist." Even
worse, by the immortal verses of his play "Nathan the
Wise," he dared to proclaim that the Jews were as good
as the Christians and should intermarry with them.
Anathema! If the old Lessing lived today, he would
be shot just as the new Lessing, the professor from Han-
nover, was shot in 1933.

The latest reports from Germany inform us that
Goethe also deserves this fate. He has been declared
an enemy of "New-German" ways and means. What
a come-down for Goethe! Until recently he had been
deified. Since the death of Bismarck and especially

since the flight of his beloved successor William II, the Germans, unable to live without some "prostration before genius" (as Nietzsche's mockery styled it) longed for a more spiritual *Führer*. Hence started the fashion of celebrating Goethe not only as poet and prophet, dramatist, novelist, and scientist, model citizen, educator and universal master of almost all professions, but also as a great statesman. At that time Hermann Bahr, who was not a Jew, declared: "Goethe is the strongest political head, that arose amongst Germans between Frederick the Great and Bismarck." The clever Jew, Moritz Heimann, protested against this exaggeration, but was willing to call Goethe "the secret emperor of Germany, whose Reich has begun to grow through the centuries." Hitler's Third Reich has made an end of the growth of Goethe's Reich. Nazi critics have found that his "Tasso could only be considered as a pathological study" and that philosophizing Faust could never more be considered as the ideal type of German man.

Evidently the Nazis despising Goethe are unjust. They ought to celebrate him, if not as their poet (he explicitly refused to write war songs) at least as their far-sighted and optimistic prophet. As to social prophecy, Goethe surely proved himself a master. He clearly recognized the deep roots of Nazism in Germany and announced that it would take centuries before they were threatened with eradication. In fact he prophesied: "Several centuries may yet elapse before so much intellect and higher culture penetrate to our countrymen that it will be possible to say of them: it is a long time since they were barbarians."

As this was said not much more than a hundred years

ago, the "several centuries" are by no means over. Yet
it may be that the Nazis object to Goethe's prophecy of
their rule, because it threatens them with an ultimate
ending of German barbarism after a few centuries;
while their leaders have definitely announced that
Nazism is to stay in Germany for a millenium.

There is another reason why the Nazis must hate
Goethe: he really belonged to them insofar as he believed in caesarism and the strong man. But unfortunately, the Caesar whom Goethe loved to call "my
Emperor" was named Napoleon. Statesman Goethe
saw no other way of subduing the German barbarism
and ending the martyrdom of the German professions
than subjecting Germany to French rule. Even as ruthless a foreign dictator as Napoleon seemed better to him
than the shameless stupidity of German rulers.

In venturing to prophesy the eventual disappearance of teutonic barbarism (which with Hitler triumphant has now taken a new lease on life), Goethe, in one
of his optimistic moods, may have fallen a victim to
the concept of continuous "progress," which is one of
the fallacious concepts of liberalism, despised so heartily—and not always unjustly—by Hitler. The concept
of progress is especially fallacious in a country without
powerful learned professions and under the control of
an aristocracy notoriously opposed to "intellect and
higher culture." It seems that one of the most ardent
admirers of these dominating "Junkers" has also made
one of the most naive statements of their utter failure
in cultural matters. It was the great novelist Theodor
Fontane, descendant of French immigrants, and by no
means a Jew, who celebrated in his numerous novels
the superior qualities of the Prussian Junkers and yet

in his old age made the following confession: "Regarding our Prussian aristocracy, which I love so well, I had to grasp the fact that all liberty and higher culture, at least in Berlin, has been brought to us by the rich Jews. This is a fact to which one must finally submit."

If Germany's "rich Jews," as Fontane avers, were essential factors working for higher culture, one may conclude that Goethe's optimistic hope for the disappearance of German barbarism has been made fallacious by the recent plundering, exiling or killing of these Jews. But since they have so valiantly collaborated with the progressive members of the learned professions to make Goethe's dream come true, and since the newspapers of February 7, 1934, reported that Hitler henceforth wants to encourage Jewish trading again, a glimpse at the alternating Jewish fates in Berlin recommends itself. The pogroms of 1933 against the Jews are just as much in conformity with old Prussian tradition and *Kultur* as the prosecution of the non-Jewish intelligentsia previously referred to. The tradition of profiting from Jewish collaboration was developed to special virtuosity by the dynasty of the Hohenzollerns.

In his historical writings, the great Frederick prides himself on having, after the annexation, exiled 4,000 "Jewish beggars" inhabiting the annexed province. He had them chased across the frontier into those parts of Poland not yet annexed. He thus managed to drive out the German speaking population from a Polish province he wanted to Germanize.

At the same time the finest philosophical mind in Berlin was that of the Jew, Moses Mendelsohn. His merits were so well recognized outside of Prussia that the royal advisors found it necessary to put his name upon the list of candidates for the Royal Academy. Without discussion the king struck out the name of the distinguished philosopher.

After the death of this great tyrant, who called himself the "philosopher of Sanssouci," the fight against the debasement of the German professions, for the first time in history, looked promising. It was then that Napoleon overthrew the Hohenzollerns. The liberated Prussians helped valiantly to overthrow Napoleon's dictatorship, which was almost as bad as that of the Hohenzollerns. During the following decades the hope of real enfranchisement transfigured the German professions. They became justly admired in all the world. It was then (1837) that Bulwer-Lytton dedicated his novel "Ernest Maltravers" with these words: "To the great German People, a race of thinkers and critics; a foreign but familiar audience, profound in judgment, candid in reproof, generous in appreciation, this work is dedicated by an English author."

It was then (1837) that the famous "seven professors of Göttingen resigned in protest against the breaking of the liberal State Constitution by the king of Hanover. It was then that professors turned liberal statesmen and prepared the German revolution of 1848. The "revolution of the professors" failed. It was during the fights preceding and following it that great German writers, artists, and statesmen like Heine, Richard Wagner, Karl Schurz, and Karl Marx had to flee to Paris, New York, and London. But although the revolution had failed, the "parliament of professors" (in Frankfurt 1848-49) had laid the basis of the German constitution which later was adopted by Bismarck in

order to win the imperial crown for Prussia, thus depriving Austria of the highest German rank she had
enjoyed for many centuries.

As soon as Bismarck had used the admirable work
of the sovereign professors, he hastened to enslave them
again. And he succeeded perfectly. His three victorious wars fascinated them. As early as the beginning
of the third one, the physicist of the Berlin University,
Du Bois-Reymond, scion of a French immigrant family,
declared enthusiastically: "The philosophical faculty of
Berlin University, quartered opposite the Royal Palace,
is the spiritual body-guard of the Hohenzollerns."

The ruin of free opinion in Germany resulting from
Bismarck's victory over France has been described by
Ludwig Bamberger, Jewish member of the Reichstag,
and spiritual founder of the German Reichsbank. In
his pamphlet "Pessimism" (1888) he gave such a pert-
inent and prophetic description of the still prevailing
political trends among German scholars that at least
some of its sentences must be quoted here in full. They
accurately describe important features of the situation
of 1933. Bamberger wrote:

"In order to appreciate the backward trend of political opinion in Germany one must study its most
perfect personification in certain types of university
professors who play in German life a rôle second only
to the army officers. From the beginning to the middle
of the nineteenth century, the university professors furnished the influential representatives of liberal ideas.
Every friend of reaction considered them as the most
detestable spoilers of public morals . . . But since the
recent political changes, one finds among the professors the most ardent worshippers of the German Chan-

cellor. It is not a myth nor a joke, but actually true that well-known representatives of scientific learning have declared: if the Chancellor would adhere to some medical or juridicial thesis which they previously had proved to be wrong, they should in future accept it as the truth."

This is exactly what has been repeated in the case of Chancellor Hitler whom nowadays German professors have raised into the place of an idealized Goethe as the "German educator" in every imaginable field. Bamberger concluded his pessimistic remarks by pointing out "the grave dangers threatening the last remainders of liberalism." He foretold such "orgies of German submissiveness" that even the Chancellor would be embarrassed thereby, because when he would want to stop enslaving the nation at the point he saw fit, he would find no public opinion to support him. The Chancellor would then be overwhelmed by an irresistable rush into ever deeper submission under the rule of the Junkers and anti-Semites. Bamberger feared that the reactionary Prussian bureaucracy and the Catholic center-party would finally prove to be the last, but inefficient, bulwark against the professional craving for submission under feudal aristocracy and fake nationalism.

This fatal craving of the university professors and their followers was also strong and permanent enough to ruin the second opportunity, when the fight against the debasement of the German professions seemed to have a chance of success. It was immediately after the World War when, instead of martyrized intellectuals, it was William II, Ludendorff, and many other objectionables who fled from Germany. The resulting Re-

public of Weimar seemed to give German liberalism
a new lease on life. But in the absence of strong free
professions, public opinion was so utterly amiss that the
parties of the left, who could have united for strong
action, surrendered to reaction.

During the war, the most violent national-socialistic
speeches had been made by social-democratic labor representatives. Heilmann, for instance, whom the Nazis
abused cruelly in 1933, outdid any later Nazi utterance.
In 1917, he wrote, (in *"Die Glocke"*): "Our final aim
is the totalitarian administrative state (*reine Verwal-
tungsstaat*). We must abandon either our fight for socialized economy or the parliamentary system. To want
both at the same time is nonsense. Our enemy is much
more the parliamentary republic than the Prussian bureaucracy or royalty." Thus Heilmann, like Bamberger, thought Prussian State bureaucracy could finally
be a bulwark against junkerism and fake nationalism.
This internationally admired bureaucracy of professional politicians ruling Germany is indeed well trained,
but so impractically and only in so narrow a field,
mostly law, that broader understanding of pressing general problems is precluded. As an example: one of
the leading bureaucrats of pre-Hitler time, a *Minister-
ialdirektor* and celebrated authority on international
constitutional law, ventured, in 1932, to give a lecture
comparing the salaries of government officials in Germany, England, and France. Upon a very interesting
array of figures, he based the claim that the German
officials are the most frugal and get the lowest pay.
Then he asked *why* this should be so and gave this in-
genious explanation: "Germany has been deprived of

capital by her almost complete repudiation of her inner state debts." Evidently a German government lawyer is not permitted to understand what the word "capital" might mean, since capital is well-known to be an invention of that Jewish scoundrel, Karl Marx.

An almost tragic alternative presents itself: must one fear that the almighty bureaucracy is going to surrender to Hitler, and, if it does, must one be sorry about it or rather praise Hitler as the long required giant-killer? Professor Max Weber (a liberal who died in 1924, but whose influence is gaining continuously even in Nazi-land) declared: "There exists no historical example of a bureaucracy which once omnipotent—as in China, Egypt, the late Roman and Byzantine Empire—ever vanished again except with the complete downfall of the civilization that had produced it."

Whether Hitler is going to surrender to the almighty bureaucracy or whether he is going to shatter it and what was left of German civilization, cannot be decided immediately. Until recently the enormous office buildings of the different ministerial departments had changed surprisingly little. Before and after the "German revolution" the same names could be found on the doors of most offices.

With parliament made impotent by Nazism, no one could any longer seriously interfere with bureaucratic productivity in the field of law-making. The new Nazi heads in charge of the few directorial offices of each department are as a rule "politicians" and therefore neither professionally trained nor capable of begetting without help what looks like a new law. And since new laws have to be produced to prove activity, nothing more is required than to insert some anti-Semitic and

other popular clauses into the various bills formerly
shelved and now awakened to new life. After signing
them, the Nazis appear as quick reformers and legis-
lators.

In a similar way the quality of reforms introduced
by Nazis depends upon the quality of the preparatory
work done by numberless bureaucratic professionals
who, in most cases, were never Nazis, but who now find
it useful and harmless to cry *Heil Hitler!* whenever
required. Their tendencies are often reactionary, for
instance in educational and criminological matters. But
some of their preparatory work was good and necessary. The plans for the abolition of the small state-
nuisance, for instance, was an old plan of the liberal
party-programs; a necessity gradually accepted even by
bureaucracy. Its realization was supported by the very
same reactionary parties that helped Hitler into power.
In the international and financial field, Hitler benefits
equally from the professional achievements of previous
governments with whose work he shamelessly inter-
fered before he got into power.

No honest man will feel sorry if the professional bureaucracy, administrators, judiciary and university professors, undergo some shocks. There is no excuse for
the manner in which they compromised with monarchist reaction and connived with the extensive system of
secret murder (*Fehme*) practised by nationalists and
Nazis against their opponents. Only in extreme cases,
the judges condescended to verdicts against the murderers. Such an extreme case was the murder of Pot-
empa (summer 1932), where five Nazis pulled an opponent out of bed and tortured him to death. In that
case the court actually gave a verdict of capital punish-

ment against the five murderers and even commented
on "the ghastly brutality with which the crime was perpetrated." Thereupon Hitler sent a telegram to the
convicted murderers calling them "My comrades!" and
assuring them "eternal fidelity." He gave similar criminal assurances in numerous speeches before audiences
of hundreds of thousands. After his coming into power
he had these murderers freed. The murderers of
Rathenau he even honored by monuments and public
meetings. What is to be expected from professional
classes willing to compromise with a *Führer* who prides
himself on being the associate of murderers of the
most contemptible kind? And how atrocious must be
the terror to force a nation to submit to such a *Führer!*

Not only bureaucracy but also the free professions,
many poets, writers and artists, have for a long time
taken collusive attitudes towards war-hungry German
nationalism. A brilliant satire of this ambiguous attitude was written by the French philosopher Ernest
Seillière. In 1924 he analyzed the latest books by
Thomas Mann, Count Keyserling, and Oswald Spengler
ler and showed their pitiful jugglery: claiming alter-
nately nothing but peaceful *Kultur* and submitting in
the same breath to military methods for spreading
its blessings. Fortunately these writers have now largely
reformed. If they had only done so sooner! If during
long decades, important sections of the liberal professions had not utterly failed uncompromisingly to up-
hold liberalism and political decency, the battle-cry
raised by Thomas Mann, a few months before the Nazi
catastrophe, could not have remained unheeded. After
the new avalanche of murder in Königsberg (East
Prussia) by which Hitler prepared his *coup d'etat* in

the summer of 1932, Thomas Mann wrote (in *Berliner Tageblatt*, August 8):

"Will the bloody crimes of Königsberg finally open the eyes of the admirers of this soulful 'movement' calling itself national socialism? Even now will the pastors, university and high-school professors stop prating approvingly about it? Will they finally recognize the true character of this national disease? Of this hodgepodge of hysteria and stuffy romanticism with its overloud claim of being German, while it is nothing but a caricature of German ideals? . . . All Germans worthy of this name are sick and tired of having the air of the Fatherland poisoned every day by the vainglorious threats of the Nazi press and by the semi-idiotic vituperations of so-called *Führers* who clamour for the beheading or hanging of their opponents, for the night of the long knives, etc. . . . It is high time that the government of the Reich strains every nerve to eradicate this barbarian degeneration of German life."

It was too late. The secular debasement of the German professions had prepared a *"trahison des clercs"* without parallel in history.*

---

* Even those who fled are not free from guilt. Many of them talk as if they would be glad to compromise with the crime if the criminals would permit it. In criticizing, in America, the attitude of the German professions the author must not fail to state that he considers the attitude of the American financiers and economists largely responsible for the German catastrophe. By indiscriminate loans of billions of dollars to Germany without being willing or capable of taking German goods in payment, and by nevertheless insisting upon rapid repayment, they have materially contributed to the economic depression without which Nazism would never have gained the power of debasing the professions as it has done.

THE ENSLAVEMENT

OF WOMEN

BY ALICE HAMILTON

THE "Woman's Movement" in Germany, the famous
"Frauenbewegung", has a very proud history, a history
of enormous courage, persistence, wisdom and of slow
but strikingly great achievement in the face of formid-
able obstacles. It was not characterized by spectacular
features as was the British struggle for woman's suffrage and to a much less extent our own, yet it succeeded so well that under the Republic, groups of women sat
in the Reichstag at a time when an American Congress-
woman was a rare and conspicuous sight. Women were
government officials, school councillors, university
teachers, and judges. The German women I used to
meet in Geneva during the years between 1924 and
1930 were unusually able and one could trust them to
take a reasoned and practical stand on controversial
matters affecting legislation for women which was in
strong contrast with that of the women of some national
groups.

German women had had a long and hard fight but
they had won a fair measure of equality under the Republic. Now all seems to be lost and suddenly they are
set back, perhaps as much as a hundred years.

It would be wrong for me to quote any woman by

name. I can only say that I talked with some who
were leaders in the suffrage movement before Germany
had woman's suffrage and whose organization had continued as the General German Women's Union (*All-
gemeiner Deutscher Frauenverein*). I met also officials
of the General Federation of Women's Clubs, of the
German branch of the International Association of
University Women, and of Women Physicians, and of
the Union of Women Teachers of Germany, an extensive and influential organization. Inside these groups
were women who had been members of the Reichstag;
others had held office in various universities or municipal governments; others were lawyers, physicians, journalists. These wise, experienced women saw their impending fate—the program of the Nazis against women
did not move so rapidly as the one directed against
the Jews—and saw no possible way of averting it. They
were courageous; they told me that rather than submit,
which meant expelling all members with Jewish blood
and declaring themselves in sympathy with National
Socialism, they would see their organizations dissolved.
And it did come to that. For weeks we could not find
out what was happening after we left Berlin, only that
the *Königin Luise Bund,* which corresponds to our Colonial Dames and D.A.R., had bowed to the command
from above and been absorbed in the new organization
of Nazi women. The fate of the others was not published, but we saw the announcement that from then
on there would be but one association in Germany, composed of Nazi women, Aryans all, with a leader appointed by Hitler. There was no delegation this year
to the International Council of Women, for there was
no organization left to send one.

Now at last comes an authoritative statement concerning the women's clubs, which is issued in English by a propaganda society in Berlin (*Wirtschaftspolitische Gesellschaft*). Here we learn that the two large organizations, the German Women's Union and the General Federation of Women's Clubs, together with the teachers' union, voluntarily dissolved early in the year. All the other organizations declared themselves ready to co-operate in the new state and have been combined with the Nazi women's associations into one organization, the *Deutsches Frauenwerk*, or German Women's Work.

So the liberal women's organizations kept their word and did not yield. This is really a proud record. No woman of any prominence in the woman's movement is connected with the Nazi régime. I was told of a spirited young woman who said to her brother, an ardent Nazi, "How can you ask me to join your party when you are turning the finest women in Germany out of the teaching profession?" And he answered, "But what can we do? They will not join us and we cannot let them build up an opposition."

The new Nazi women's association has a man at its head, appointed by the government, State Councillor Krummacher, with a woman as assistant, Dr. Paula Siber, who is also consultant for women's affairs in the Department of the Interior. An irreverent young woman sent me from Germany Dr. Siber's recent pamphlet on the woman question, plentifully adorned with exclamation points, which, however, were not needed to make me see the really appalling silliness of this influential lady. It is a piece of flowery sentimentality such as might have been written in the early

part of the last century, without a touch of realism.
Woman is a mythical figure, a throbbing heart, while
man, equally mythical, is embodied intellect. "To be a
woman means to be a mother . . . All womanly knowledge springs from the deep roots of the woman's soul,
while the special mental power of man arises in the
colder atmosphere of the absolutely intellectual. The
coldness and hardness of the man longs for the softness
and warmth of the woman."

This pamphlet cannot be dismissed as merely silly,
for it bears the imprimatur of a powerful man, Frick,
Minister of the Interior, who, indeed, contributes the
preface. We are obliged to treat it as the authoritative
expression of the Nazi leaders and so we must delve
through the syrupy sentimentality for the hard core
that lies inside.

Dr. Siber proclaims at the outset an absolute break
with "liberalistic-Marxistic democracy" and all its
works, and repudiates the *Frauenbewegung* as a movement among middle-class women for intellectual emancipation and among working women for material com-
forts, both of them contrary to woman's true nature,
and in accordance with Jewish doctrines of sex equality and sex freedom, which render woman rootless.
There is much about motherhood and its glories, child-
bearing and its joys, and we are told that the motives
for limiting the number of children in a family are
only materialistic, liberalistic, Marxistic, and egotistic.
The State is all-important, not the individual child nor
the mother; the State needs children, therefore the refusal to bear children is treason to the State. "To
awaken and renew the will in men and women for large

families is the pressing task of the new woman's movement."

It follows that the education of girls is to be for
motherhood and is to be quite different from that of
boys, nor are the two sexes to be allowed to become accustomed to each other—decidedly not, for this leads to
the loss of the finest womanliness. Girls must have the
best of physical training, sports and play, but always
with duty in mind, and sacrifice, "yes, with so much
joy in their hearts that they will be able to make sacrifices all their lives in the service of duties gladly accepted." Such sacrifices are not required of men and
therefore in this, as in all things, the two sexes are different and their training must be different.

The last year of schooling is to be passed in a compulsory labor camp, but the provision for these camps
has not yet been made and for the present the voluntary camps must be used. The inference is that the
latter are Nazi institutions, but this is far from true.
They grew up under the Republic and were founded by
Eugen Rosenstock of Breslau, now teaching in this
country. The universities are still open to women but
the number of women students must not exceed ten
per cent of the whole student body and the latter is
now limited to 15,000. Formerly it ran from 23,000
to 30,000 and there was no restriction on the number
of women students. The schools of law are closed to
women but they may study medicine for "who would
forbid women to be doctors when the woman's heart
is needed at the bedside, as much as is the man's scientific knowledge?"

Dr. Siber recognizes the problem of the superfluous
women of whom there are said to be 1,900,000; indeed

she says that "the large disproportion of women and the bitterness of the lot of the unmarried is at the bottom of women's restlessness and it drove them under the liberalistic régime to strive for equality with men." But she offers no solution for those who under the Nazi régime are being ousted in favor of men except to say that under National Socialism everything is woman's work that concerns womanhood and motherhood, and goes on to enumerate the wonderful callings open to them, the care of all the helpless, of those sick in mind and body, of the old and the delinquent, and the education of little boys and of all girls. But surely this was true under the Republic and it is hard to see why it should be called "the real liberation of woman from the prison of self and family into the glorious freedom of work for the nation." This is her concluding paragraph:

The woman's movement of National Socialism claims for itself the honor of being the most advanced expression of the movement for the renewal of womanhood. Its foundation and its driving power are in the heart of woman; its determination is to recognize pure womanhood; its aim is the highest development of woman's nature and her incorporation in the service of the National Socialistic Commonwealth.

Nobody would say that the plan to remove women from industrial work and return them to home and family would spell hardship for the majority of German women. It is true that there are women of the educated class who would much rather do professional work than housework and who wish to be self-supporting even if they are married, or at least to supplement

their husband's earnings, but I very much doubt if
that is true of women of the working class. I believe
the vast majority of working women would be thankful
to have only their homes to manage, not to do the double task of factory-work and housework. Hitler's program for women would doubtless be hailed with joy
and relief by millions of them if it could be carried
out, but they know it cannot be, and apparently the
leaders are discovering this too.

It was quite evident during the first six months or
so of the Nazi régime that the relegation of woman to
her position of a century ago was carried on with vigor
and with German thoroughness. Not that the newspapers told us much about it, but rumors came of
wholesale discharges, first of married women, then of
women in families where there were male money-earn-
ers. Sometimes we were told that employers were ob-
jecting to the substitution of young men for experienced
typists and secretaries, and that the telephone exchanges
were in a sad way after the girls were turned out. The
brochure from Berlin which I mentioned above gives
interesting sidelights on this phase of the Nazi régime,
not by telling what happened but by assuring foreigners that certain things are not to be permitted any
longer. Thus we read that although the Nazi ideal is
to place woman in the family it has been found that
this ideal cannot always be realized. A woman of
mature years who is not yet married probably will not
be able to marry and she must not be crowded out of
her job, for that simply means that she swells the number of unemployed. So a woman who cannot marry
has a right to a job. To be sure it has been laid down as a
principle by the Nazis that in case of competition be-

tween a man and a woman for a position the man is to
have the preference if he is equally suited to it, but women who are better qualified than men are not to be displaced, e. g., saleswomen, stenographers, clerks, and
secretaries. Wherever, in the excessive zeal of the first
months, women have been dismissed from such posts,
failure has resulted and the government has now issued
orders that the ousted clerks and stenographers must
be reinstated because the men who replaced them were
so inexperienced as to considerably affect the smooth
conduct of business.

The same thing was true of the dismissal of women
welfare workers and teachers and the Reich Minister
of the Interior forbids such dismissals, even of married
women, unless there is a qualified man to take the place.
He also recognizes the fact that many women work
because they must and he decrees that no woman is
to be discharged unless her economic future is assured.
However, the Nazi government hopes to bring it about
that women shall be employed only in womanly work,
domestic service—which is to be increased by making
it cheaper—and welfare work including nursing, play-
ground and gymnastic work, while young women of
course are to be encouraged to marry.

Women doctors, lawyers, teachers, all expressed
grave apprehensions at the impending outlook for them
in the Germany of today. More than one told me that
in a few years not only would they have been driven
out of the professions but even excluded from the universities and from all but a rudimentary intellectual
training. And anyone who has read Hitler's discus-
sions on the woman question in *Mein Kampf* must
admit that their fears are well founded.

It is true that the Nazis promise new professions for women: assistant heads of girls' schools—apparently the head is always to be a man—leaders of the compulsory labor camps for girls, heads of the motherhood schools, mothers' helpers, "spiritual advisers" and so on, but the women who have not been trained under the new system may find it hard to substitute such work for their independent professional life.

Women are entirely excluded from parliament. The National Socialist party has never had a woman on its list of candidates and when Hitler dissolved all the other parties and the question arose as to which of their members were eligible to join the Nazi party, it was decided that no woman and no clergyman was eligible. Still as the propaganda pamphlet naively says, since the parliaments of the various states have been dissolved, and in the Reichstag only one party exists, the elimination of women is of no practical importance.

The urge to raise the birthrate, so important a part of Hitler's program, was seen in several measures which were passed in the first three months of his rule. There is a tax on the unmarried, which applies also to the widowed and divorced, but not to those over fifty-five years of age or if they are supporting children or helping support relatives. The government has made it easy for overburdened mothers to employ more domestic servants by abrogating unemployment insurance for those servants and by permitting the head of the family to claim exemption from his income tax for as many as three servants, just as if they were his children.

Young couples are loaned 1,000 marks to buy furniture and cooking utensils, and this can be repaid in monthly instalments of one per cent (no interest is charged) and on the birth of each living child 25 per cent of the debt is written off. Large families are to be encouraged in every way. The new head of the organization of women doctors—the old was dissolved and all officers were asked to resign—who was of course appointed by the government, urged in her inauguration speech the necessity for doing everything to increase the population of the country and condemned all measures of family limitation as treason.

The attitude of the Nazis toward women is, therefore, frankly and avowedly a reversion to the past. While all other countries move on toward a greater degree of equality between the sexes, Germany deliberately turns back to the ideals and standards of a less civilized era.

Two motives seem to be back of this systematic plan to relegate women to a position of entire subordination to men. One is frankly economic. As is true of much in the Nazi program, the decisive factor was unemployment and the imperative demand for jobs on the part of adherents who had been promised work when there was no increase in work and who must be satisfied at the expense of people who, it was thought, would submit in silence.

The second motive is far more important. In the Germany Hitler is planning, women count for nothing except as they bear children, care for them in childhood, nurse the sick, the wounded, the aged, and help in the work on the land. For in the Germany of Hitler's dream, a glorious, conquering Germany, the people who are needed are strong peasants to provide food, so that Germany will never again starve under a block-

ade by her enemies, and strong soldiers to restore her
prestige and bring under one Reich all the Germans
in Europe. Hitler will therefore have the education
and sports of boys directed toward the production of
soldiers who are to liberate Germany, while the training
of girls is to be directed toward fruitful motherhood so
that the supply of Germany's soldiers shall not fail. If
girls are to be trained with healthy motherhood as the
goal, a strong physique comes first in importance, then
character-building, last intellectual training. No more
is stress to be laid on the individual, that fatal error of
progressive education. The State is all, the individual
counts only as he serves the State, and the girl is to be
taught that the State requires of her child-bearing and
child-rearing, not work which men can do as well as
she or better. Competition between the sexes is to be
abolished by the elimination of woman.

That all Nazi women will accept this position of de-
pendence and helplessness may be doubted. We were
told that there were some stirrings of revolt among
them, that at one of the first meetings of the new Nazi
"Women's Work" they were bold enough to announce
their adherence to all the Nazi program except that
part which deals with women. American journalists
reported that there was considerable resentment
among the women who came in thousands to the great
Nazi rally in Nüremberg last Summer when they found
that they were being completely ignored. One of the
former leaders of the Womans' Movement (*Frauenbewegung*) told me that the work for sex equality in
Germany must be begun all over again, but she did not
despair, though she felt that her group could do nothing. The Nazi girls, she said, would not long submit

to a system which would mean hopeless drudgery and poverty for the great majority, and there would come a new revolt of women under new leaders.

Just now that seems a dim and far-off hope. Revolt of any kind seems futile and a revolt of women is always especially difficult. But German women can look back on a history of a splendid movement for their own emancipation and surely they may hope for another in the future. It will not be possible for one country, in the center of the civilized world, to turn her back on the march of time and deliberately re-enter the eighteenth century. Yet, it must be admitted, the place assigned to women by Hitler is the place women have always held in a strongly militarized state and the only place they can hope for in such a state. Therefore, until Germany turns from her glorification of physical force and her dream of a great German Reich won by the might of the sword, it is hard to see how there can be any change in the lot of German women.

THE DEGRADATION OF

CULTURE

BY I. A. HIRSCHMANN

Gleichschaltung has become the keyword for analysis
of the state of the New Germany. Yet "standardiza-
tion" or "bringing into line" cannot in themselves explain the nature of the Nazi revolution. They are, in
themselves, not fatal to cultural life. We can very
well imagine or dream of a present-day literature standardized to the level of Shakespeare. *The Saturday Evening Post*, for example, filled with stories by Goethe,
verse by Shakespeare, and humor by Cervantes would
be an example of literature brought to a level by
Gleichschaltung. There might be objections. Some
people, many people in fact, might not prefer "great
literature" all the time. Yet it is patent that such a
unified and standardized literature could make a nation
immortal in the annals of cultural history.

The tragedy of Nazi Germany lies rather in the
level at which thought and artistic expression are
to be pegged for the greater glory of the Third Reich.
The silencing of unco-ordinated voices is not a temporary measure such as it has been in most Western
lands in times of war. The program of repression, expulsion, and unification is a logical consequence of a

false philosophy of history and society, held with fanatic conviction by the men who rule present day Germany. Nazism is not new in Germany. Its philosophy of culture roots in the mass of pseudo-scientific literature and fragmentary distorted interpretations on the subject of race, culture, and history which have been current in that country during the last and present centuries. For example, in a speech reported in the *Voelkischer Beobachter* on September 3, 1933, Hitler stated, "It is the sign of the sinister-souled decadence of the past period, that they talked of styles without acknowledging their racial limitations. The Greeks did not build internationally but in the Greek way—that is, every purely cast race has its own handwriting in the book of art."

Now every book on Greek art starts off with the indebtedness to Egypt and Crete, both inhabited by non-Grecians. The "purest caste" racially, among the Greeks, were the Spartans. They produced no art whatsoever. The Athenians, the most artistic of the Greeks, were racially highly mixed. To the original mixture of Doric invaders and pre-Doric inhabitants who gathered in Attica during the conquest by the Doric peoples, were added a large number of people, of varying racial origins, who settled and inter-married in Athens. They were given full citizenship rights up to the time of Pericles. So much for the Hitlerian theory of cultural history.

In the lengthy addresses and prophecies of Goebbels, Hitler, and other leaders, one hears echoes of Chamberlain's and Gobineau's racial theories as applied to concrete situations. These two men attained a large following among the people of Western Europe by theories, well advanced and highly pleasing to the members of that following. Their theme was the history of Race and it was evolved by the delightful system of rejecting all history and anthropology that did not further their preconceptions. Gobineau advanced the thesis that race, and race alone, is the creator of civilization. Yet only pure and superior races, he says, can build civilizations and the tragedy of human history is that the purity of superior races has been constantly adulterated by cross marriages with members of less gifted groups and today even the Aryan branch of the white race (*la crême de la crême*) is on the downward path to cowlike mediocrity and contentment, which all humanity is treading. Nothing can be done about it now, for inter-mixture has gone too far and humanity is doomed to degradation: "Human herds, no longer nations, weighed down by a mournful somnolence, will henceforth be benumbed in their nullity, like buffaloes ruminating in the stagnant mire of the Pontine marshes." Such is the theory of Gobineau.

Chamberlain is, however, more cheerful. Perhaps he felt the hideous injustice of Aryan-descended buffaloes ruminating cud by cud with non-Aryan types. He therefore devises a new conception of race as a creative factor. He belittles purity as the cause of creativeness, instead he elevates limited inter-breeding among homogeneous groups. There have been many great races, many more may yet evolve in the passage of time. Western culture is the result of the peculiar contribution of the Teuton races (and he is generous enough to include Celts and Slavs under that name) on the basis of the heritage from the Greeks, Romans, and Jews. Within this culture there is a struggle between Teutonic

and non-Teutonic groups for supremacy. It transpires
on the battlefield as well as within the heart of peaceful societies. His weapons include "marriage, shifting
of wealth, the birth of new influences and the disappearance of others." Thus, Chamberlain.

While the Nazi view on race in relation to Culture
is definitely the result of the thought and resourcefulness of these two men, it shows changes and variations made with an obvious eye to establishing a Germanic myth. The same insistence on race as the determinant of a civilization obtains, but the theory is modified. Thus purity of race is stressed as a necessity for
real culture. Yet it is conceded at the same time that
the Germans are not a pure race. The superiority of
the Aryan is proclaimed but Aryanism becomes a special Germanic privilege, for the term is modified and
glorified to "Aryan Nordic."

The Germanic *"geist"* is one of strength. Dr. Rosenberg who is held to be an authority on the concrete
manifestations of the Nazi *Weltanschauung* declares:
"The ideal of the poetry of our time must be the strong
and healthy man." Works of art, states the special
commissioner for the Munich German Art House, must
express the "greatness and loftiness of the German
soul." Writing in the *Voelkischer Beobachter,* Flor-
entine Hamm sets up mysticism as the fundamental
trait of German art. "If artistic creators become wholly
seized by this mystic feeling of the community of blood
and work, then there will be no need to ask what is
German art—it will speak for itself."

Characteristic of most of these new-sprung prophets
of culture is the tacit admission of ignorance as to
what in German art is distinct from, and superior to,

the art of the faded era of the Republic. Certainly
its half-educated view of artistic production as being
something holy *per se* because it is "national," cannot
be considered adequate expression of thought on the
subject. Thus Goebbels emphatically, if vaguely, declares that "only consecrated hands have the right to
serve at the altar of art."

The conception of German art is a confused one,
not solely because this art is yet to be born, but rather
as the result of the whole Nazi conception of the nature
of art. Here we see the views of a lower middle class
group set up as law for those who would do creative
work. Anything which represents culture beyond their
comprehension is distrusted and suspiciously removed.
Art is a sacred concept, the artist a mystic prophet of
a mystic idea. The type of people who speak of Goethe
in hushed tones but never read him, and cannot even
understand him, are the ones who are to designate the
artist, assign him his task, and pass judgment on his
work. "Perhaps the worst offense of the artist of the
bygone era," Goebbels claims, "was that it (art) stood
no longer in organic relation to the people itself and
thereby lost the roots which had brought it new nour-
ishment daily." Who are those people? Not the mob.
Not the intellectual classes that found delight in the
now *verboten* works of Mann, Heine, Hindemith, and
Reinhardt. The people are rather those who condemn
all that transcends their limited understanding. The
people are the little men with petty ideas—their insistence on the smallest of conventions, their unthink-
ing worship of the old because of its age, and fear of
the new because it has not been stamped as good. The
people are mediocrity. They are those whose mental

stock in trade consists of a few old saws, dim memories of school texts, and the glittering theories and generalities of a cheap press.

Where can one find a richer collection of clichés on the subject of culture and art than in the speeches of the Minister of Propaganda? "Art is not an absolute conception, it first attains being in the life of the people . . . Culture is the highest expression of the creative powers of a people . . . German art, freed from the power of the people, lost itself in the thickets of modern civilization and soon became *nothing but experiment, tomfoolery, and bluff.*" Surely this last statement—typical of the smug narrowness which condemns or ridicules all it cannot comprehend—neatly epitomizes the pitiful, underlying dread in the Nazi mind.

In the light of such ideas, the significance of the book-burnings and proscriptions, the barring of new music and celebrated musicians, the removal of pictures from art galleries, assumes a new significance. It is, comparatively speaking, a matter of minor importance to know that authors and musicians cannot hold governmental or even private positions of a certain type because of their racial or political makeup. It is true, of course, that present-day German literature without Jews and liberals sinks into absolute insignificance. Yet the tragedy lies in the fact that aside from race, aside from politics, the work of these men would be forbidden or disapproved even if they were not Jews.

Wassermann is proscribed not merely because he, as a Jew, should not write in German or about Germans, not because he writes as a mystic when mysticism is the hall-mark of the Aryan-Nordic. He is proscribed chiefly because the emotions he describes are not those

felt by Nazi cultural leadership, because the seeking
and pain of this character are alien to "strong men."
Surely, neither Göring nor Hitler experience such sen-
sations.

Aside from the actual atrocity reports, probably no
single incident in the Nazi "revolution" impressed the
world so much as the burning by students of some
25,000 books in Berlin on May 10, 1933. The writings of philosophers, scientists, novelists, musicians and
poets were consigned to the flames like so much kind-
ling. The bonfire, however, was not limited to books
by German authors. Writers from many other countries were to be found in the proscribed list, including
the Americans, Upton Sinclair and Helen Keller.

As a matter of record in one of the darkest and most
fatuous pages in the history of civilization, the authors
of the books consigned to the flames are listed:

The Bible
Ernest Aassirer
Peter Altenberg
Berthold Auerbach
Georg Bernhardt
Eduard Bernstein
Ivan Block
Ludwig Boerne
Moritz Bonn
Max Brod
Constantin Brunner
Martin Buber
Hermann Cohen
Albert Einstein
Kurt Eisner
Arthur Eloessen
Lion Feuchtwanger
Sigmund Freud
Ludwig Fulda
Fritz Gundolf

Fritz Haber
Maximilian Harden
Heinrich Heine
Theodor Herzl
Moses Hess
Georg Himmel
Rudolph Hilferding
Magnus Hirschfeld
Edmund Husserl
Hugo von Hofmannsthal
Ludwig Jacobowski
Siegfried Jacobson
Helen Keller
Alfred Kerr
Ferdinand Lassalle
Moritz Lazarus
Emil Lederer
Max Liebermann
Samuel Lublinski
Emil Ludwig

Karl Marx
Felix Mendelssohn
Giacomo Meyerbeer
Hugo Munsterberg
Franz Oppenheimer
Hugo Preuss
Otto Rank
Arthur Schnitzler
Arnold Schoenberg
Upton Sinclair
Ludwig Stein
Heyman Steinchal
Carl Sternheim
Ernst Toller
Jakob Wassermann
Otto Weiniger
Franz Werfel
Theodor Wolff
Arnold Zweig
Stefan Zweig

Coincident with the burning of the books in Germany, Nazi vandals mutilated a number of books in

the New York Public Library. Those of Heinrich
Heine had an especially low ignition point. At the
same time, anti-Jewish propaganda leaflets were placed
in many books in branch libraries in New York City.

Probably the best possible comment on the German
literary suppression was penned by Heinrich Heine
more than one hundred years ago, in the second volume of his *"Reisebilder"* in which the entire twelfth
chapter consists of the following:

CHAPTER XII

The German censors of the press........

. . . .

. . . .

. . . .

. . . . blockheads . . . .

. . . .

. . . .

. . . . !

Everyone is quick to protest the hounding of men.
But hounding the spirit is even more inhuman. We
smile when we hear of attempts to rewrite the Bible
because it is too Jewish or insufficiently manly. It
seems childish. We feel reasonably certain that the
Bible will live on. But transfer this ghoulishness to
the assault on the hearts of living men, and the animal
essence of the Nazi spirit is revealed. Of what will
the poet sing when he dare not reveal his soul? Who
can discover new beauties when state-glorification and
war-worship are the sole objectives? To the civilized
mind there can be no art in Germany as long as the
spirit of man is in torture.

Bronislaw Huberman, replying to Wilhelm Furtwäengler's request that he continue his artistic occupation in Berlin, expresses more poignantly and with deeper effect a spirit of repugnance against the efforts of the state to limit art and artists than any published document since the upheaval. He stated:

The government deems it necessary to emphasize the selective principle of highest achievement as the decisive one for music, as for every other form of art. This underscoring of something that ought to be self-evident would be meaningless if it did not imply a determination to apply the principle of selection on a racial basis—a principle that is impossible to apply to all other realms of culture.

I should like a definite rendering of music as a sort of artistic projection of the best and most valuable in man.

Can you expect this process of sublimating, which presupposes complete abandonment of one's self to one's art, of the musician who feels his human dignity trodden upon and who is officially degraded to the rank of a pariah? Can you expect it of the musician to whom the guardians of German culture deny, because of his race, the ability to understand "pure German music"?

In reality it is not a question of violin concertos nor even merely of the Jews; the issue is the retention of those things that our fathers achieved by blood and sacrifice, of the elementary pre-conditions of our European culture, the freedom of personality and its unconditional self-responsibility unhampered by fetters of caste or race.

Let us consider the progress of the new government in unifying and co-ordinating the music of Germany within the limitations of these theories. It is the pattern of destruction by which all the arts are cut. As an initial step in the reorganization of German music, a commission was set up by the Prussian Ministry of Culture with a view to controlling the programs of all public concerts, whether state-subsidized or privately financed. Thus, the Nazi baton conducts all the music of Germany. The commission is composed of Wilhelm Furtwäengler, Wilhelm Bachaus and Georg Kulenkampff, with a fourth member to be named later. The chief aim of the committee is to foster German works. The commission is endowed with full authority to decide all questions pertaining to musical programs within the Prussian jurisdiction. Professional German musicians of every category will be under the control of the *Reichskartel der deutschen Musikerschaft* (National Union of German Musicians), with the sole power to grant licenses and concessions for performances, in co-operation with the Ministry for Propaganda and Public Enlightenment.

The movements in the great symphony of control over the musical life of Germany and the elimination of individuals not sympathetic towards the politics or proscriptions of the new government follows:

In April, 1933, Fritz Busch, who is not a Jew, was forcibly removed from his post as general musical director of the Dresden Opera, despite reported intercession on his behalf by Chancellor Hitler himself. The local opposition to Busch was too strong even for Hitler.

The Prussian Minister of Culture in Berlin forbade the scheduled series of Brahms chamber music by Artur Schnabel, Bronislaw Hubermann, Gregor Piati-

gorsky and Paul Hindemith, each the most eminent
in his particular branch of music. The only conductor admitted besides Wilhelm Furtwäengler was
Gustav Havemann, a prominent Nazi musician. Furtwäengler would not yield to the demand for the dismissal of the three leading solo players in the Berlin
Philharmonic Orchestra, all Jews.

The world premier at Freiburg of Franz Schreker's
new opera, "Christophorus," was postponed indefi-
nitely. Schreker is a Jew.

Adolf Busch withdrew from participation in the
Hamburg Brahms Centennial celebration as a protest
because his friend and protegé, Rudolph Serkin
pianist, was refused permission to take part in the
festival, in accordance with the present anti-Jewish
policy. Serkin, a concert artist of some reputation
in Germany, had appeared widely with the Busch
Quartet. Busch sailed for America shortly afterward, arriving April 21.

In June, 1933, Wilhelm Furtwäengler was appointed "first state conductor" of the Berlin State
Opera for a period of five years. The title is a new
one. Furtwäengler previous appeared as a guest
conductor.

Otto Klemperer, Arnold Schoenberg, and Franz
Schreker were dismissed from their posts in Berlin.
Klemperer's contract as musical director of the State
Opera extended until 1937, but under the "non-Aryan" section of the Civil Service Act he resigned and
is now director of the Los Angeles Symphony Orchestra. Schreker and Schoenberg received indefinite
"leaves of absence" from the Prussian Academy of
Arts where they were directors of composition.

(Schoenberg is now a member of the faculty of the Malkin Academy of Music, in Boston).

Others dismissed from Berlin State Opera are Fritz Zweig, conductor, and his wife, Tilly de Garmo, soprano; Lotte Schoene and Marcel Noe, singers, and five other members of the staff. Leo Blech, conductor, who had been associated with the State Opera for some twenty-five years, was retained, although he is a "non-Aryan." Chancellor Hitler is reported to have insisted that he stay.

Hans Gal was removed from directorship of *Musikhochschule* in Mainz, and succeeded by an unknown composer. Dr. H. Mersmann, editor of *Melos*, a forward-looking German musical magazine, was removed from his post by pressure from the *Kampfbund für Kultur*.

In August, Paris reported a continued influx of German artists and intellectuals; that it was rapidly becoming a *Lieder* center in Brahms, Schubert and Schumann; that a full-fledged German theatre was anticipated for the coming season, ministering specially to German refugees, with a repertoire of works forbidden by the German Government. Max Reinhardt, the theatrical producer, ousted from the directorship of Deutsches Theatre, Berlin, by the Nazi régime in April, applied for French citizenship and contemplated producing plays at the Theatre Pigalle, Paris.

Professor Carl Schuricht succeeded Bruno Walter as chief conductor of the Gewandhaus in Leipsig, and also succeeded Otto Klemperer as conductor of the Berlin Philharmonic Chorus.

Emanuel List, American Jewish baritone, was retained at Berlin Staatsoper despite his race.

Gleichschaltung was extended to the Annual festival of the Association of German Musicians at Dortmund. Modern music was banned.

Dr. Karl Muck (not a Jew) resigned from conductorship of the Hamburg Philharmonic in opposition to the plan of the Hamburg Senate to merge the Philharmonic with the municipal theatre orchestra and "coordinate" the two politically. His resignation stirred all Germany, since he qualified racially for a German musical post.

Wilhelm Furtwäengler, conductor of the Berlin Philharmonic, was unable to induce foreign artists to play in Germany. Among those to refuse were Fritz Kreisler, Pablo Casals, Artur Schnabel, Adolf Busch, Vladimir Horowitz, Bronislaw Hubermann and Yehudi Menuhin. Kreisler, in refusing, said: "Art is international, and I oppose chauvinism in art wherever I encounter it." He said he would not appear in public in Germany until his colleagues in the musical world, irrespective of nationality, race, or creed, were not only tolerated, but actually welcomed.

Unquestionably the most significant event in connection with German music under the Hitler régime was the refusal of Arturo Toscanini to conduct at the Bayreuth Festival. On April 1, 1933, Toscanini headed a group of eleven famous musicians in a protest to Hitler against the persecution of their colleagues in Germany. It was reported at the time that Toscanini was considering withdrawal from the Bayreuth Wagner Festival as a protest. Hitler never acknowledged the cable from Toscanini, but on April 4 the Government forbade broadcasting of musical compositions by musicians in the United States who had signed the cable.

On June 5, Toscanini formally cancelled his engagement to conduct at Bayreuth, stating his reasons in the following message to Frau Winifred Wagner, who had repeatedly insisted that he would not withdraw:

> The lamentable events which have wounded my feelings both as man and as artist have not up to this moment changed, despite my hopes. It is my duty today to break the silence that I have imposed upon myself for the last two months and to inform you that for my, your, and for everybody else's tranquility it is better not to think any more of my going to Bayreuth. With unchanged sentiments of affectionate friendship towards the entire Wagner family, I am yours,
>
> ARTURO TOSCANINI.

The cancellation created an international sensation and was a terrific blow to German music and the Hitler Government. Toscanini was to have been the star attraction at Bayreuth. He had always been held in the highest esteem there, and had only recently been made an honorary citizen of Bayreuth, being presented with a flowery testimonial of regard by the local Burgomeister.

Toscanini was to have conducted eight performances of "Die Meistersinger" and five of "Parsifal" between July 21 and August 19 at the Bayreuth Festspielhaus. His place at the opening performance of "Parsifal" July 21 was taken by Richard Strauss, while Karl Elmendorff replaced him for "Die Meistersinger" July 22.

Fritz Busch, who lost his post as general director of the Dresden Opera when the Nazis came into power, declined an offer to conduct a performance of *"Die Meistersinger"* at Bayreuth in Toscanini's place, and shortly afterward left Germany to conduct German works at the Color Opera in Buenos Aires.

The wholesale discharge of musicians and conductors has made the world feel that Germany is giving up her place in the musical world. Yet the musical greatness of a nation is but partially dependent on the number and ability of her interpreters of established music. Rather in the proscription of such men as Hindemith, Schoenberg, and Schnabel, is Germany denying *herself* a musical future. A consistently dreary picture of German music in 1933 has already been painted by Herbert F. Peyser in a dispatch from Berlin to the *Musical Courier*. In December, the height of the concert season, he reported not one worth-while concert.

In another dispatch, describing the *Kultur-Politik* of the moment, Peyser told how the conductor, Werner Janssen, had arranged to conduct a program including several modern works, among them one of his own compositions, only to discover on his arrival in Berlin from Italy that the program had been almost completely changed without his knowledge or consent. He was eventually permitted to retain his own composition, but the other pieces of his choice were thrown out. Of the concert itself, Peyser reported that it was "disastrous, owing chiefly to the startling unmannerliness of some of the orchestral players, who not only talked and sniggered among themselves during the progress of the pieces, but disregarded the American conductor's beat with such obvious wilfulness that they almost succeeded three or four times in effecting a complete derailment."*

Joseph Paul Goebbels' official title, that of Minister of Propaganda and Culture (sometimes given as "art") reveals the curious marriage which German culture is being forced to undergo. The final results are interestingly foreshadowed in the state of criticism, the art of which has been thoroughly "co-ordinated" under the Nazi Government. In fact, the *"Gleichschaltung"* affects the press perhaps more than any other cultural or quasi-cultural medium. The *"Zeitschrift für Musik"*, an old and liberal German musical journal founded by Robert Schumann, has gone completely Nazi. In a bitter tirade against modern and foreign influences on German music, this publication celebrates: "Even at the twelfth hour an end is to be made of a music that Juda-izes (*verjudet*), be-niggers (*verniggert*) and is without soul."

The state of music criticism under the Nazis is most aptly described in an article written last May by Herbert F. Peyser, Berlin correspondent of the *Musical Courier*. Peyser wrote:

> German music critics will learn how to toe the mark and acquire the habit of uniform thinking on a number of matters if the lately organized Working Committee of Berlin Music Critics can enact its wishes into a law of the land. That should not be difficult just now, for the Working Commit-

---

* It is perhaps worth noting that the signing-off signal of Berlin radio stations, which formerly consisted of a metronome tic-tac, has been "co-ordinated" like everything else, and now consists of characteristic measures from the fighting-song, *Volk ans Gewehr* (The Nation to the Guns).

tee is Nazi from top to bottom and is greatly concerned in fostering "national" culture. The committee is an outgrowth or by-product of the *Kampfbund für deutsche Kultur* (Militant League for German Culture), a body which is rapidly obtaining a preponderating influence in musical matters. The *Kampfbund* has an orchestra which gives concerts under a certain Gustav Havemann. When the Berlin Philharmonic requires substitute players, they are as likely as not these days to come from the ranks of the *Kampfbund* orchestra.

The Committee of Critics is under the chairmanship of Dr. Fritz Stege. Dr. Stege is one of the editors of the monthly *Zeitschrift für Musik*, which Schumann founded a century ago and conducted on the most liberal principles but which has now gone over, bag and baggage, into the reactionary and anti-Semitic camp. If the new committee can enforce its decrees legally, it will mean that music critics will have to obtain a license before they can be engaged by German newspapers. And licenses will be granted only to such critics as are willing to stand squarely back of the musical ideals and policies of the present government. It is further proposed that all executive musicians and teachers be subjected to a test and be duly licensed before they are allowed to make public appearances or to practise pedagogy.

Thus German criticism is compelled to abandon all the grounds it previously held and to judge art in terms of its contribution to national unity or the Nazi *Weltanshauung*. Critical vitality in Germany and its significance then become limited in two senses; it can have meaning for those who hold the Nazi ideal of state and society, and it can treat only works which deal with the problems and life of such a society. The second limitation is perhaps merely formal, for the Nazi attitude to the writer and his task precludes any other serious productions.

The theatre, closely dependent on the state and being the most easily censorable of art forms, suffers the most. The old playwrights will be presented insofar as they are inocuous. For even the classics must come into line, and not even Goethe is sacred. On July 1, Herr Esser, Bavarian minister without portfolio, reproved Goethe for being "internationally minded" and a "stranger to his people." Goethe is guilty of not having contributed to German "liberation." In writing plays, the literary craftsman must construct very carefully. He cannot allow vicious un-Germanic thoughts or feelings to triumph over duty and the readiness to perform it. The true German exists for the nation and racial posterity—all others are probably descended from non-Aryan grandparents. As a result of this attitude, the theatre in Germany is witnessing an unusually great revival of standard musical operettas. Of course Gilbertian satire and irreverence are *verboten*.

Will the stream of German culture dry up? Will the penetrative and elevated thought which was Germany's priceless contribution to Western progress cease to flow from a nationalized fountain-head? Certainly, in the last year, nothing of scientific or academic importance has come out of Germany. The works which are published are no longer read in this country because the people in American universities feel that the German scholars who remain in Germany are under such repression that everything they write must perforce be colored and falsified by the Nazi outlook. Even so politically remote a field as science can no longer be pure in such a country. Where the purity of race becomes the alpha and omega of progress, all that serves the ends of civilization must be mongrelized.

By the same token, it is significant that no book of scientific or academic importance has come out of Italy in the last ten years. Nor any creative work of significance. Italian culture, under Mussolini is in a state of moral decay.

There is this difference, however, between the situations in Germany and Italy; scholars are intellectually no less hampered in either country, but in Italy it is done more subtly. You can publish a distinguished scientific work in Italy without regard for the régime in power, but it will not be reviewed by any magazine or newspaper, and it will not be displayed by any bookstore. The effect of this is to stifle creative work by choking it at the source. In Germany you cannot even publish. The effect is the same in both countries, and as a result academic and scientific circles in this country no longer recognize anything written by German or Italian professors.

This is not only true of science and research. In literature it is the same. Only members of the German Writers' Guild can publish in the Reich, and the members are picked by Göring, an aviation expert.

It is the same in art. Everything modern is rooted out of the museums and exhibitions. Nothing experimental is tolerated. German art is now run by Hanf-staengl, who accepts nothing later than Dürer as German. We have traced the decline of music. It is the same in architecture. The modern German architectural school, which originated in the purely functional building methods of American engineers, is not tolerated by Hitler, who insists on what he conceives to be the neo-Gothic. The *Bauhaus*, nucleus of German modern architecture, is now closed.

And so history, art, sociology, and politics are to be based on a racial theory of the type enunciated by Goebbels and Rosenberg. Any thought in these fields contrary to that theory constitute treason to an all-powerful state. Hitler's historical and sociological pronunciamentos in his autobiography are an amusing example of the "new thought." Yet it is sad humor when we recall that the man behind these ideas holds sixty million people under his authority and is in a position to set Europe afire! And so the New Germany marches on, marches on over the men, the ideas, and the impulses which are the basis of civilization in the Western World. And at the head of this terrible army is the little man, mediocre, strangled, intolerant, fearful of all wisdoms but his own.

THE FATE OF

THE WORKER

BY LUDWIG LORE

M AY DAY, 1890. Labor in Hohenzollern Germany
demonstrating for the international brotherhood of
man, for world peace and labor protection. As if it
had happened yesterday that first day of May still lives
within me as one of the most memorable events of my
boyhood days. Its observance in the friendly little
Silesian city was neither large nor dramatic. A cheery
band of workingmen, women, and children with red
flags flying had marched through sunny streets to the
nearby woods, singing revolutionary airs and rejoicing
in the daring that had made this holiday their own.
There was no talk of revolution. Not once did the
speaker of the occasion refer to the "overthrow of the
capitalist system." It was all very safe and very innocent. The element of melodrama that impressed the
celebration so deeply on my memory was furnished not
by the celebrants themselves, but by a thoroughly
frightened bourgeoisie. Soldiers stood at arms in the
garrisons. Police and gendarmes moved watchfully
about, acutely conscious of the sharply loaded revolvers
in their holsters. The knowledge that staid and super-
cilious burghers were trembling behind closed doors
that day, gave the occasion a thrill it would otherwise

have missed. Not until the day was long ended did
their hearts beat evenly once more and their lives re-
sume their normal course. The revolution had passed
Germany by. . . .

May Day, 1933. Labor in National Socialist Germany celebrates its May Day as a national holiday,
demonstrating its allegiance to Fascist principles and
furnishing its oppressors with the stage effects for a
demonstration of popular fealty to the National Socialist state. Compared with the small groups that celebrated that other first of May forty-three years ago, an
impressive sight. But the difference between these outward manifestations then and now was no greater than
the divergence of sentiments which they expressed.

On this May Day of 1933, German labor dug its own
ignoble grave. At the behest of their trade union leaders, class conscious German workers had flocked to
these Nazi demonstrations, hoping against hope that
this last indignity, this final self-abasement, might save
their organizations from the fate that had already over-
taken the Communist and Social Democratic Parties.
But too late they discovered that the leaders of the
free trade unions had made their last great mistake. To
the new rulers of Nazidom their acquiescence was
merely another demonstration of organized labor's
spineless inability to hold its own. On the following
day all trade union headquarters in the Reich were
occupied by SA and SS troops, trade union treasuries,
records, books, and paraphernalia were confiscated,
trade union buildings became the property of the state
and trade union officials were replaced by Nazi bureaucrats. Hundreds of trade unionists whose only crime
had been their faithful service to the labor movement

were sent to prisons and concentration camps where they were tortured by half-grown sadists.

The trade unions themselves continued to exist, but as organs, now, of the German Labor Front, "the total- itarian organization of all German citizens who play a part in the country's industrial process, (a) workers, (b) salaried employees, (c) employers." "Trade unions," announced Dr. Ley, head of the Labor Front, "are necessary and must continue to exist." "The trade union," reiterated Walter Schuhmann, National Social- ist Director of the Federation of Salaried Employees, in the name of the government, "is the essential repre- sentative of the worker in the productive process. The National Socialist German Labor Party is convinced of the importance of the trade union and will defend its existence to the utmost."

In his autobiography, "My Battle," the Bible of every good National Socialist, Hitler had likewise em- phasized the need of trade union organization. "The necessity of trade unions must be taken for granted," he had written, "so long as employers included among their numbers men who had of themselves no feeling for social obligation, nor even for the elementary rights of humanity . . . In the present state of affairs I am convinced that the trade unions cannot possibly be dis- pensed with. In fact they are among the most impor- tant institutions in the economic life of the nation . . . The National Socialist movement which aims at the National Socialist state for the people may entertain no doubts that every future institution of that state must be rooted in the movement itself. It is the greatest of errors to imagine that possession of power by itself will allow any definite reorganization . . . without the help of men who have been trained beforehand in the spirit of the enterprise . . . Thus no one could propose suddenly dragging out of his portfolio the draft of a new constitution and expect to be able to 'introduce' it by an edict from above. It might be tried but the result would not survive . . . The National Socialist state must avoid all such experiments; it must grow out of an organization which has already long been working . . . In the hand of the National Socialist trade union the strike is not an instrument for ruining the nation's production, but for increasing it and causing it to flow . . . For it is absurd and also untrue to claim that the trade union movement is essentially hostile to the Fatherland; the opposite is the more correct view. If trade union action aims at improving the condition of a class which is one of the pillars of the nation and succeeds in doing so, its action is not against the Fatherland and the state but it is 'national' in the truest sense of the word. In that way it helps to forge social principles, without which general national education is unthinkable. It earns the highest merit for, by eradicating social cankers, it attacks the causes of disease both mental and bodily and so adds to the general welfare of the nation . . . If unsocial or unworthy treatment of men provokes resistance, then, until the lawful judicial bodies are prepared to do away with the evil, this struggle can only be decided by the side which is the strongest. It is evident that any large group of employees, face to face with an individual employer supported by the concentrated strength of his business, must unite in a single body if they are not to give up all hope of victory from the very start."

But when the smoke of battle cleared, the Nazi union

was found to differ radically from the trade union pos-
tulated by the Leader and his appointed followers. Its
important functions had been delegated to official Arbitrators (*Treuhaender der Arbeit*), appointed by the
Chancellor. The regulation of wage disputes, when
and under what conditions to strike, the settlement of
disagreements—all these and other duties that had once
been the warp and woof of trade union activity were
now settled by these Nazi appointees. The name of
those who had once directed the free trade unions were
published on a "List of the Despised." "He whose
name appears on the 'List of the Despised'," said the
new trade union statutes, "shall not be given any kind
of work. All organs directly connected with German
industry will receive a copy of this list that not one of
these traitors may make his devious way into our German jobs or places of work to continue his subversive
activity." Indeed, the National Socialist government,
having risen to power on the shoulders of the industrial overlords of the nation, was prepared to go further still to protect their interests. On May 25 a proclamation signed by Dr. Ley and Dr. Wagner, Reich
Commissar for Industry, forbade all "strikes, stoppages,
and lockouts." This was followed on July 31 by an
edict curtailing the powers of the National Socialist
Shop Council Organizations (NSBO) because on several occasions they had ventured to oppose the decisions of the "Arbitrators." On July 22 mine workers
in the Ruhr district were forbidden to demand wage
increases, and on August 23 a similar order was given
to the Metal Workers of Berlin.

The final blow fell on January 23, 1934, when the
Reichsgesetzblatt published a "Law for the Regulation

of National Labor" signed by six Ministers of the Cabinet, consisting of seven paragraphs and seventy-five sections. This law which goes into effect on May 1, 1934, now orders the dissolution of the aforementioned Fascist, Government controlled unions and in their stead gives the individual employers what amounts to undisputed control over his establishment while it dissolves all "collectivistic and cooperative organizations of labor on the industrial field." The official German news bureau describes the purport of the new law as follows: "The basis of the new social system is the factory. The Leader is the employer. He decides for the Following (employees) in all questions concerning the management of the plant . . . The Following shall render faithful service to the Leader in all things related to the conduct of the undertaking . . . This law revokes all previous laws of basic significance relating to shop councils, wage agreements, arbitration and strikes and lockouts and similar questions." The Leader thus becomes the absolute monarch over his plant. He posts wage announcements on his factory walls without previous negotiations, and in the same arbitrary manner extends the length of the factory's workday. The law seeks to conceal the naked truth of labor's total subjection to the dictatorial power of its industrial masters by the establishment of three institutions (1) Trustees (*Vertrauensrat*) (2) Arbitrators (*Treuhaender der Arbeit*) and (3) the Social Court of Honor. Trustees exist only where there are at least twenty workers. They meet under the chairmanship of the Leader and have no executive power, acting merely in an advisory capacity, and that only if and when called by the Leader or if at least one half of the Trustees request him to call them into session. These Trustees are appointed by the Leader (employer) with the advice of the Nazi Shop Council, and may therefore be relied upon under all circumstances to safeguard the rights of the employer, rather than the interests of the Following. In wage questions the Trustees have not even advisory powers, indeed, not even the Arbitrator is qualified to interfere in the settlement of wage rates for a single establishment. He is empowered to regulate wages for industrial groups but only "if there can be proven a real need" for such interference in the rights of the Leader. Obviously such occasions will not often arise; the existence of such a situation must first be determined by a Commission of Experts (*Sachverstaendige*) consisting of employers, experts appointed by the Arbitrator and employees. But as there is only one Arbitrator for every large industrial district, wages and working conditions, with but few exceptions, will be determined arbitrarily by the individual employer or group of employers. Both employers and workers may appeal from the decision of the Arbitrator to the Social Court of Honor, but such an appeal must be submitted through the Arbitrator himself. The employer may charge employees with having violated "social honor" by "deliberate attempts to foment dissatisfaction," or "by the presentation of unjustifiable complaints (as in the case of Trustees for instance)" while a worker may accuse his employer of undue exploitation, reflection on his honor as a worker, etc. These Courts of Honor consist of a judge, who acts as chairman, an employer of the plant in question and a third person chosen by the other two. It is hardly necessary to describe the brand

of justice that these Courts of Honor will mete out to
the workman who dares lodge a complaint.

Though this "Labor Law" does not take effect officially before the first of May, the trade unions are
practically out of existence. In their stead The Labor
Front, heretofore composed of labor unions and employers' organizations, has been reconstructed, and
will, when the new law is enforced, consist of individual members only, a vertical structure in which all
persons connected as workers, salaried employees, and
employers with the industrial life of the nation, are, in
theory at least, members of equal standing. This new
organization is totally devoid of those responsibilities
and privileges that are generally associated with the
idea of a labor organization. So far as we have been
able to discover, its functions are merely passive, i. e.,
it is the recipient of whatever propaganda, obligations
and duties the government chooses to place upon the
backs of a supine working class.

The employer, on the other hand, has every reason
to be satisfied with his rôle in the co-ordinated industrial system. The New Year's Day issue of the
Deutsche Bergwerks-Zeitung, always notorious for its
anti-labor stand, expressed this jubilant satisfaction of
the capitalist with things as they are in the Nazi world
as follows:

> It is self-evident that the National Socialist state
> cannot free the employer over night of all the heavy
> loads with which the trade union state of the past
> burdened its industries. Fundamentally it is the pur-
> pose of the National Socialist state, however, to res-
> cue the employer as it will rescue all other estates,
> from that inner political squandering of the nation's

resources which the trade union state with its excessive taxation, its system of high wages and excessive social services and its systematic promotion of the class struggle foisted upon the nation.

This was written, it should be noted, before the issuance of the new labor law. But the gentlemen of the press were well informed of what was going on behind the scenes. "Now," the article continues, "new forms will have to be found within which those differences which will arise even under a system of closest co-operation between all industrial groups can be overcome in a true National Socialist spirit, without friction and without reopening old enmities. Calmly and with serious reflection we will arrive at a new system of labor regulation . . . The preliminaries for such a system are already accomplished."

With the dissolution of the trade union the German worker loses the last organ that might conceivably have served to defend his rights and solve his problems. A proclamation issued late in November and signed by three Cabinet Ministers and Dr. Ley outlines the aims and functions of the Labor Front: "It is the will of our leader Adolf Hitler that the German Labor Front shall not decide on the material problems of the worker's daily existence, nor shall it concern itself with the conflicting interests of individuals in the economic process. For the regulation of conditions of labor, forms will presently be created which will give to the leader and his staff in every plant the position and functions that a National Socialist conception prescribes. The exalted aim of the Labor Front is the education of all Germans who participate in our industrial life, for the National Socialist state and to a National Socialist con-

ception. It aims particularly to train those best fitted
to exert a directive influence in the branches of our
social institutions, our labor courts, and our social services. It will strive to make the social honor of the
leader of industry and that of his following a driving
force for a new social and economic order."

The destruction of the trade union movement wiped
out only one, albeit the most important of German
labor's economic organizations. The Workers' Co-operatives, once the most highly developed and most ef-
ficiently managed co-operatives in the world, founded
and developed to an unexampled degree of perfection
under the guidance of the Social Democracy, still continue to exist. When Hitler became Chancellor, the
Workers' Co-operatives had more than 50,000 retail
stores in the Reich with an annual turnover of $425,-
000,000. They controlled more than five per cent of
the country's retail trade and worked with an overhead of seventeen and one-tenth per cent as against the
average retailers' twenty-four and two-tenths per cent.
These co-operatives which did a thriving business
among the better-paid workers and their families, had
always been a thorn in the flesh of the small retailer,
wherefore their destruction became one of the early
promises made by the demagogic Nazis to their middle-
class following. But after they had taken possession
of the machinery of the co-operatives it occurred to
the Nazi leaders that this organization with its hundreds
of thousands of salaried posts could be used to better
purpose. The Co-operatives remained, and National
Socialists, most of them heretofore without visible
means of support, were given the jobs of the ousted

"Marxists." The National Socialist Party discovered that the co-operatives, far from encroaching on the rights of the middle class are in reality "its natural allies" (quotation from a Nazi leaflet entitled "National Socialism and Consumers Co-operatives") The co-operatives were co-ordinated, every trace of democratic management and control disappeared, and local managers, officials, and employees who had formerly held office at the pleasure of the local membership are now appointed by a central board in Hamburg.

But the Nazis are finding that they made their reckoning without their host. The initial campaign against the co-operatives damaged these organizations severely. Thousands of members, executives and employees withdrew, the public feared to buy in the co-operative stores while Social Democrats and Communists, once their most active patrons, now pointedly avoid these strongholds of Nazi retail business. A sales slump of considerable magnitude was the result, and the situation is developing serious aspects. If the co-operatives break down, the hundreds of thousands of workers who have invested their money in these undertakings will hold the National Socialists responsible; worse still, creditors will lose their money and many bankruptcies will follow all over the land. For such situations there is only one answer—the public must be forced to support the co-operatives. The Nazi directors have already issued a leaflet to all "Party Comrades" which contains the following gem of National Socialist consistency: "The co-operatives are not only theoretically, but in actual daily practice an effective weapon in the fight against capitalism. There are many today who, either through fear, or stubbornness or for other reasons, oppose the co-operatives. This is not in accord with our fundamental principle: Common interests before private interests." But the class conscious worker who once gladly gave his talents, time and untiring effort to the co-operative movement is not interested in the Fascisized organization, consequently the co-operatives work with an overhead, not of seventeen per cent, but of twenty-nine per cent and have long since ceased to compete successfully with private wholesale and retail establishments.

Most tragic, because most far-reaching in its after-effects, has been the suppression of the German political labor movement, the guide and mentor of all other proletarian organizations in the Reich. In no other country in the world had the political ideology of the labor movement so permeated every phase of working class activity. Proletarian singing societies, sport organizations, chess clubs, free thinkers' societies—all were crushed under the heavy hand of the National Socialist dictatorship for their close connection with the political movement. Even the numerous Esperanto Clubs were doomed to suppression because, as one Nazi organ quaintly put it, "Esperanto is a Hebrew derivative."

The Communist Party which, because of its militant opposition to the National Socialist movement, had incurred the hatred of the new régime to a far greater measure than the Social Democracy, was the first victim of Nazi suppression. Its deputies were ousted from the Reichstag in the first days of the new régime to give Hitler an absolute majority over the combined oppositional forces which the election had just failed to give. The party itself was dissolved after the Reichstag fire forced the Hugenberg Nationalists to consent to its suppression. Though much smaller than the Social Democracy and less firmly rooted in the masses, the Communist Party with its large army of young and courageous fighters and its almost 300,000 members, was a force to be reckoned with in the political life of the nation. It published thirty daily and weekly newspapers, and in the last election before its suppression polled 4,000,000 votes, a loss of only one million votes, despite the suppression of its organs and a campaign of unexampled Nazi terrorism. In 1932 it had elected more than 1,500 of its members into the various municipal councils of the Reich. Psychologically as well as organizationally it was far better prepared for illegal work than the Social Democracy. In spite of a system of espionage that penetrated into its innermost organs, and a daily growing list of arrests, imprisonments, murders and death penalties which is decimating its ranks at a terrifying rate, its members still publish newspapers, leaflets, pamphlets in incredible quantities though by far the larger part of this material which is produced under such tremendous dangers and sacrifices, never reaches the public, "thanks" to the faultless workings of Göring's Secret State Police. Organizationally little remains of the Communist Party. Sporadic attempts in Berlin, Upper Silesia, Saxony and in the industrial districts of the Rhineland are all that is left of the largest and most influential Communist movement outside of Soviet Russia.

The same is true of the right-Communist Brandler-Thalheimer Opposition group, the Left-Communist Opposition group, commonly known as the Trotzkyites,

and of the Socialist Workers' Party, a leftist organization that split from the Social Democratic Party almost
three years ago and drew many "outlaw" Communists
into its ranks. These and other smaller groups are
still anchored here and there in the Reich in more or
less active groups. But nowhere is there a possibility
of effective political work. The terror of the SA and
SS, the horrors of Nazi barracks and concentration
camps, have decimated the ranks of these once proud
organizations to such an extent that only isolated groups
remain to tell the story of a once almost invincible
labor party.

The Social Democratic Party was allowed by the Hitler government to continue a much curtailed activity
for two months after the Communist sections of the
labor movement had been wiped out. In the March,
1933, elections it polled 7,000,000 votes, a loss of 2,-
000,000 since previous elections. The last report of
the National Executive of the party listed 1,080,580
members in 9,972 local branches. In the municipal
councils the Social Democracy had not less than 55,271
representatives and 662 of the 2,148 deputies in the
various state parliaments belonged to the party. The
SDP of Germany published 19 monthly periodicals
and 234 daily and weekly newspapers; its daily press
boasted of more than 7,500,000 subscribers.

Practically nothing remains of this imposing structure. The majority of its former—and present—
Executive Committee, recognizing after the catastro-
phic pro-Hitler vote of their party group in the Reichstag that their usefulness in Germany was at an end,
is now living in Prague. Wels, Breitscheid, Scheide-
mann, Vogel, and Künstler saw that to remain in Ger-

many would offer them only two courses of action—to place themselves and their party unreservedly at the disposal of the Hitler régime or to continue a futile opposition at the daily risk of life and liberty. Those well-known Social Democrats who preferred to remain in the Reich are living a sort of extra-legal existence—i. e., they are never for a moment certain that they will not be arrested and thrown into a concentration camp. Thousands of others have been in these places of torture for months, and new arrests are constantly being made, although the Social Democracy is much less active than the Communist Party. Its illegal apparatus is poorly organized and still ineffective. Its chief activity consists in the sporadic distribution of the *Neue Vorwaerts* (Karlsbad) and the *Neue Freiheit* (Saarbruecken). For the coming months the regular distribution of short propaganda pamphlets has been planned. Several Left Wing Socialist groups, some of which are receiving strong moral support from Communist elements dissatisfied with the tactics of their own party, are unfolding an organizational activity that is bearing fruit, although, or rather because, they carry on no outside propaganda.

What has the "National Revolution" given the German proletariat in return for this wanton destruction of all it held sacred? The government insists that it has reduced the number of unemployed by millions. In November, 1933, the number of workers receiving unemployment benefits was 530,000 less than in the same month of the previous year. But this does not prove that fewer people are out of work in the Reich or that a greater number has found employment. Other factors play a part that cannot be disregarded. Rigid economy has been practiced by the social service agencies of the government to reduce expenses. The tens of thousands who are in prisons and concentration camps, tens of thousands who have fled across the borders, the thousands of "Marxists" and Jews who have been blacklisted—they all had jobs and are no longer counted as unemployed. Thousands of women and older men have been forced out of the industries and younger men given their places. 700,000 persons, according to a report recently issued by the Reich Minister of Labor, Franz Seldte, have found employment on public works and in the labor camps, which "without this measure would probably have added considerably to the number of unemployed." Indeed, the official figures of the Labor Ministry prove beyond a doubt that unemployment figures have not dropped but risen.

No discussion of German labor in the new régime would be complete without a word concerning its voluntary labor service. These labor camps are not a National Socialist institution. They were first inaugurated under Bruening, and at that time were what they claimed to be, places in which young unemployed workers and students were given work by the government. To call the camps that exist under that name today either voluntary or labor is a conscious mistatement of facts. The young unemployed youths of Germany must serve in these camps or starve. Young men between the ages of eighteen and thirty who refuse labor service receive no unemployment benefits. In many cases they are permitted the choice between work in a labor camp or on one of the large estates in the

Eastern parts of Germany where miserable food and living conditions for farm help are proverbial. Often the Junker landowners refuse to give the "noble" pay of 50 Pfennig (10 cents) for a long and hard day when the work is done; the laborers rebel and are sent to concentration camps.

The Hitler authorities are conspicuously reticent concerning the question of wages paid to the workers in the new era. The "co-ordinated" "*Institut für Konjunkturforschung*" offers some information on this point. It estimates that the total paid out in the form of wages and salaries to workers, salaried employees, and executives increased in the second quarter of 1933 approximately half a billion marks. But, it adds, this increase is due to a rise in the number of those gainfully employed, not to a rise in the income of the individual. According to official figures the second quarter of 1933 brought an increase of 1,114,000 gainfully employed. Yet for that same period the sum total paid in wage taxes remained almost stationary: 182,-226,000 mk. in the first and 182,384,000 mk. in the second quarter. Since this wage tax is subtracted from the wage or salary of the employee at the time it is paid, it furnishes an accurate gauge for the actual status of wages paid. Manifestly there must have been a radical reduction in the wages paid to the individual when 13,307,000 employed workers earn no more than 12,193,000 in an earlier period. A comparison of these figures with those for 1932 shows a reduction of the income from wage taxes of 44,163,000 mk., indicating that the total wage for 1933 was approximately 400,-000,000 mk. below that of the previous year, and that this reduced total was divided among a much increased army of wage earners. But the *"Institut für Konjunk-turforschung"* places other figures at our disposal, which throw a revealing light on industrial conditions during the first months of the Hitler régime. According to these figures income from industry was 19,073,-000,000 mk, from January to September, 1932, and 19,300,000,000 mk. for the same nine months of 1933. In other words the income of the German worker during the first three quarters was 230,000,000 mk. greater than in the same span of the preceding year. During the same period (again according to official figures) the number of persons employed was increased by 2,434,000. This would mean, assuming that wages remained stationary, a monthly income of ten marks for every man or woman newly employed. The following figures from the report of Germany's Old Age and Invalid Insurance Service, to which all workers must contribute, give an idea of the actual wages paid by German industry. The employees enrolled in this state fund reported the following weekly wages for the second quarter of 1933: 4% received up to 6 marks; 22% from 6-12 mk.; 22% from 12-18 mk.; 15% from 18-24 mk.; 11% from 24-30 mk.; 9% from 30-36 mk.; and 17% over 36 mk. On the other hand the new government's striving toward industrial and agricultural self-sufficiency by the introduction of prohibitive tariffs, particularly on food stuffs, so raised prices that the real wage of the worker has fallen to an even greater extent than the above figures indicate.

But this the Hitler government has given to Labor—the uniform of the German Labor Front. "The German Labor Front—the organization of those who create," says a decree by Dr. Ley, "knows no difference between workers, salaried employees, and employers. It knows only creative work. Outwardly this disappearance of all social and economic differences will find expression in the gala uniform of the German Labor Front, that uniform which will be worn on festive occasions by all who are members in its ranks." The decree then describes the garment in detail and orders that all tailors who desire to make such uniforms apply for permits to their guild organization. "These guilds," so closes the decree, "are responsible to the Reich Bureau of Supplies that only tailors of Aryan extraction will be permitted to manufacture such uniforms." Thus far a uniform for German labor "produced by Aryan tailors" has been for the worker the sole fruit from the tree of Hitler achievement.

PART TWO

AN INTERNATIONAL MENACE

THE THREAT TO FREEDOM

BY JOHN HAYNES HOLMES

I NEVER denounce the Hitler horror but what sooner or later I am myself denounced for believing the current reports about Nazi Germany. I am charged with inconsistency for accepting so-called "atrocity stories," when I steadfastly rejected such atrocity stories in the days of the Great War. After twenty years of resisting anti-German propaganda and anti-Bolshevik propaganda and anti-radical propaganda in this country, I am accused of falling easy victim to anti-Hitler propaganda. My hour of intellectual and moral collapse, I am told, has come. I am just as gullible, prejudiced, and hateful as any of the 'phobists who busied themselves in spreading lies and fomenting ill-will during the vast upheavals of war, revolution, and disaster which have convulsed the world during the past two decades.

It might be sufficient to answer these charges, if I
were so minded, by referring to the record. If I could
go through the excitement of the Great War and the
furore of the Russian Revolution without being deceived, why should it not be presumed that I could
keep my head under the impact of the Hitler régime?
My years of experience in observing cataclysmic events,
and in successfully training myself to sift evidence, analyze reports, recognize facts, and detect propaganda,
must have taught me something about the nature of
truth and error in times that try men's souls. As for
my critics, why should I trust them today when I could
not trust most of them yesterday? If I know that they
were swayed during the Great War not by reason but
by emotion—a pro-German devotion to their native
land which led them to defend even the wrong of the
Belgian invasion and the horror of the Lusitania sinking—why should I not suspect that they are now driven
by the same emotion to the same apology for ill? I
see nothing in the record, in other words, to persuade
me that these critics may be right, or that I must be
wrong.

But I do not want to rest my case upon any such personal and therefore biased grounds as these. I make no
claim to infallibility. I have been mistaken before in
my time on many a crucial matter, and may well be
mistaken again in this Hitler Business. So I propose
to begin over again, and judge this present situation
on its own merits. What are the factors in my judgment today? What are the influences which have
moved my mind in this latest convulsion of the nations? What reason have I to believe that I am not
deceived in my conviction that Hitlerism is a reversion

to barbarism, and a menace therefore to every precious
thing in our civilization?

As I survey the data which have been determining
my opinion of Nazi Germany, I note the following:

(1) The fact, undisputed and indisputable, that refugees, Gentile and Jewish, rich and poor, men, women
and children, have been pouring out of Germany like
a flood ever since Hitler came to power! It is con-
servatively estimated that not less than 200,000 persons have exiled themselves during the past year. The
Geneva commission on refugees announced some time
ago that people are escaping from Germany, as from
a burning building, at the rate of 10,000 a month.
This fact speaks for itself. Citizens do not run away
from their native land except under conditions of terror and despair. When we saw refugees pouring out
of Russia in the early days of the Revolution, we did
not hesitate to draw the inference. Why hesitate with
Germany? I find awful significance in the fact that
for the first time in history, in time of peace, it has
been necessary to appoint an international commission
to take care of the refugees from a so-called civilized
government.

(2) Personal contacts with refugees! I have met
and talked with a certain number of refugees from
Germany, and have heard directly or indirectly from
many more. I have looked into the faces of these refugees, heard their stories, read their letters and testi-
monies. I never believed the old "atrocity stories,"
because I never saw a child with its hands cut off, or
a woman without her breasts, or a Canadian soldier
nailed to a cross. I have refused to believe the worst

of the anti-Bolshevik yarns because I have yet to see a nationalized woman or a butchered priest. But I have seen with my own eyes and touched with my own hands some victims of Hitler's troopers, and I believe, even as Thomas believed when he touched the wounds of Christ.

(3) Nazi data—documents, books, literature. By documents I mean transcripts of laws, decrees, constitutions, and other official state papers adopted, published, and enforced by the Hitler Government, and thus as incontrovertible as the Constitution of the United States and its statute laws. By books I mean, for example, Nazi textbooks used in the public schools, anti-Jewish pamphlets and volumes issued by the Party or the Government, other publications of official propaganda, copies of which I have seen and handled. By literature I mean Hitler's *"Mein Kampf,"* Rosenberg's "The Myth of the Twentieth Century," Graf von Reventlow's organ, *Reichwart,* and speeches by Hitler and other leaders. All of this varied material has one unvarying characteristic—it convicts the National Socialists out of their own mouths.

(4) Books about Germany written by trusted scholars and trained observers. These run all the way from Edgar Mowrer's "Germany Turns Back the Clock," published shortly before Hitler gained office, to Dr. Charles S. Macfarland's "The New Church and the New Germany," which has just come from the press. The most valuable and important of these books is Professor Calvin B. Hoover's "Germany Enters the Third Reich." This last volume is objective, good-tempered, moderate, impartial, authoritative, and utterly damning.

(5) First-hand despatches of newspaper correspond-

ents, some of whom I know personally, and all of whom
I know by reputation. From the beginning of the
Hitler régime, there were posted in Berlin such men as
Birchall and Enderis of the New York *Times*, Elliot of
the New York *Herald-Tribune*, Knickerbocker of the
New York *Evening Post*, Mowrer of the Chicago *Evening News*, Lochner of the Associated Press, and the
German representatives of the London *Times* and the
Manchester *Guardian*. These men are all of them journalists of world-wide fame and unimpeachable integrity. Daily they have been sending despatches to their
papers which constitute the current history of the Nazi
revolution. Never has any such world event been
"covered" by so numerous a body of experienced and
trusted observers. In the Russian Revolution, the
newspaper despatches bore the date-lines of Riga and
Helsingfors; in the Great War, they were stories written under the control of the military censorship, and
frequently manufactured by the official propaganda bureaus. "Now it can be told," cried Sir Philip Gibbs,
with infinite relief, when the War was over, as though
truth, long repressed, must now at last explode! But
in this German cataclysm, truth has been told right
along in day-by-day reports from those who have seen
with their own eyes and heard with their own ears. Like
light breaking out of darkness is the story of Germany
(1933) as compared with the stories of Russia
(1917-22) and of Europe (1914-18.)

(6) First-hand accounts of impartial visitors and observers—not tourists who find hotels comfortable,
streets quiet, and trains on time, not Germans or German-Americans or pro-Germans who think everything
is right because it's "made in Germany," not Jews, or

Socialists, or Communists, or intellectuals who have
suffered and therefore are stricken and offended, but
spectators who are interested in the scene and know
how to report it. Of these, who have been many, I
name two by way of illustration—Robert Dell, of the
Nation, a veteran English journalist, and Alice Hamilton, a medical scientist of Boston. If I knew nothing
about Nazi Germany except Dr. Hamilton's description,
in her three articles in the *Survey-Graphic,* of what the
Hitlerites have done to the Jews, the trades unionists,
and the intellectuals of Germany, I should know
enough to know that the Nazis, tested by every standard of modern civilization, are savages.

These are the sources of our information about Germany today. Let no one say we do not know or have
been deceived about what is going on in the Reich. We
know with a certainty which makes the Hitler règime
the most terrifying experience since the Great War itself. What have the Nazis done?

They have destroyed self-government, freedom of
speech, freedom of the press, freedom of asesmbly, freedom of petition, and all the civil rights of a free people.

They have abolished all political parties, and made
it a crime to organize any new political group.

They have pursued and persecuted, with fierce fe-
rocity, all Socialists, Communists, pacifists, free-think-
ers, and other radicals antagonistic to the iron régime
of a totalitarian state.

They have liquidated the trades unions, confiscated
their property, bank deposits, printing presses and
headquarters, and exiled, imprisoned, and in some cases
killed their officers and leaders.

They have abrogated the social legislation of the Reich—the insurance, pension and other protective systems built up by the workers through a half-century of struggle and sacrifice, and long since become the model for our western world.

They have transformed a collapsing capitalism into a new economic feudalism dominated by industrial lords and served by proletarian serfs.

They have inaugurated a persecution of the Jews more terrible in its rigor than anything known since the Middle Ages—a "dry" pogrom of political disfranchisement, social outlawry, and economic ruin which dooms Israel to extinction or the ghetto.

They have outraged the church, both Catholic and Protestant, in a deliberate attempt to subdue the conscience of Christendom to autocratic rule and pagan ideology of the Nazi state.

They have ended the emancipation of women, returning one-half of the human race in Germany to the subjection of an older and darker day.

They have withdrawn the writ of *habeas corpus*, exposed homes to invasion and persons to arrest without warrant, and decreed *ex post facto* laws for cruel and unusual punishment of crime.

They have re-established duelling, restored the medieval rite of execution by the headsman's axe, and honored assassination.

They have made war on science, art, literature, and culture.

They have burned books, torn down monuments and buildings, and defamed and defiled the names of immortal Germans.

They have turned universities into training-schools,

colleges into military academies, and a world-famous public school system into a régime of Nazi discipline.

They have prostituted opera-houses, symphony orchestras, art galleries, learned societies, laboratories, libraries, museums, and research institutes to the base uses of party prapaganda.

They have dismissed, degraded, insulted, herded in concentration camps, and driven into exile, the intellectual and spiritual leaders of the nation.

They have driven writers, artists, actors, musicians into a so-called Chamber of Culture, controlled and censored by officials of the Nazi Government.

They have infected an entire people with the virus of Aryanism, and with all its attendant ills of prejudice and passion.

They have re-established war as the pathway to glory.

They are militarizing a new generation to the lust of arms.

They are unsheathing "the German sword—to give sod to the German plow."

They are plotting, planning, and preparing for "the next war."

And over all this work of force and violence, brutality and barbarism, they are casting the veil of an impenetrable censorship, so that the Germans, alone of all peoples in the world, know nothing of what is going on.

These are the deeds of the Nazis! We know these deeds are done. We know what these deeds mean. They are a denial of civilization. They are a repudiation of what enlightened men hold precious. They are a betrayal of all that glorifies and vindicates mankind.

These deeds are not in this sense to be confused with events in Russia. In bloodshed and suffering, the sheer agony of the flesh, the Bolshevist revolution was undoubtedly more terrible than the Nazi. But the former upheaval was never a repudiation of progress, nor an attack upon the mind and spirit of the race. Thus, there was no reversion in Russia. At their worst, the Soviets simply took over the traditional practices of the Tsars, and continued a repression to which the people had been inured for centuries. There was no loss of civil rights in Russia, for the reason that one cannot lose what one has never had. Liberty did not give way to tyranny, since there was no liberty. But in that one area of human experience which is most important to the welfare and happiness of the great masses of mankind—namely, the economic—there has come during the last decade a liberation of the Russian people so pervasive and so potent as to constitute the one most stupendous act of emancipation that is known to history. One cannot hope to understand the work of the Bolsheviki unless one sees that the revolutionists took a vast welter of men and women, ignorant, superstitious, degraded, existing on the lowest levels of human subsistence, and are now raising them, step by painful step, toward the highest levels of comfort, culture, and enlightenment. The peasants, the workers, the intellectuals, the Jews, the nationals, ninety percent of the population of Russia, are now for the first time free. The people of this enormous land, untouched by the Renaissance and the Reformation which delivered the peoples of Western Europe from the bondage of the Dark Ages, have at last been quickened into life, and thus started upon the way to progress.

Whatever the terror of the early years, there began in Russia, in 1917, a movement destined to achieve a larger and nobler liberty than man has yet known upon this earth.

But Hitler has gone backward. He is retracing the progress of a thousand years. He is destroying the liberty bought at a great price through ages of struggle for the light.

It is not difficult to describe what man has been doing, or trying to do, through all these centuries gone by. Popular treatises like H. G. Wells's "The Outline of History," and Hendrik Van Loon's "The Story of Mankind," have made familiar the trends of social evolution. We feel the impulse of the movement like the theme of a symphony, growing, expanding, caught in mad intricacies of discord, lost in chaotic cadences of sound, but always emerging and rising into the prophetic paean of final and exultant triumph.

What man has been doing is to find himself, to discover and fulfill his essential being. He has been hunting out the inner qualities of his genius, and then expressing them in outward manifestations of thought and life. History is the record of the human struggle to give man a chance, each man to do his work, to speak his word, to exalt his soul, and therewith to prove his kinship with the divine. In the beginning, man was immersed in the mass. He was little better than one drop of water in the flood, one animal in the swarming herds of animals. His task was to discover his individuality, and to develop it for the enrichment of the race and the vindication of his own spirit.

Very early it was found possible for the few to es-

tablish conditions which would favor the satisfaction
of their desires and the fulfillment of their powers.
The strong, the aggressive, and at last the intellectual
could gain ascendancy over their fellows, and subdue
them to their purposes.   In one short and glorious period in ancient Greece, a chosen class of aristocrats,
supported by a slave population, demonstrated for all
time the supreme capacity of the human mind. But opportunity enjoyed by the few has been inexorably demanded by the many.   Steadily, through the ages, has
spread the pressure of the masses for larger liberty.
In periods of ignorance and superstition, under reigns
of tyranny and oppression, man has been restless and
resistless.   Instinctively he has felt his powers and demanded freedom for their expression.   Thus, at long
intervals, he has broken out into rebellions and revolutions; and at great climactic moments of release,
achieved liberations which have marked the milestones
of his progress.   This has been the spirit of liberalism
at work—the spirit which has ended slavery, destroyed
kings, established democracy, public education and the
popular franchise, emancipated women, sought international peace, and today, in vast experiments of col-
lectivism, is laying deep and sure the foundations of
that economic security which will at last give freedom
to mankind.

It is from this point of view that the roots of our
contemporary civilization, which have blossomed into
this enlightened liberalism of our day, go far back into
the past.   It might be argued, in no wholly fantastic
sense, that the prophets of Israel were liberals, also
the seers of Greece and Rome, and the apostles of
Christianity.   The Middle Ages had their nascent the-

ories of popular rights. The Renaissance was a flower-
ing of the free mind, and the Reformation of the free
soul. The Puritan revolution in England, for all its
grim terror, had the liberal spirit in its heart; and the
second revolution of 1688 was accompanied by what
John Morley called "the reasoned vindication of liberal
principles" in the writings of John Locke. It was this
movement of democracy, accompanied by the influences of the French Illumination, which precipitated
the American Revolution, and then widened, like a
spreading flood, until it engulfed the western world.
Frenchmen, Englishmen, Germans remade their nations in the wake of Napoleon's vast upheavals. A generation of reaction served only to bring the outbreak
of 1848, and the far-flung liberation of the '60's and
'70's, which penetrated for a brief moment even the
dark fastnesses of Russia. By the last quarter of the
nineteenth century, liberalism had achieved a civilization. It had consolidated its victories and was preparing a final triumph, when forces which it had itself
released and not yet brought under control, produced
the incredible catastrophe of the Great War and its
aftermath.

If we ask what this liberalism was, and still is, we
may find it set forth in Thomas Carlyle's famous proclamation of "faith in the imperishable dignity of man,
and in the high vocation to which, throughout his
earthly history, he has been appointed." This faith
reveals itself in certain virtues—self-respect, self-re-
liance, tolerance, charity, justice, freedom, and brotherhood. It avoids certain vices—race prejudice, national
pride, class consciousness, intolerance, tyranny, and
violence. It seeks with single eye the establishment

of such social conditions as shall most speedily and permanently liberate men for the full and free expression of their essential individuality. The great success of liberalism has been in the political field, where effective institutions have been established for the organization and proper functioning of the common life. The great failure of liberalism has been in the economic field, where autocracy has enslaved man to poverty, and therewith undermined and destroyed all other liberties. The tragedy of liberalism has been its collapse under the impact of the surviving barbarism of war. Yet there endures the dream of that ideal commonwealth where war shall be no more, and poverty done away, and man shall no longer "labor in vain, nor bring forth for calamity," but live and love in the free expression of his own native being.

It is this dream which Hitler would destroy, this progress of the ages which he would undo. If life is worth living for enlightened men today, it is because of these ineffably precious possessions which have come to us from the free spirits of the past. If history can justify itself, it must be through the achievements of that liberal tradition which has slowly but surely emancipated the race. If there is such a thing as progress, it is to be found in that steady movement toward social stability and economic security which combine to release men for the "filling of their day." But all this Hitler would deny. He would go not forward, but backward a full thousand years. He would abrogate all modern liberties, restore all ancient tyrannies, and therewith destroy, as though by one fell blast of doom, all that man has achieved since he emerged, with infinite pain and loss, from out the abyss of the Dark

Ages.   And as though by the will of ironic gods, this
Nazi *Führer* has been let loose to work his spell upon
the most intelligent, enlightened, and highly cultured
people of contemporary Europe!

What Hitler would do, and as a matter of fact is
now doing, is to restore *the horde* of primitive and
savage days. We speak of the Nazi movement as nationalistic in character—a rebirth of an intense passion
for the separate nation as over against the single body
of humanity. But the nation is the product of a long
process of evolution. It contains within itself a myriad
differentiations of thought and life which are the sure
evidence of progress. While not the end of the historical process, which must be the ultimate production
of the world state, the nation represents a far stage of
advancement in this process. But Hitler would undo
the nation, as he would undo every other late achievement of man's days upon this earth. For what he is
concerned with is not nationalism, but tribalism. He
seeks to bring back upon the stage of history *the horde,*
which swamps all individuality in the human mass,
which lives one uniform life of iron discipline and
rigid custom, which yields obedience to one great chief
or lord, which marches armed with lust and hate against
the world, and which moves to destroy all evidences
of beauty, enlightenment, and culture.

If Nazism be not *the horde* rampant and triumphant, how else may we explain the repudiation by the
Nazi leaders of historic Christianity, pre-eminently in
its spirit a religion of liberal idealism wherein man
perhaps was first discovered in the full dignity of his
essential divinity, and the revival by these same leaders of the pagan faith which possessed the ancient Ger-

manic tribes when they roamed the trans-Rhenish and
trans-Danubian forests, and later broke the frontiers
to overwhelm the Empire? I find a supreme significance in this remarkable recrudescence in the modern
world of these primeval Nordic cults. On July 30 last
(1933), for example, more than 100,000 Hitlerites,
gathered in convention at Eisenach, declared their responsibility "for our Germanic origin before the divine
reality," and sought the restoration of Odin, Baldur,
Freia, and other Teutonic gods to the altars from which
they had been hurled by Christendom. Such reversion
to Wotan in place of God, and to Siegfried in place of
Christ, is not nationalism at all. It is something far
back of nationalism, back to the shadows of the dark
days and savage peoples. It is tribalism alive in our
world again—the return of a whole people to forms
of primitive paganism from which we had fondly imagined that mankind had escaped forever.

Hitler, I repeat, is bringing back *the horde*, restor-
ing the days and ways of barbarism. It is in this sense
that his movement is so terrible a menace to liberalism,
so ghastly an assault upon all the rich intellectual and
spiritual treasures of our age, a frontal attack upon civilization itself. In Hitler and his storm troops we find
the fulfillment of Lord Macaulay's famous prophecy
that, whereas the ancient civilizations were destroyed
by barbarian hordes which overwhelmed them from
without, our modern civilization may well be destroyed
by barbarian hordes bred deep within the womb of our
own life.

If Germany were alone in the hands of the Nazis,
we would not be disturbed, though the Hitler horror

would still remain one of the supreme catastrophies of modern times, and Germany itself a tragedy as terrible as Troy. But Germany is not alone, and cannot be alone. For weal or woe, she is a part of a close-knit modern world in which "whether one member suffer, all the members suffer with it." What is her present calamity, for example, but the harvest of the dragon's teeth sown in her soil by the pitiless victors of Versailles? And what may be her final disaster but a world disaster in which she drags down mankind in ruin with herself?

Since the Great War, Fascism has been darkening upon the West like a day of doom. Democracy has steadily retreated before the onsweeping hosts of tyranny and terror. Nation after nation has been engulfed by this advancing flood of fierce fanaticism. In Germany the crowning culture of our age has succumbed; and from Germany now spreads a pestilence to infect the world. This is a fight against the modern Black Death. Liberalism, democracy, civilization hang helpless in the balance. Helpless unless, before it is too late, there rallies to the defence of humanity's dearest treasures the awakened conscience and courage of mankind! A war, not of the flesh but of the spirit, is now our lot—reason against madness, culture against anarchy, civilization against barbarism, that mankind may at last survive the hour of its most dreadful trial.

THE REVOLT

AGAINST CIVILIZATION

BY LUDWIG LEWISOHN

My FRIEND, a blond and blue-eyed specimen of the
Nordic race, had come back from a three-weeks visit
to his native Hamburg. He walked up and down clasp-
ing his head. "The frontier of Europe and of civilization," he said in a voice hoarse with horror and grief,
"has been shifted from the Vistula to the Rhine. My
people is possessed by a demon." He did not know
how aptly, using a common phrase, he had chosen his
symbol. For a good many years now vast numbers of
Germans have been possessed by a demon. We shall
come to the psychological, to the more or less scientific background by and by. What justly horrifies the
world today is that demon, whose character is ill understood; it is what Thomas Mann, in a great warning
addressed to his people three years ago, called the "St.
Vitus dance of fanaticism," which since he spoke has
raged and ravaged—as such spiritual infections have
done before in history—like a forest fire or a pestilence.

The demon by which the German people is possessed is no night fear of the Middle Ages. To say, as
has been done, that National-Socialism is a throw-back
to medievalism is to misunderstand the movement. The

Reprinted by courtesy of Harper's Magazine.

demon is the old pagan demon which the Christian
Middle Ages sought to exorcise and to drive out forever. German nationalism today is a revolt against
Christianity in its broadest as well as in its deepest
sense; it is a pagan revolt against the whole of Christian civilization; it dreams, spinning like a dervish,
of Nordic armies overrunning the earth, of berserker
rage in battle, of the ecstasy of death and blood. To
think of the Nazis merely as hoodlums and fools stung
into action by hunger and demagogues is gravely to
under-estimate both the force and the menace of the
movement, which has its mad but highly articulate
prophets, which has at the core of its inner circle as
its ultimate leader (*Führer*), of whom the Hitlers and
Goebbels are only vulgar echoes, that extraordinarily
gifted poet, Stefan George. Many years ago George
prayed for Sicilian Vespers; in 1922 he called to his
disciples that it was too late, according to the decree
of heaven, for "patience or potion." No,

> Ten thousand must the holy madness seize,
> Ten thousand must the sacred pestilence slay
> And tens of thousands more the holy war.

Well, we are witnessing the "holy madness" and the
"sacred pestilence," are we not? Let us beware of the
"holy war."

I am not one of those who blankly assert that there
was no Jewish problem in Germany. Both Jews and
Gentiles had made mistakes. But there was no problem that decent and intelligent co-operation could not
have gradually solved. The "holy madness," however,
the demon of pagan revolt, had to wreak itself upon an
immediate and accessible object. And that object had
to be, however unconsciously, a symbol of all that was

to be destroyed; it had to be the symbol of peace and forgiveness; it had to be the symbol of the free personality alone with its God; it had to be the symbol of the critical intelligence, which the "holy madness" holds in especial abhorrence; it had to be non-pagan, anti-pagan, non-Germanic. It had to be the Jews. It had to be Jesus, the Jew. They could not crucify Jesus. They crucified the Jews. And that is the reason why Jews are not permitted freely to leave the hell that is made for them. If the Jews were not there to be tortured, upon what symbolical object could the "holy madness" wreak it self-justificatory pagan rage? Let no one say that I am being fantastic. The Catholic Church is profoundly aware of the pagan character of the German revolution and of its symbolical re-crucifixion of Christ. It was not for nothing that the Prince Bishop of Cologne pleaded for the Jews up to the last possible moment; it was not for nothing that the Cardinal-Archbishop of Paris commended the persecuted Jews of Germany to the prayers of the faithful of his diocese. These prelates were motivated by no shallow humanitarianism. They protested in the name of the human catholicity of the Church against the pagan-racist particularism of the Nazis; they protested against the symbolical pagan attack upon the very roots of the Judæo-Christian ethical and humane tradition.

Now let us examine the specific content of the "holy madness" of this pagan revolt. The chief article of its creed is the fanatical belief in the superiority of the Aryan-Germanic racial strain. All of the ills of Germany are due to the biological and spiritual contamination of this race by alien, specifically Mediterranean races, and their slavishness of soul. According to cer-

tain extremists of the neo-Nationalist movement, such
as Hielscher, author of *"Das Reich,"* the Mediterranean
Judæo-Christian contamination and corruption of this
Germany of today have gone so far and are so hopeless
that it were best to plunge the land into war after war,
to make it the battleground of the world, so that in
"nine times one hundred housand years" the pure German "substance," preserved in a few specimens, may
come into its ultimate triumph and apotheosis. (Please
understand: I am not caricaturing, but soberly report-
ing and translating.)   The most serious philosopher of
the movement, the late Professor Friedrich Wolters,
who taught at the universities of Marburg, Frankfurt,
and Kiel, who was the personally appointed chief disciple of George and who wrote two enormously influential books, *"Herrschaft und Dienst"* and *"Vier Reden
über das Vaterland,"* stopped short of Hielscher's epi-
leptic contortions. He was the more dangerous in that
he proposed definite aims: "We are and shall be forced
again to engage in a combat for life or death, survival
or annihilation, with those barbarian Gauls, whom
Cæsar described and overthrew, that people which
for some centuries has eaten away the Roman and Germanic racial substances, has wasted it in its revolutions
and now seeks to hurl itself upon its flourishing neighbor with all the vengefulness of subject and inferior
races, with all the bloodthirstiness of re-barbarized
Celts." This insane racial arrogance, it will be observed,
is directed not only against the Semitic or the colored
peoples, but against Latin and Celt as well.

Now the first step toward these wars and tumults
and conquests must be the re-purification of the German race from foreign blood and foreign faith, specific-

ally, from the Jews and from Christianity. The churches, keeping the superficial traditional nomenclature, are re-organizing from this point of view as Aryan, as Germanic churches. This is inevitable, since the Nazis openly repudiate the ethics of Jesus in favor of the virtues of their pagan ancestors. Thus the speech that Franz von Papen made at Münster the other day, and which rather horrified readers of newspapers everywhere, was nothing but a frank popularization of current Nazi doctrine: "Pacifist literature . . . does not understand the ancient Germanic horror of death in bed. . . . The representatives of the national revolution are men and soldiers who are physically and morally warriors." In so far as perhaps they are not yet all "morally" warriors, it will be seen to it that they become so by racial purification, by re-paganization, by conditioning their reflexes through blind obedience into the militarization of a whole people until the Germanic ecstasy of death in battle is the highest ideal of every German.

Again readers may think that I exaggerate. Luckily for our knowledge and for our being warned, Germany has professors. And one of these, Professor Alfred Bäumler, who holds the newly created chair of Political Pedagogics (!) at Berlin, has left no doubt concerning the aims of the Third Reich. "To the type of the educated man, which philosophy has hitherto sought to create, is to be opposed the type of the soldier. The soldier used to be considered as unintellectual (*ungeistig*), and it was not recognized that the army was an integral part of the education of our people. It was no idealistic and humanistic philosophy that won the battles of the World War; it was the inarticulate philosophy of the army. The aim of our new philosophy is to be the transcendence of the false antithesis: Spirit—Force." The treacherous misuse of philosophical terms can go no farther. The plain meaning of "the transcendence of the false antithesis: Spirit—Force" is the worship of naked brutality, when exercised by pure Nordic Germans, the repudiation of every moral scruple, of compassion, of shame, of humility. The universal goose-step of a slavishly obedient soldiery, psychically and physically taught to regard murder and rapine as the highest good, is the frankly avowed ideal of the Third Reich.

How very deep this pagan revolt with its worship of brutality goes is illustrated by the fact that the universities of Germany, once the strongholds of research and intellectual freedom, have been swept by a new theory of knowledge which justifies all the outrages of the Nazi student organizations and automatically eliminates all that has hitherto been known as either thought or science. According to this theory, there are no objective criteria of truth. Truth is arrived at by feeling, specifically by the feeling of uncontaminated Germans. Reason is to be "strictly in the service" of these Germanic institutions. Woe to him who sets up his reason against the Germanic intuition of his "leaders." And indeed, it is a fundamental principle of the redoubtable Wolters and his disciples that the new Germanic relation of absolute obedience to absolute command excludes independence of thinking. "The utter self-subjection of him who serves to the hero"—such was Wolters' definition of the spirit of the new Germany. That spirit, be it observed, is now leaving the studies of Nazi professors and is being embodied in every institution, in every organization in the Reich. The entire structure of German society is being recast with an astonishing rapidity. Everywhere parliamentary forms and technics of self-government have been abandoned. The nation has constituted itself into a mass of robots who roar and foam at the mouth and reel with berserker rage as the leaders, the *Führer*, the "heroes," press the emotional Germanic button. All non-Germans as well as all German political opponents are simply to be excluded, save as objects of just destruction, from the field of the true German consciousness. It is the duty of the German from now on, according to Hitler, the great popularizer himself, "not to seek out objective truth in so far as it may be favorable to others, but uninterruptedly to serve one's own truth."

Among the various consequences of this return of an entire society to a pagan, pre-Christian level, let me select one of very profound significance—the re-subjection of women. The principle of the slavish obedience of all males to their leaders evidently eliminates woman as a spiritual and intellectual factor in society. That she is to be so eliminated is the practical tendency of the Third Reich. This, like all the other fundamental traits and principles, was also announced long ago by the poet Stefan George:

Woman

Bears but the beast: man creates man and woman,
She being cursed or kind as his rib.
Leave her the mystery of inner order
Who on the marketplace is lawless outrage.
As in the book of books speaks the anointed
At very crisis of the world: "I am come
Utterly to destroy the woman's work."

"Woman bears but the beast—*Das Weib gebiert das Tier*"—that announces not only the lower merely physically generative function of woman; it announces equally the repudiation of Christian romantic love with its mutual respect and faithfulness. In actual practice many, many thousands of the younger National-Socialists are in fact substituting love and loyalty toward male-comrades and toward their leaders for the love of woman, who is limited to breeding and caring for the very young. As in Greece (note again the return to paganism) and as among certain very primitive peoples with their "men's houses," this society of heroes and henchmen, of leaders and blindly obedient warriors is to be an exclusively male society. After that it is scarcely necessary to add the notorious fact that the entire neo-nationalist movement has been from the start both deeply and broadly tainted by sexual perversity and its accompanying sadism.

That completes the picture of the results of the "holy madness" by which Germany is to be delivered and the world to be redeemed. Germans are, in quite the sense of the old-fashioned British colonizer, the only really "white men;" Germany is the land, according to George again,

> Where the all-blossoming Mother first revealed
> To the white race (corrupt since and grown wild)
> Her genuine countenance.

Well, the Christian-Mediterranean corruption is to be "cleaned out." The Germans, the "white men," the conquerors, welded together into an indistinguishable mass of heroes with but one impulse and but one will, glorying in the death of battle, ruthless to others by

the divine right of their Germanic purity, will set out
sooner or later to conquer and to save the world.

How, the reader may ask in our pleasant American
phrase—how did they get that way? How did it come
to pass that a good half of one of the very great and
spiritually productive contemporary peoples could fall
into a group-madness so brutal, so stupid, and so menacing to the rest of the world? No answer and no explanation can be complete. For we are back to the
old conundrum: which came first, the egg or the hen?
So we ask and have no answer: Does a people's character shape its history or does its history shape its character? Was it untoward circumstance or that character which *is* fate that kept the German people from
uniting as the French and the English did and entering
two centuries earlier the competition for world-trade
and colonial expansion? The fact remains that, especially since the founding of the Empire in 1870, the
German people have had the sense of having been unjustly and to their detriment left out of the great game
of the conquering powers and of having been somehow
wronged and disinherited. But always they had the
suspicion, whether conscious or not, that the facts they
deplored were rooted in some weakness of the national
character, some failure in the ability to unite, to show
a common front to the world, to concentrate their energies. The Nazi Government of today emphasizes and
condemns these old inner divisions and their consequences; it proposes, as I have shown, to weld all Germans into an indistinguishable mass; from the same
point of view it is hectically eliminating all traces of
Federalism from the structure of the German state, and

has reduced even Bavaria to the status of a Prussian Province.

Bet let us go back to that inner doubt which the Germans harbored, to their deep suspicion that it was something in their own character that had caused them to fall short when compared with the French, with the English. They have been for a long time a nation unsure of itself, infirm in self-esteem, harboring within the core of consciousness a profound self-distrust. But even as the individual will not admit a conviction of inferiority either to himself or to his fellows, but seeks to make up for it, to compensate and to over-compensate for it, and answers every doubt of his own worth by declaring that he is much better than the next man, so did the Germans from 1870 on seek—and in a thousand ways worthily and brilliantly—to compensate by achievement, by power, even by waving plumes and glittering arms for that rankling suspicion of inadequacy in their own breasts. But, again like a neurotic individual, they had no fortitude, which is the fruit of a calm selm-esteem. Whenever things went a little wrong, whenever the compensatory mechanism did not work perfectly, they lost their heads. Thus when the so-called *Gründerjahre* after the Franco-Prussian War —the fat years, in a word—were followed by lean ones and depression succeeded boom, there arose an anti-Semitic agitation which sought to fasten on the Jews (who lost—as I happen to know from the history of my immediate ancestors—their fortunes as quickly and thoroughly as anyone) the responsibility both for the crash on the exchanges and for the growth of Socialism among the masses. This agitation increased in fire and fury for a number of years, years which also included

Bismarck's notorious proscription of the Socialist Party in 1878. Returning prosperity brought a calmer and more reasonable state of mind. But the whole situation, a miniature counterpart of today's, made it clear enough that these modern Germans were afflicted with a neurosis that made it impossible for them to shoulder the responsibility for their own errors and misfortunes. They had to have a goat, a scapegoat, someone to whom to impute guilt and an evil eye. The Jews were handy and convenient, then as today.

Now it is a matter of common observation as well as of scientific fact that individuals who harbor a deep and wounded suspicion of their own inferiority cannot bear to assume responsibility for their own errors or sins, and hence are incapable of either humility or expiation. Desperately afraid that they will whine and creep, they clamor and strut; in their agonized practice of over-compensation they will be madly arrogant. But since they must hide the nature of this process from themselves, they must assign apparently rational causes and motives. Hence they must believe themselves to have been outrageously maltreated, especially in view of their extraordinary superiority to their fellows. The real superiority, which they often possess, does not suffice them. They must invent unheard-of virtues and merits for themselves; they must at the same time invent a mystic and malevolent author of their ills to serve them as enemy and scapegoat. Unable to bear the hard world of reality within which they are, like everyone else, a mixture of virtues and vices, of strength and feebleness, of good sense and folly, and in which it would behoove them to accept with a measure of serenity and good sportsmanship the conse-

quences of their errors and their sins, they withdrew
into a fictive world in which *they* alone are well-born
and virtuous and handsome and clever but in which
the conspiracies of evil and inferior forces corrupt
their wills and render vain their virtues. Into this neurotic world of their escape they will often incorporate
details from reality, a fact which makes it especially
difficult to clarify them concerning their delusions. It
is the structural and moral *pattern* of this fictive world
of theirs which so hopelessly falsifies and caricatures
the fact and patterns of reality. Who has not met such
individuals—so-called arrogant Jews, very often, into
whose soul has crept the universal disesteem of their
race, sensitive women unable to recover from some early
slight or moral mishap that his disturbed their psychical equilibrium?

The reader who has followed me so far already sees,
of course, the analogy and the lesson. What happens
to individuals can evidently happen to groups of individuals. And it is well understood by psychologists
from Gustave Le Bon on that in groups all psychical
mechanisms or technics are intolerably intensified and
coarsened at the same time. Many, many years ago,
leaning upon the absurd theories of the Frenchman
Gobineau, the Germans invented the defensive myth
of their racial superiority which dark and corrupt
races were seeking to destroy. They invented this myth
as a safeguard for the future. Nor is it without the
greatest significance that precisely toward the year
1914, as though out of a deep inner distrust and pre-
sage of its necessity for them, large numbers of Germans embraced this myth with a new intensity. The
War came, and the confidence in victory was, at least

in the upper strata of consciousness, sincere and universal, and William II declared that he knew neither races nor parties nor religious groups—only Germans. The Jews rose as one man to that apparently generous declaration; thousands volunteered before being called to the colors; before the War was over twelve thousand of them had laid down their lives in Poland and in Flanders. But 1916 came, and it was evident now that no easy victory was to be achieved. In anticipation of defeat and guilt the scapegoat was selected. An anti-Semitic member of the Reichstag named Werner demanded that the Jews be counted, to find out where these "slackers" were. The humiliating and discriminatory census was carried out. Its results were, from a militaristic point of view, supremely honorable to the Jews. Half of the more than sixty thousand Jewish soldiers were in front-line trenches. That made no difference. It was from now on at least subconsciously determined who was to bear the burden of Germany's defeat and shame, who was to be scapegoat and crucified one; to whom, in our good popular phrases, the buck was to be passed in order that the Germans might let themselves out. The thing clicks like a typical case-history out of the records of a psychiatrist.

The rest of the story unrolls itself easily. Defeat approached. A Jew, the late Albert Ballin, implored the Emperor to make peace on reasonable terms and committed suicide when his council was harshly rejected. Hunger came on account of the blockade and the cries that the Jews be crucified rose higher and higher. And the humiliating peace came with its nefarious war-guilt clause and its stupid and inhuman reparation clauses and its inexcusable tearing asunder of the eastern provinces of the Reich. Now the Germans had, as all the world was ready to acknowledge in recent years, genuine grievances. But alas the neurotic, individual or group, responds to real grievances not otherwise than to fancied ones. He will not deal with them directly and honorably. This is what the leaders of the German Republic from Ebert and Rathenau to Stresemann and even Brüning sought to do. And for that they were hated more and more bitterly by the increasingly soul-sick masses of the National-Socialist movement, who in ever-intensified frenzies finally persuaded themselves that Germany had been in actual fact not defeated at all, that neither the hunger blockade nor America's troops had had anything to do with the case, but that the gleaming unsullied warriors of the North had been betrayed and "stabbed in the back" in their homeland by these Republicans and Jews who alone were responsible for the otherwise impossible defeat of the Empire.

Incredible as it may appear to sane people elsewhere in the world, this myth is *believed*. On April 1, the Association of Nationalist-Socialist Women issued an announcement to its membership: "It is your duty to enlighten German women concerning the fact that Jewish propaganda was responsible for the outcome of the World War, for the two millions of our dead, for the old people, the women and the children who died of hunger, for Versailles and Dawes and Young." Not German mismanagement of the War nor a world in arms against them, but Jewish propaganda and the Republican-Socialist "stab in the back" were responsible. This myth is believed because it is fanatically believed that the superior Aryan German *could* not have been defeated except by treachery, and that even

this treachery served to undo him only because he had
consorted with Latins and with Jews and had permitted his lordly virtues to be tarnished by the slavish morals of Christianity (a vile Jewish invention) and by the
republican and libertarian fallacies of the West, introduced into Germany by international Jewry and unworthy of the noble descendants of the Nibelungen.
The whole thing would be more like a ghastly farce if
it did not constitute so grave a danger for human civilization, if it were not corrupting the souls and hopelessly addling the brains of a whole generation of the
German people. For it is clear today that they will
act according to their myths. They have begun. The
scapegoat is being slain; the Jew is crucified.

The repercussion of Germany's pagan revolt against
civilization in the sphere of practical politics and world-
peace is already very clear. Those who were most profoundly convinced of the utter stupidity and wicked-
ness of the provisions of Versailles are now afraid to
propose or support revision. Who would dare to place
one additional Pole or Jew under the Nazi heel? Who
would dare to favor equality of armaments for a nation
fanatically convinced that it would be helping to save
the world for the savior race of the Germans to "gas
in" (*einzugasen*) foreign provinces and exterminate
life where inferior races live and then replace them?
German politicians, even Hitler, will not use such language. They will repudiate with a certain superficial
sincerity the extremes to which their own mad myths
lead them. They will even play the game of international political decency when it suits their purposes.
But it will be a game. Nor will the cool heads of the

party—and there must be such—be able to restrain
the terrible forces of fanaticism which they have first
fed and next unleashed. It is possible, of course, that
the whole regime will crash through economic catastro-
phes. Meanwhile we are dealing with a people which
has indeed (this was *not* true in 1914) made both a
philosophical doctrine and a religious duty of ruthlessness.

It is this fact that constitutes the revolt against civilization. Take quite dispassionately the economic aspect of the Jewish question. Five hundred thousand
German citizens are being gradually but mercilessly
forced out of the economic life and structure of the
country. Nakedness and hunger are already very close
to thousands of them. The question was raised: "But
what, even on your own ground, do you expect these
people do do?" The *Völkischer Beobachter* of Munich,
the official organ of the Nazis, replied blankly that it
was nobody's business, and that these accursed "No-
mads" would manage, as they always did. But what
is actually happening is this, that Paris and Amsterdam and Zürich are flooded with penniless fugitives,
men, women, and children, and that Jews in all these
countries, as well as in England and America—Jews
who are integrated with the economic systems in which
they live—are forced in this poverty-stricken time to
give and give again and give more than they can afford to help their stricken brethren both within Germany and without. In brief, the Nazis are forcing the
other economic systems of the world to pay for their
jamboree. For since help is brought by civilized people to earthquake sufferers in Japan and famine-strick-
en coolies in China, it is clear that we cannot let a

group so highly civilized, so close to us in habit, speech,
sensitiveness, taste, and culture as the German Jews
simply die of hunger.

But it is precisely this order of sentiment, it is precisely this great classical tradition of the Christian
world that the neo-Nationalists of Germany are theoretically and practically repudiating.   In a hundred
manifestoes one hears again and again the summons
to be "hard"!   "We must once more learn to punish!"
is the slogan of the new ministry of justice.   So one
can well imagine the fate of those thousands of Republicans and Liberals and Socialists who are crowded in
the concentration camps.   To be hard on principle in
the name of one's own madly and neurotically con-
ceived superiority, to take delight in punishment, to
be unashamed of insane pride and the cruelty that it
engenders—is that not a pagan revolt against the whole
inner meaning of Western civilization, however, im-
perfectly, however haltingly that meaning has been
wrought out by us in practice?   Is it not an unbearable
repudiation of all that constitutes the one faint hope
of humanity? For that hope may be said to have arisen
when the unknown scribe recorded in Leviticus the
words: "Thou shalt bear love unto thy neighbor (I
translate the dative of the Hebrew text) as to thyself."
And this became the groundwork of the prophets from
Amos of Tekoa to Jesus of Nazareth.   And all the
sages of the Talmud and all the doctors of the Catholic
Church and all leaders of Protestant revolts and all
republicans and liberals and humanitarians and who-
soever in all our Western civilization had any vision of
goodness and the good life, any hope of better things
for mankind—all, all, whatever differences divided

them, united on this fundamental principle of the duty of love, of mercy, of forgiveness between man and his brother.   It is this foundation that the German neo-nationalists repudiate and seek to destroy.   They must meet an unbroken front of moral resistance in which all civilized men, irrespective of nation, race, or creed, wholeheartedly unite.

NAZI ECONOMIC POLICY

BY MAX WINKLER

WITH a peculiar disregard for cause and effect; a complete ignorance of the sequence of events or a marked paucity of information concerning them; a sad lack of familiarity with the philosophy of Hitler and his disciples; and perhaps also undue reliance on the word of those interested in the disposal of German bonds, issued primarily to facilitate the rehabilitation of the Reich, rendered bankrupt by the war and the economic consequences of the conflict, it has often been suggested that Nazi ruthlessness was a direct result of harsh treatment accorded to the vanquished by the victorious Allied Powers.

The exact contrary is the case. Whether or not the terms of the Versailles Treaty were commensurate with the enormity of Germany's guilt, need not be argued, because the victors did not hesitate to make a series of concessions which resulted ultimately in complete repudiation of reparations, with deplorable consequences to international amenities.

When, at the Spa Conference, the first reduction was made, Hitlerism was born. When the Dawes Plan authorized a still larger reduction and paved the way for dollar loans, the Hitler party registered substantial gains. When Germany was admitted to the League of Nations, and the sum of reparations cut still further, the Nazis became the third strongest party in the Reich.

When payments were suspended for one year, as a result of the so-called Hoover moratorium, Hitler's party advanced to second place; and when reparations were virtually eliminated at the Lausanne Conference, Adolf Hitler was called upon to guide the destinies of the Fatherland.

Now that the first year of the Hitler reign has come to a close, it is time to ask how he has kept the promises made to the German people and, indirectly, to the rest of the world.

Under date of December 6, 1933, in a copyrighted article published in some of America's leading newspapers, he boasted that "one of my chief aims is to restore the world wide credit of German commerce, industry, and finance," adding that he was "confident the world will soon feel vastly different about Germany when it is proven that her sole aim is to reconquer and create confidence in our entire business dealings."

To what extent Hitler, in the first year of his rule, has achieved these aspirations, may be gathered from the comment of one of Great Britain's leading statesmen, Sir Arthur Samuel, in connection with Germany's repudiation of contractual commitments almost immediately after the advent to power of the National Socialists. Says Sir Arthur: "Germany will not be able to raise money again in Great Britain, France, or the United States during our life time...Abuse of credit... has developed into abuse of confidence, amounting to nothing less than vulgar dishonesty ... Cold and selfish disregard of post-war obligations by the Prusso-German authorities . . . shocked all honest men . . . The arrogant trampling on the rights of others is all of a piece with the German mentality that led up to the World War and constitutes one of the worst cases of debt default."

Repudiation of debt contracts, one of the earliest demonstrations of Hitlerite policy, destroyed the ten-year growth of international friendship in as many weeks. A ruthless and exultant exercise of sovereign power made this act possible, but was powerless to save the country from suffering the consequences, even though it may for the moment enjoy the dubious benefits derived from the withholding of funds rightfully due its foreign creditors.

While it may be possible, by means of special decrees, to deprive certain citizens of their rights; to suppress public opinion; to torture those who hold views at variance with the men in power; or to send people to concentration camps solely on racial and religious grounds, even the most despotic ruler has not been able to issue an edict or promulgate a decree which could defy the laws of economics. These are far more cruel than the cruellest of tyrants, and while a despot may succeed in effecting a change in a nation's economic and fiscal structure, such change cannot but be transitory in character, and those who are responsible for it will, sooner or later—and as a rule sooner than is generally anticipated—be called upon to pay the inevitable penalty.

Germany must be converted into an economic paradise! Such was the decree issued by Adolf Hitler, who failed to appreciate that in order to make a people prosperous, it is necessary to consider all sorts of factors over which even a Hitler has no control. By rea-

son of its position, the Reich depends to a very large
extent on foreign trade. Germany's economic status
can, therefore, best be appraised in the light of statistics
pertaining to foreign commerce.

If the country buys and sells in increasing volume,
the nation prospers, and conversely, if trade is stagnant,
the nation suffers. It may, of course, be possible for
a time to divert the attention of the masses from the
difficulties which confront them. It may be possible
to keep hundreds of thousands of youths occupied with
marches, parades, and torchlight processions; to amuse
them by frequent changes in the color of their uniform; to arouse their patriotic instincts by referring
to the grandiose victories which German armies have
to their credit, and that the World War would surely
have resulted in the complete defeat of the Allies, had
not Germany been betrayed at home by the liberals and
Marxists and pacifists; to excite their racial enthusiasm
by reminding them of Thor and Wotan, and Loki and
all other deities in Valhalla; to assure them of the superiority of the German soil and of the German race—
all this may be possible for a time, but even the most
patient are bound to tire of the sameness of the act.
They will tire of the circus and will demand bread.

In the commercial history of practically all nations,
1932 was a very sad year indeed. No country proved
immune from the economic onslaught. All suffered.
America, with all her resources, was just as much subject to the crisis as was impoverished Germany. The
advent of the Nazis was to put an end to Germany's
plight. Let us see how they have succeeded.

While sales of German goods during 1932 averaged
473,100,000 marks a month, the first year of the Hitler

reign witnessed a decline in the monthly average to
405,900,000 marks, a shrinkage of well over fourteen
percent. Her imports, that is, Germany's purchases
abroad, declined during the first Hitler year approximately ten per cent, while total commerce registered
a shrinkage of about twelve and one-quarter per cent
compared with 1932. These losses would not appear
particularly distressing, were it not for the fact that
1933 was characterized by material improvement the
world over. Furthermore, the losses would be much
more marked, if German trade were carried on as hon-
estly as is that of other countries. This statement
should not be interpreted to mean that German trade
statistics are not reported accurately. The accuracy of
the figures as furnished by the German Government
or the various Government-controlled agencies is not
questioned. Owing to the ban on the export of capital
from Germany, regardless of who may be the owner,
and owing to the refusal of the German Government
to meet contractual engagements abroad, notably those
outstanding in the hands of the American public, merchants in countries dealing with Germany are placed in
a position where they may acquire German goods at
distinctly advantageous prices.

The scheme is approximately as follows: Funds held
in Germany, belonging either to Germans or to foreigners, and which cannot be taken out of the country,
are designated as blocked marks—that is, marks which
belong to the owner, but which he cannot obtain. If
one wishes to dispose of them, regardless of price, the
German Government makes such transaction possible
on two conditions: First, that the sale is effected at a
price substantially below the figure at which the Ger-

man currency is officially quoted; and, second, that the purchaser employ the marks so acquired for buying German goods, for traveling on German boats, for living expenses in Germany, or for staying at German resorts. Since the discount on blocked marks varies from about twenty to as high as fifty per cent of the official price, it is possible to purchase German goods at half the actual price.

Is it not, therefore, most astonishing, to say the least, to find that in spite of the abnormally attractive price at which one may shop in Germany, the country's sales abroad have not only not gained over 1932, but have actually declined by about one billion marks?

A novel instance of government interference, probably unique in the annals of finance, is the offer made recently to American holders of German bonds, outstanding at about one billion dollars, by the German Government through Hjalmar Schacht, head of the Reichsbank, Germany's Central Bank of Issue. Pleading that the Government is lacking sufficient foreign exchange to meet payment in full, Americans are asked to accept thirty per cent of the amount due them in cash, and a check for the remaining seventy per cent in marks, which the Government would repurchase from the owner at sixty-seven per cent of the face value, with the understanding that this transaction will result in the purchase of "supplemental" German goods. In other words, the Government is unwilling to redeem its own promise to pay at more than two-thirds. Financial integrity, thy name is Hjalmar Schacht!

If it were possible to ascertain with accuracy the amount represented by German goods purchased with money acquired at a huge discount, an even more discouraging story would have to be told. The importance of foreign trade on the Reich's status may be gauged by a recent statement by the *Berliner Handels-Gesellschaft*, one of Germany's leading financial institutions, as follows: "The question whether it will be possible in the coming year (1934) to reduce unemployment at as rapid a pace as during recent months depends to an appreciable extent on foreign trade developments. For Germany, even a modest improvement of export figures which, in turn, will lead to a further increase of imports, would in the circumstances afford a particularly welcome stimulus."

The above policy of juggling with the nation's money has been instituted by the same Doctor Schacht, pre-eminent amongst financial tricksters, who in the early years following the Great War originated and adopted a deliberate policy to wreck the German currency, thus reducing to the vanishing point, not alone the mark, but also all bonds and shares the value of which was expressed in marks.

Carried to almost inconceivable lengths, this holocaust came to an end only when the cost of printing fraudulent paper money exceeded the amount for which it could be sold. Into it were thrown two billions of gold dollars, largely by Americans, including many of German descent whose faith in the Fatherland's financial integrity was so ingrained that no warnings could shake it.

Even after this infamous campaign had proved successful far beyond Dr. Schacht's fondest hopes, a powerful section of public opinion in the United States continued to commiserate with the lachrymose German Government and was particularly outspoken in its criticism of the victorious Allies who, knowing Germany far better than America knew her, had imposed an indemnity which was large enough to warrant the belief that the country would think twice before provoking another conflict.

Demands for the rehabilitation of the Reich became insistent and clamorous, provoked doubtless in part by holders of neat packets containing hundreds of million-mark notes, who believed that therein lay their own chances of enrichment. And, so it came to pass that Americans became the prime movers for the restoration of Germany's fallen credit. It was American bankers who underwrote upwards of one and three-quarter billion dollars of the obligations of the Reich, the various German states, cities, and corporations, and it was the American public who absorbed the bonds, proceeds of which were employed to rebuild Germany, to replenish the working capital of German enterprises, to restore German shipping, and to revive German trade.

Oblivious to the tremendous sacrifices imposed by the war, and to the staggering losses incurred in more recent years by foolish reliance on the contention of German spokesmen, such as Hjalmar Schacht, that the Reich would always honor the sanctity of international commercial obligations, American investors, through their dollars, converted into a solvent and relatively prosperous nation a country which, up to only a short while ago, has been hopelessly insolvent and completely at the mercy of its surrounding foes.

So blindly infatuated were American investors nine years ago with the fixed idea that any German bond offered in New York was a security of the highest order, that the most diffident expressions of doubt regarding its sanctity were received with contumely.

This sanguine expectation endured until the actual consummation of default last year. As late as April 7, 1933, that "reliable" Nazi spokesman, Doctor Hjalmar Schacht, told the Reichsbank shareholders: "Whatever may be the effect of the Reichsbank's policy as a result of the shrinkage of Germany's export surplus and the consequent depletion of the nation's gold reserves, Germany must stand by her commercial foreign debt to preserve confidence abroad, which she will need in future trade relations."

Contrast this noble attitude with Doctor Schacht's utterance exactly eight months later, as reported by the press:

"Maintaining the well-known stand that the decision about the payment of her debts *was the sovereign right of Germany herself,* Doctor Schacht notified the creditors that some time before the end of December he would announce new terms of the moratorium applicable for the next six months.

"According to an official communique, these terms will depend on whether 'in *his* opinion the Reichsbank is in a position to maintain the transfer of interest payments at its present level or not.' "

Have the creditors of Germany no voice in the matter? Has the German debtor the sole right to decide on the type of treatment which is to be accorded those who loaned the funds? One thing is clear: *In two gigantic raids, Doctor Schacht despoiled those who trusted him. In the first of these, his fellow countrymen were included among the dupes; but in the second*

they were given an opportunity to recoup their losses.
Americans were the victims on both occasions.

It would seem futile to speculate as to what would
have occurred in Germany, had the former government been permitted to continue. Is it not within
reason to assume that the gains which have been recorded practically everywhere might also have been
registered in Germany? In other words, the interference resulting from the political transformation of the
Reich has not only not helped conditions, but has actually retarded and delayed the progress of which there
was considerable evidence in the latter part of 1932.

Great Britain which was not blessed by a government
of the Adolf Hitler type, for example, reported for
1933 an increase in exports compared with 1932, while
the country's total trade last year declined from the
previous year's figures somewhat less than two and five-
eighths per cent. France, another important nation,
whose problems are being solved without the aid of
Hitler, reported in her 1933 trade a loss of only about
five and one-third percent, compared with 1932, while
her sales abroad declined less than five and one-half
percent. In the United States, last year's total trade increased almost four per cent over the previous year
while sales abroad declined only eight-tenths of one
per cent.

German-American trade for the past year is particularly enlightening. The figures presented hereunder
pertain to American purchases from Germany, as reported by the United States Bureau of Foreign and Domestic Commerce, converted into marks at the average
rate of exchange for each month. Values for 1932 are

shown at par, or 23.8 cents to the mark. The period under review is that of the Hitler administration until the end of last year.

AMERICAN IMPORTS FROM GERMANY
(In Reichsmarks)

Month	1933	1932	Decline (In %)
April	18,900,000	27,300,000	30.77
May	18,500,000	22,000,000	15.91
June	23,700,000	20,900,000	13.40*
July	23,300,000	18,800,000	23.93*
August	26,200,000	23,900,000	9.62*
September ...	23,900,000	28,400,000	15.85
October	21,700,000	30,000,000	27.67
November ...	17,200,000	26,800,000	35.82
December	18,300,000	19,900,000	8.04
Total....	191,700,000	218,000,000	12.16

In the face of general business improvement the world over, American purchases from Germany registered a decline of well over twelve per cent for the last nine months of the past year; but for the four months, September to December, the shrinkage amounts to nearly twenty-three per cent.

Reference to the same high statistical authority yields an exceedingly imposing disclosure of trade advancement during the entire year 1933, as compared with the preceding year, in respect to six leading nations and Germany.

America's imports from Argentina for 1933 show a gain of more than one hundred sixteen per cent over

* Denotes increase.

the 1932 figures. The gain in American purchases in Great Britain amounted to almost forty-nine percent. Imports from Sweden increased twenty-six and one-half per cent; from Russia, slightly less than twenty-five per cent; from Switzerland, about sixteen and one-quarter per cent; and from France, more than eleven per cent. The gain in American imports from Germany in 1933 amounted to only six and one-third per cent compared with 1932 figures. These statistics would seem to suggest that American purchases which have heretofore been taken care of in Germany, are now being effected in other parts of the world.

The new Government and its spokesmen point with pride and satisfaction to the marked decline in the number of unemployed, reported officially a year ago at about six millions. At the beginning of the current year, one-third, or two millions, are said to have found employment. Although it is a known fact that, during the past year, a good many unemployed were simply taken off the unemployment lists, it is of interest to observe that the number of those reported out of work is somewhat at variance with the number of those who are said to have found employment.

To illustrate: At the beginning of November, 1932, the number of unemployed was given as 5,109,000; at the beginning of the same month last year, the number declined to 3,745,000, a reduction of 1,364,000. At the same time, according to official statistics, the number of those who were employed at the beginning of November, 1932, amounting to 12,915,000, increased to 14,062,000 by November, 1933—a gain of 1,147,000. What has become of the 217,000 who, according to the above report, should have found new employment, a fact which is not apparently corroborated by another report? Is it perhaps an oversight on the part of one of the numerous governmental bureaus which are to enlighten the world as to the progress registered by the Fatherland while under the overlordship of Hitler?

Leaving out of consideration the measures adopted, as well as the method of computation employed, the number of Germany's unemployed, on the basis of one set of figures, shows a decline of twenty-six and one-half per cent. One may, however, inquire whether Germany is the only country which has been successful in reducing unemployment, and whether the achievement, even assuming the accuracy of statistics, is unique among nations. Has not during the same period, unemployment in the United States declined thirty-three per cent? Has not unemployment in the United Kingdom declined twenty-two per cent? Has not the Kingdom of Denmark succeeded in reducing the number of its unemployed more than thirty-two per cent?

The significance of the above figures relating to German trade is further attested to by a set of statistics contained in a recent issue of the *Institut für Konjunkturforschung* pertaining to industrial production and consumption in the Reich for the past two years. Total industrial output for 1933 is given as 19,400,000,000 marks, compared with 17,500,000,000 marks, an increase of 1,900,000,000 marks or about nine and three-quarters per cent. On the other hand, consumption declined from 21,400,000,000 marks in 1932 to 21,000,000,000 last year, a shrinkage of 400,-000,000. Is it to be wondered at that Germany is desperately trying to dispose of a steadily growing inventory?

Commenting on this state of affairs, Joachim Haniel, a prominent European economist and interpreter of economic phenomena, has this to say: "Nothing illustrates more clearly the whole artificiality and inner weakness of the economic structure created by Hitler. The Government is handing out important orders by greatly expanding the budget, by resorting to the printing presses (à la 1919-1923?), and by the utilization of all public and semi-public bank credits. As a result of extreme pressure, the Government compels industry to produce on a large scale goods which are not needed, and the output of which is therefore uneconomical. The result of this effort is the equalization of a decline in consumption, brought about by heavy taxation and exploitation of the laboring classes. In order that the decline in consumption may not exert too great an influence upon labor, industry as a whole, from the heads of the important enterprises to the smallest merchant and storekeeper, is compelled senselessly to accumulate unnecessary inventories."

The extent to which labor is being exploited may be gathered from a Berlin report, according to which an employee of the Berlin Elevated Company received his wage, but not without various deductions including *Krankenkasse* (sickness insurance), *Gewerkschaft* (organization contribution), *Winterhilfe* (Winter relief) . . . (and) *Für das Feuerwerk am 1, Mai* 1933, *Mark* 1 (for fireworks on May 1, one mark). One wonders whether Americans who helped finance the Berlin Elevated by a $15,000,000 bond issue, placed with investors through a syndicate headed by Speyer & Company, ought not to raise a protest against what appears to be a disregard of their privileges as creditors.

What is also most difficult, if not altogether impossible, to explain, is the fact that in spite of a marked reduction in the unemployment figures, the wage index has not changed correspondingly. Statistics for August, 1933, show a decline from August, 1932, of about two per cent. In other words, the aggregate wage paid German labor has only not increased, but has actually declined.

Were the improvement in the Reich of a genuine, that is, permanent character, statistics relative to production would be accompanied by corresponding gains in consumption. This is not the case. On the contrary, the consumption of goods has definitely gone down. The same is true of the national income, as officially estimated. The latest figures are those covering the first half of 1933, amounting to 22,350,000,000 marks, which compares with 23,670,000,000 for the same period in 1932, and with 22,800,000,000 for the first half of 1932.

With foreign trade declining, with wages lower, with the national income shrinking, and with consumption receding, one is curious to find the reasons which prompt the thoroughly Nazified German press to talk of an improvement in Germany's economic status, or rather an improvement in the position of the German people. The question one is temped to ask is: Where do funds come from which enable the Government to carry on the work? Who is taking care of the distinctly non-productive outlay of from three to five million marks a day required to house, feed and clothe the hundreds of thousands of marching Germans led by Hitler.

The economy of the Reich does not permit of, nor can it stand an expenditure of about one and one-half billion marks a year. Some of the funds are doubtless derived from moneys belonging to the creditors of Germany, from whom interest and amortization are now being withheld. This, however, accounts for only a part of the total outlay. Is it possible that the balance, or most of it, is being financed by the same method which Germany employed in the early post-war period, and which, thanks to the assistance rendered by the same Hjalmar Schacht who runs German finances today, resulted in the deterioration and ultimate collapse of the mark, costing Germans and non-Germans (notably Americans) hundreds of millions of dollars, which became irretrievably lost? The desire on the part of owners of marks tied up in Germany, to dispose of them, despite the large discount, may bear out this hypothesis.

That commentators on German conditions are much bewildered by what is going on, is evident from the experience of a prominent American economist. After pointing out that "Nazi official statistics are to be received most cautiously (especially as to employment)," that "a most generous scope must be allowed for dubitation," and that one ought to discount "manipulation of statistics" and make allowances "even for downright mendacity," the observer in question, realizing the futility of giving too much credence to Nazi reports, concludes a none-the-less illuminating review of "the first instalment of the Hitler four-year plan" as follows:

"It is with much regret that I must omit further discourse concerning the debts (how, for example, Germany is immensely profiting by the devalution of the dollar), the foreign trade (with so many fascinating facts), unemployment (a study in bunkum), the Reichsbank (balancing on a razor edge), and the fisc."

The next few months are bound to furnish more dependable information.

THE BROWN

INTERNATIONAL

BY EMIL LENGYEL

"THE German Reich as a State," wrote Adolf Hitler in *"Mein Kampf"*, "must embrace all Germans in the service of the task of collecting and preserving the most valuable ingredients of the primordial elements (*Urelemente*) of the race, slowly but surely guiding them to a dominating position."

National Socialism is based primarily on the race, and not on the idea of the State. Its leaders owe their position not to their citizenship, which many of them acquired in recent times, but to the "quality of their blood."

Adolf Hitler is an Austrian by birth and he became a German citizen only in the Spring of 1932. His representative and next in command in the National Socialist Party, Rudolf Hess, a Minister of the Reich, was born in Alexandria, Egypt, and was taken to Germany at the age of fourteen. Dr. Alfred Rosenberg, cultural chief of the Third Reich, head of the "Foreign Office of the Brown House," and editor of the *Voelkische Beobachter*, was born in Reval, then in Russia and now in Estonia, and he became a German citizen after the war. Walther Darré, Minister of Agriculture in the Hitler cabinet and organizer of the Nazi farmers, was born in Belgrano, Argentina, and was taken to Germany at the age of ten. Ernst F. S. Hanfstaengel, liaison officer of the Third Reich with the foreign press, and more recently head of the *Nationalgalerie* in Berlin, is the son of an American mother.

National Socialism is thus a misnomer and its correct name should be "International" National Socialism. Since it is the race that counts, and not one's citizenship, all Germans and other Nordics should belong to the Third Reich, irrespective of the place of their residence. Nearly fifteen million "Germans" are in Austria, the Baltic lands, Czechoslovakia, and Switzerland. "We demand the union of all Germans in a greater Germany according to the right of self-determination," says the first article of the program of the National Socialist German Workers' Party.

About twenty-four million "Nordics" live in the adjacent small countries: parts of Belgium, Holland, and the Scandinavian peninsula, and their place is in a racially pure Third Reich. "Germany from the Alps to Upsala" is the dream of some big-wigs of the Nazi party, especially of Dr. Alfred Rosenberg, a champion of the blond man's supremacy.

Before coming to power, the Hitlerites showed great resourcefulness in devising plans to draw their fellow Germans and Nordics into the orbit of the Third Reich. Some of the leading Nazis suggested that the *Auslandsdeutsche*, foreign citizens of German blood, should be granted the right to vote at the Reich's elections. This plan had to be dropped, however, when it was realized that in the Third Reich not even German citizens would have the right to vote. More extreme partisans hoped for a general uprising in the neighboring countries in

favor of a Greater Third Reich.   Under the Nazi racial
theory, the ancestors of an *Auslandsdeutsche* may have
lived abroad for centuries without their offspring losing their right to be called Germans.

It was after the great Nazi Reichstag victory of September, 1930, that the idea was first broached in Hamburg to unite all Germans living abroad.   Less than a
year later the Foreign Section of the party was in full
operation.   Its story was told by Ernst Wilhelm Bohle,
leader of the Foreign Section.   Its first object was to
build up a system of propaganda key points, *Stütz-*
punkte.   In the middle of 1933, it had about 230 national groups and key points in all parts of the world,
which were supplied with Nazi news items and editor-
ials by the central propaganda department. In addition
to this, every German ship was drafted into service as
a floating center of Hitlerite propaganda.

What is the present status of the Brown International?   What measures have the continental governments
taken to combat this menace?   We shall speak of Hitlerism in every case where the racial element predom-
inates, leaving out of account the Mussolinian variety
of Fascism.   Since the Fascist movements in England,
Ireland, Spain, and Portugal are not dominated or to
any serious extent tinged by the Nazi concept of race,
we shall not discuss the Brown International in relation to these countries.

Austria with her nearly seven million Germans, is
domestic territory, so far as the German Nazis are concerned.   For years after the World War, the Alpine republic had sought union with the Reich, the *Anschluss,*
which the Peace Treaties had outlawed.   As soon as

the Hitler Government assumed power in Berlin, the
Nazis set about "co-ordinating" Austria. *Gleichschaltung* was of vital importance to them, as it would increase German territory by more than thirty thousand
square miles at eastern central Europe's most strategic
point, from where they could dominate the Danube
valley and guard the approaches to the Balkans. Thus
Germany's *Drang nach Osten* would be gratified. Austria's possession would give an inestimable advantage
to the Reich over Czechoslovakia, which it would embrace as the tongs embrace a nail. For Hitler the
Anschluss was also a matter of personal prestige. He
wanted to exchange his status of a naturalized citizen
of Austrian origin for that of a full-fledged German.

Austria, however, reversed her former attitude toward the *Anschluss.* Catholic Austrians did not relish
the idea of being trampled underfoot, as were Catholic
Bavarians. Nor did Austria fall in love with the prospect of becoming an appendage of Prussia, realizing
that this would be her fate after the Hitler Government
had set up a strongly centralized government, and had
done away with the individual States. At the same
time, the Austrian politicians were not slow in realizing
the danger for their own interests of the Hitlerite
hordes descending upon Vienna and capturing the
choicest jobs. The Socialists of the capital, who form
the largest part of its population, and the Jews of
Austria, who are highly influential, had their own excellent reasons for fearing the victory of Hitlerism.

The German Hitlerites went to work in Austria with
their high-pressure methods. The propaganda bureaus
of Munich began to work overtime, devising new
schemes for the conquest of Vienna. The wireless sta-

tion of the Bavarian capital invaded the air with martial music and patriotic speeches in order to win the kinsman's heart. In the Tyrolean mountains the flames of burning swastikas lighted the night and on the top of Hafelekar, across Innsbruck, the Hakenkreuz defied the inhabitants of the valleys. University youth displayed its Nazi emblem and the personnel of the railways, the police and even the judiciary was honeycombed with Hitlerites. The streets resounded with the cries: *Heil Hitler! Dollfuss verrecke!*

If foreign countries had not taken an interest in Austria's case, she would long ago have been engulfed by Hitlerism. Since the beginning of 1933, a Second World War has been fought on Austrian territory—a diplomatic World War. The idol of the German Chancellor, Signor Mussolini, entrenched himself behind the Treaty of Versailles, which forbade the *Anschluss*. Even though Herr Hitler claimed him as his master, Il Duce saw the danger of a militaristic Germany becoming Italy's neighbor on the Brenner Pass. He had to think of South Tyrol, with her race-conscious German population, now belonging to Italy. Besides, the dictator of the Italians has his own dreams of a *Drang nach Osten*, which can become a reality only by his having access to the Balkans.

France also showed great interest in keeping Hitler from Vienna. The sanctity of the treaties was involved, not to speak of the safety of her eastern allies: Czechoslavakia and Yugoslavia. Even England was concerned, because of the balance of power which London was afraid would be disturbed by Germany's occupation of Austria.

Dr. Engelbert Dollfuss, Austria's miniature Chancellor, knew how to capitalize foreign fears. From the London Conference he obtained forty million dollars for his country. He had the sympathetic attention of Mussolini, the affectionate interest of the French Premier and the respect of Downing Street. At home, he countered Hitler's high-handed methods with simliar measures. Taking advantage of a mistake of the Socialist opposition, he dismissed parliament and assumed dictatorial powers. He put the press under rigorous censorship and abolished the freedom of speech and assembly. After having outlawed the Nazi party, he copied Hitler's concentration camps and deprived Austrian Nazis of their citizenship. He re-discovered Austrian nationalism, which he tried to instil into his fellow countrymen with methods learned from Dr. Joseph Goebbels, the Reich's Minister of Propaganda.

At the time of writing, in February, 1934, Austria is still under Chancellor Dollfuss' dictatorship. He has all but smashed the organization of the Austrian Social Democrats, who had formed the largest party of the republic. The Chancellor's own Christian Socialist Party seems to have gone into eclipse. He is working with the *Heimwehren*, a Fascist organization *à la* Mussolini, whose leaders detest the Marxists and hate the Jews, although their emotions are less violent than those of the Hitlerites. At the last parliamentary election, in November, 1930, the *Heimwehren* returned to the *Nationalrat* only eight deputies out of a total of 165. This shows that the Dollfuss dictatorship has no basis, and it is being kept alive by the opposition of foreign powers to German National Socialism's encroachments upon Austrian sovereign rights and the fear of a large part of the city population of Hitler terror. Meanwhile, anti-Semitism which was never lacking in Austria, is assuming more serious proportions.

What is the Nazi situation across the Austrian frontier, in Czechoslovakia? It was in those parts—known before the World War as Bohemia—that the original National Socialist Party was fathered by two German bookbinders, Ludwig Vogel and Ferdinand Buschofsky, in the nineties of the last century. Hitler's Nazism is the successor of their movement. How has National Socialism fared at its birthplace?

The two original Nazis had little luck. Soon after they had begun to co-operate with Georg von Schoenerer's anti-Semitic All-German Party, they dropped out of sight. A few years later, in 1904, a German Labor Party was founded in the Moravian parts of Austria with a somewhat similar program, and it succeeded in electing to parliament a young engineer, Rudolf Jung.

In the last year of the World War this group adopted a new name: "German National Socialist Party of Austria." Rudolf Jung was among the first ones to teach Adolf Hitler the hatred of the Jew—the enemy of Germany and friend of western democracy. Then Bohemia became Czechoslovakia and Jung also became a Czech citizen. He is a member of the Prague parliament, a National Socialist at heart, although he has not followed his former disciple all the way. Jung's anti-Semitism is less violent and he is not opposed to democracy.

In August, 1933, Professor Theodor Lessing, formerly of the Hanover Technical College, a German émigré, was assassinated in the Czechoslovak city of Marienbad by two German Nazis of the neighborhood. This aroused public opinion, which until then had been inclined to minimize the Hitler danger, and the Prague government took recourse to dictatorial measures. The number of National Socialists among Czechoslovakia's three and a half million Germans has never been ascertained. Most of the Germans of the republic are Socialists and Agrarians, who are opposed to Hitlerism.

The German Nazis of Czechoslovakia sought to escape the government's punitive measures by forming a sporting club, the *Volksport,* but the authorities were not deceived. Then the leaders of the club made an attempt to transform it into a so-called National Front, uniting all non-Marxist German parties in Czechoslovakia. When this manoeuvre also failed, they made a last minute move to form a Patriotic Front. This also proved to be a fiasco and the Hitler party was dissolved, several of its leaders arrested and their newspapers suppressed. In the middle of January a few Nazi leaders made an effort to resurrect the movement, but were tracked down by the Prague police.

Switzerland, with her 2,700,000 German-speaking Swiss, seemed to offer excellent opportunities for Nazi propaganda. Fascism took there the form of *Fronten,* which are facing the difficulty of reconciling the national and linguistic diversities of the Confederation in the interests of political and anti-Semitic reaction. The Front of National Socialist Confederates (*Eidgenossen*) is closest to Hitlerism. Members of this Front call themselves Confederates, because the designation "Swiss" does not convey to them the idea of a community of blood. The Confederate symbol is the swastika which, they like to explain, is not a German but an ancient Nordic emblem. Their slogan is: *Schweizerland Wach' Auf!* Although they want to exclude the

Jews from Nazi Switzerland's community life, they have
not yet adopted the Hitlerite slogan: *Juda verrecke!*

Students, intellectuals, and young peasants are among
the originators of the Front movements, the best known
of which are: *Eidgenoessische Front, Jungbauern,
Kampfbund Neue und Nationale Front, Neue Schweiz,
Ordre et Tradition, Union Nationale.*

"Shall Switzerland or our canton be our fatherland?"
asked *Ordre et Tradition,* the Front of the Canton of
Vaud. "Only the canton may be considered our fatherland," it answered its own question, "since it unites the
totality of all moral and economic forces, and has a
well-developed and full-grown civilization which
Switzerland herself lacks."

A fat Jew, representing the Capitalist, and a wild-
eyed Jew, representing the Bolshevist, looked down
upon Zurich from the posters of the *Vaterlandische
Front* at the autumn elections of 1933. The hoardings
of a German city could not have looked more anti-
Semitic. Yet the Front was beaten badly and its enemies, the Socialists, gained. The Hitlerites lost also in
Geneva and Lausanne, where the Marxists scored important victories.

If it had not been for the revelations in the English
press of a German plan to march through Switzerland
in the Second World War, the *Fronten* might have had
a measure of success. These revelations were officially
brought to the country's attention by Rudolf Minger,
head of the War Department. In October, 1933, the
Swiss National Council appropriated twenty million
francs for the army, representing the first part of an
appropriation of a hundred and twenty millions, asked
for by Minger. Even the Socialists declared their will-

ingness to abandon their pacifist attitude in an effort
to ward off the Nazi menace. German raiding parties
into Swiss territory were countered with instructions
to the frontier guards to shoot the invaders.

On the night of December 29, 1933, a young Hitlerite, shot dead Ion G. Duca, Prime Minister of Rumania,
as he was awaiting a train at the Sinaia railway station,
after an interview with King Carol. His murderer,
Radu Constantinescu, turned out to be a member of
the Hitlerite Iron Guard. He boasted that he had committed the crime because Duca was a friend of the
Jews. The search of Iron Guard headquarters brought
to light a blacklist of some of the most prominent statesmen of the country, such as Foreign Minister Nicholas
Titulescu, who were also to be assassinated. Although
the King's mistress, Mme. Helen Lupescu, is also a
Jewess, her name was not on the list.

"Jesus, King, and Nation," was the slogan of the
Iron Guard. Its head was Cornelius Zela Codreanu,
who had qualified for this position by murdering the
prefect of Jassy "because he favored the Jews." The
original name of the Rumanian Hitler organization was
"Guard of Archangel Michael," and their emblems were
the pistol and crucifix. In order to keep up with current fashion, they wore green shirts, Hitlerite belts,
and red brassards with blue swastikas on yellow ground
—the Rumanian national colors.

"The basis of our program is a hundred per cent
anti-Semitism," said Professor Paulescu, a Rumanian
Hitlerite, in an interview with a representative of the
Paris *Excelsior*. "The Jewish element is destructive
of State and society."

"What would you do with the Jews if you came to power?"

"I would expel them all, without exception."

The French publicist, Pertinax, charged in the *Echo de Paris* that previous to Duca's murder, the German Hitlerites had spent about thirty million lei in Rumania. He also made the charge that N. Jonescu, editor of the Bucharest Nazi newspaper, *Conventul*, which had made a nuisance name for itself by propagating Nazi doctrines, was often seen at court, so that Rumanian students, forming the bulk of the Iron Guard, were under the impression that their movement was under the King's protection.

Anti-Semitic sentiment has been strong in Rumania since the foundation of the Kingdom. It was the German plenipotentiary, Prince Bismarck, who was the most ardent champion of Jewish rights in Rumania, at the Berlin Conference in 1878. After much wrangling, these rights were granted the Jews of Rumania in theory, but not in practice. In 1907 the Kingdom witnessed a bloody peasant riot, directed against the Jews and the landed barons, the *boyars*. Hitlerite agitation has intensified this sentiment.

It was among the Germans of Rumania that Hitlerism first found a fertile soil. The Saxons of Transylvania, who, according to legend, had been lured into leaving their ancestral homes centuries ago by the magic tones of the Pied Piper, responded with alacrity to the Pied Piper of the Reich. They organized their own storm troop detachments, sat in awe before Nazi propaganda films, listened in hushed silence to Hitlerite agitators, and transmitted to the *Führer* in Berlin the expression of their most reverential homage.

Late in 1933, the German inhabitants of Cernauti, capital of the formerly Austrian Bukovina, allied themselves with the local Rumanian and Ukrainian anti-Semites, and plundered the Jewish shops. The *Czernowitzer Post* began to expand miraculously. Another German-language newspaper, the *Scharfschütze*, blossomed forth as the official organ of the *Führer* of Wilhelmstrasse. The *Siebenbuergische Tageblatt* in Transylvania joined forces with the Hitlerites. At the election of the Saxon National Council in November, 1933, the Nazis scored important victories in several cities.

The Rumanian Nazis were known under different names, but the most aggressive of them were in the Iron Guard, which staged street battles with the police and built barricades on at least one occasion. On both sides a few combatants were killed, and in February, 1933, the government proclaimed a state of siege in the more vulnerable parts of the Kingdom. Alexander Vaida-Voivod, who had become head of the cabinet in the summer, did not proceed against the Nazis with sufficient energy, and the King withdrew his confidence from him, entrusting Duca with the formation of a new government. Duca outlawed the Nazi newspapers: *Calendarul* and *Facla*. Riots broke out in the Danubian port of Constanza and also in Jassy, where the Iron Guard resisted the police for three days. On December 10 the Guard was dissolved, and was thus prevented from putting up its candidates at the national elections. After Duca's death, the government proclaimed martial law and promised a policy of the mailed fist in exterminating the Iron Guard.

The Baltic countries seem to have learned from Ru-

mania's tragic experience with Hitlerism. The governments of Estonia, Latvia and Lithuania are swinging
into action against the Nazi menace. Since Dr. Alfred
Rosenberg, a leader of the Third Reich, comes from
these parts, he seems to have led one of the major of-
fensives of the Brown International against this front.
It is one of the pet obsessions of Munich's Brown House
that the Baltic seacoast must be drawn into the German
Nazi orbit, and possibly be used in a grand crusade
against the Russian neighbor.

The police of the Estonian capital, Tallinn, found at
the end of 1933 that the Nazi movement of the country
was being run by the local "German club." The *Führer*
of the Hitler party was Arved von Zur Mühlen, better
known for his hunting and drinking exploits than for
political sagacity. His house was designated as "National Socialist Provincial Headquarters in Estonia."
The government closed the "German Club," and prohibited its publication, *Der Aufstieg.* Parliament liquidated all National Socialist organizations as inimical to
the State, and demanded the dismissal of Baltic-Ger-
mans from public offices beyond a certain percentage.

Estonia and her neighbor, Latvia, proceeded jointly
against the secret organization of the *Baltische Brüd-
erschaft* (Baltic Fraternity), founded by the local National Socialists and Nationalists in 1929. The pre-
amble of the Fraternity's Constitution stated its object
was the maintenance of old traditions by helping the
Germans remain the ruling class in the Baltic land.

The Latvian authorities found out that their Hitler-
ites were sending their sons to the National Socialist
Youth School in the East Prussian city of Königsberg.
The formerly democratic *Jaunukas Sinas*, heretofore

a poor but honest newspaper, had become suddenly
affluent and switched its allegiance to the so-called Liberation League, which is in Hitler's service. Finally,
parliament decided to dissolve the *Pehrenkrusts,* the
local Fascist organization. At the beginning of 1934,
the Latvian Foreign Minister visited the Swedish and
Finnish capitals, presumably in an effort to organize
concerted action against the economic terrorism of the
Hitler régime, which had declared a tariff war on some
of the Baltic countries.

So aggressive were the Hitlerites in these northeast-
ern regions that at the end of 1933, both Moscow and
Warsaw were reported to have inquired at the Baltic
capitals about the chances of an omnibus treaty, guar-
anteeing their independence and neutrality. While
the Latvian press observed that there would not be
much sense in exchanging the Hitler threat for the
Stalin menace, Estonia and Lithuania showed some interest in the project.

Anti-Semitic reaction was at one time considered a
serious menace in the northernmost Baltic country,
Finland. In March, 1932, General Mart Wallenius,
former chief of the General Staff, led the rebellion of
the Lapuan Fascists against parliament, Marxism, and
the Jews. There are altogether about 1,500 Jews in
Finland's population of three and a half millions. The
rebellion was beaten and the Lapuans were so much
ashamed of their failure that they changed their name
to "Patriotic People's Movement." The new organization decided to hitch its policy entirely to the German Nazi star.

The Finnish Hitlerites have copied the religious mysticism of the German Christians, and they are propa-

gating the worship of a racial God, Hiomojomula, the
heavenly ruler of all Finns, Estonians, and Hungarians,
the three nations supposedly related by blood. The
Nazis of the Land of the Thousand Lakes have re-
served, however, their most poisonous epithets for Finland's Swedish minority, whom they class with the Jews
as a racially inferior nation. Since the Finns are not
Nordics, the racial policy of their Hitlerites against
the Nordic Swedes furnishes an illustration of the
adaptability of Nazi doctrines to all conditions. At the
parliamentary elections of July, 1933, the Finnish Nazis
suffered a great defeat, while the representation of
their enemies, the Socialists, was materially increased.

Russia—Finland's neighbor—too, has her Nazis, but
they are outside of the Soviet Union. From time to
time the Soviet press publishes sensational reports about
the alleged activities of Hitlerite White Russian troops
and of other émigré organizations in the Reich. The
Polish newspaper, *Kurjer Warszawszki*, has given a detailed account of White Russian and German Hitlerite
fraternization. It seems that the White Russian troops
are receiving a thorough military training in preparation for the Czarist *Tag*. On the first German Labor
Day of the Third Reich, May 1, 1933, the White Russian storm troops of the swastika, wearing their Cos-
sack caps, kept company with the Hitlerite Brown Army
on Berlin's Tempelhofer Field.

It was through the good services of Dr. Rosenberg,
always anxious to promote the cause of world reaction,
that Adolf Hitler became a patron saint of the Russian
émigrés. The Leader first met the White Russian en-
voys a few years after the war, when Grand Duke Cyril,
self-appointed Czar of all the Russias, was holding

court at Coburg, in northern Bavaria. The émigrés founded the *Rond*, an association for national freedom, a favorite occupation of which, after Hitler's coming to power, was to blackmail wealthy German Jews. The German Nazis placed Henry Pelchau, a former actor, in charge of the *Rond*, and he announced that he was responsible only to Russia, God, and his own conscience. At the same time, Pelchau, a Baltic German, assumed the name of Swietazarow. The Russian Embassy in Berlin protested against his organization, and so did several real Czarist émigrés, who threatened to move to France if their grievances were unheeded. Pelchau thereupon had a few White Russian leaders—such as the Ukrainian Hetman Ostranitsa and Colonel Lampe —arrested on charges of espionage for France and the Soviets.

Finally, Pelchau was replaced by the military expert of the Russian Nazi movement, Bermont-Avaloff. Internal troubles arose in the organization and the émigrés seemed to be more interested in fighting one another than the common enemy. The Russian Nazis were deprived of their own picturesque uniforms, but their storm troopers were given the right to don the uniform of the Brown Army.

The rumor spread in the summer of 1933 that the Russian émigrés were ready to set up a small anti-Soviet army of twenty-one "half regiments," partly out of their own ranks, and partly by inducing the unemployed Russian émigrés of France to move to Germany. A mysterious American uncle appeared in the person of A. Vonsiacki, who was said to have married into a fortune of several million dollars, a part of which he seemed to want to spend on the Russian Hitlerite cause.

Meanwhile, Dr. Alfred Rosenberg and General Hermann Göring were frequently seen in the house of Pavlo Skoropadsky, former Hetman of all Ukraine and head of the military dictatorship set up there by the Germans in 1918. They were said to be devising plans for the amputation of the Ukraine from the Soviet Union, with the object of giving this territory to Poland in exchange for the Polish Corridor.

Poland's case, so far as Hitlerism is concerned, does not require much comment. The Land of the White Eagle anticipated Hitler many years ago by annihilating the Jews economically and reducing them to the status of pariahs. Warsaw muzzled the opposition, emasculated parliament and all but exterminated Marxism. The Polish National Democrats of Roman Dmowski are no better than the Nazis of Adolf Hitler. If oppression and persecution is done more thoroughly in the Reich, it is because of the German national character.

Official Germany does not admit having any designs on the Scandinavian countries, but unofficial Germany does. Nordic blood is, after all, thicker than diplomatic water. General Hermann Göring, one of Nazi Germany's strong men, is particularly interested in Sweden, which he remembers from the time when he was a patient of the Lunatic Asylum of Langbro as a morphinist.

Unofficial Germany's main attack is, however, concentrated on the Danish neighbor, because Denmark is less adequately protected than the others and because she received a slice of German territory after the World War—North Schleswig, otherwise known as South Jylland. This territory of some two thousand square miles and a population of less than two hundred thousand was detached from the Reich after a plebiscite. By concentrating their attacks on Denmark, some of the Nazi extremists seem to be seeking those laurels which the Hitler régime could not gain in the strongly fortified Polish Corridor.

"Denmark need not fear us," the Brown House of Munich assured the world while some ten thousand German Hitlerites were parading in brown uniforms just south of the Danish boundary during the Easter holidays of 1933. Nazi agitators were despatched to South Jylland and with them came shipments of storm troop uniforms. The Danish government thereupon forbade the wearing of uniforms, including even those of the boy scouts.

A Socialist deputy declared in the Danish *Folkething* at the end of 1933 that the German National Socialist Party had about five thousand enrolled members in South Jylland, and that it had also its marine troops, ready to seize the harbors of southern Denmark in case of a Hitlerite revolt. The headquarters of the organization is in Flensburg, on the German side of the frontier.

"We want to return to Germany," wrote the new Nazi editor of the *Nordschleswigsche Zeitung* immediately after taking charge of the paper. A philosophically-minded clergyman, the Reverend Schmidt, who likes to talk about *Weltanschauung* and metaphysics, is aspiring to the position of the *Führer* of the local Nazis. The Third Reich has sunk large amounts in the local German clubs and in scholarships. The German teaching staff of the minority schools have gone over to the Nazis.

"Our border is patrolled by the military and police," Theodore Stauning, Denmark's Socialist Premier, told an American newspaper correspondent. "We must protect our people by all means at our disposal . . . There is of course unrest. The German contingent is in sympathy with the new movement in the Reich."

Denmark had been the first European country to go ahead with disarmament plans without waiting for the other powers to fall into line. Military conscription was to be abolished and a corps of seven thousand frontier guards was to be set up in place of the regular army. The Disarmament Bill had passed the Lower House but was stopped in the Upper House, and now the Stauning government has withdrawn the bill, in view of the Nazi menace, and ordered a considerable number of bombing planes.

The native Nazi movement of Sweden seems to be somewhat stronger than that of Denmark. "We must tear up the Communist weed by the roots," declared Admiral Lindman in the greatest reactionary demonstration Sweden has ever seen, which took place in May 1933. The Swedish Nazi group is composed mostly of non-commissioned officers, who were adversely affected by the economy program of the ruling Socialist party, and of elderly gentlemen, yearning for the good old times. The Nazis of the country have about half a dozen newspapers, which have made themselves very obnoxious.

M. Furugaard, the Swedish Nazi leader, told in the early summer of 1933 a fantastic tale of his trip to Germany, where he had called on General Göring. According to Furugaard, Prussia's strong man offered his Nazi group a liberal subsidy if he consented to turn

over Sweden's northern territories for German colonization, after their coming to power, but Furugaard, he
said, rejected the offer indignantly.

Since then General Göring paid a visit to Sweden,
with the object, according to *Sozialdemokraten*, a government organ, of creating a Brown Army and engi-
neering a march on Stockholm.

"Nationalist propaganda would become dangerous
only if we were to lose our fight against the crisis," said
Per Albin Hansson, Socialist Premier of Sweden. "Seeing the partial results already achieved, I think we
shall win."

The Minister of Public Instruction, M. Engberg, is
one of the leaders of the anti-Nazi forces. The government has taken strong measures against the Hitlerites,
especially since two Nazis were elected in the place of
two Socialists in the Town Council of Skanör, on the
extreme southern tip of the peninsula.

The countries described so far are in the front line
of Nazi attack. Let us see the second line.

"*Français, Réveillez-Vous!*" a Hitler leaflet admon-
ished Alsace-Lorraine some time ago. "International
Jewry, a dishonest and rapacious race, tells you to boycott German merchandise, but forgets to tell you that
its stores are crammed with non-French goods. . . .
Frenchman, Awake! Time presses! Don't take your
money to the Jewish vermin!"

"Hands across the Rhine," says the propaganda department of the Munich Brown House, but both banks
of the river should be occupied by brown hosts. French
Nazis must cast out the shame of Negro blood and de-
throne Judea.

"The Hitler mark is rolling in France," wrote Emile Buré in *L'Ordre*, quoting a member of the French government. "It is a sad thing," stated a writer in *Petit Parisien*, "that we have often felt the effect of this nebulous and all-pervading propaganda." *Le Temps*, which is supported partly by the *Comité des Forges*, extolled Hitler's sincerity in an article published in December, 1933, and compared him to his advantage with Gustave Stresemann, creator of the Locarno Pacts. For many weeks, *l'Ami du Peuple*, of late the boulevard sheet of the anti-Semitic perfume manufacturer, François Coty, carried on a campaign for a Franco-German crusade against Bolshevist Russia, "dominated by the Jews." *Libre Parole* stands up for hundred per cent Hitlerism in France. "Back to the ghetto with the Jew! He is not, and can never be a Frenchman!" Although French Hitlerism is not serious as yet, it has had some effect by arousing anti-Jewish sentiment, and its very existence across the Rhine is a symptom of the age.

In neighboring Belgium, the Nazis have their own "Green House" in Ghent, patterned after the Munich Brown House. The emblem of the "dinazos" is the wheel and blue gulls. Whatever strength they have, is concentrated in the Flamand part of Belgium, where the German influence has nearly always been strong and where opposition against the French-speaking Walloons is bitter.

A little more serious is the Nazi movement of Holland, as was shown at a mass meeting in Utrecht, attended by some six thousand Dutch Hitlerites. Their leader, A. A. Moussart, declared in November, 1933, that in ten months their membership had increased from one thousand to ten thousand.

The *Telegraaf* of Amsterdam described such a Nazi meeting. At the entrance of the hall the black and red flag of the N.S.B., the Dutch Nazi party, greeted the audience. The leader of the movement mounted the tribune in the midst of the theatricals to which one grew accustomed in the Reich. He repeated Herr Hitler's bombastic phrases and was rewarded with explosive enthusiasm. *Hou-zee,* shouted the assembled Nazis, "Watch the Sea!" They first sang the Wilhelmus, the national anthem, and then their own march:

> For the Queen and for the Netherlands,
> The Black Troops of the N.S.B. march,
> Marxism will have no more indulgence,
> The ship of State has a new crew.

The meeting wound up in the nearby taverns, where the assembled Nazis drank throaty "prosits" for the success of the Dutch Third Reich.

In January, 1934, Dutch State officials were forbidden to belong to the Nazi party. Previously, the Minister of Interior submitted a bill to parliament providing for prison sentences up to two years for insults against the authorities or groups of citizens. The bill is meant mostly for the protection of the Jews.

Hungary anticipated Hitlerism by more than thirteen years. After the collapse of Béla Kun's short-lived Bolshevist rule in the summer of 1919, the Awakening Hungarians and their allies inaugurated their so-called "Christian-Magyar" régime. "Out with the Jews!" they shouted, and this also meant "Out with the Socialists!"

Police powers were usurped by a group of sadists,

who killed and beat up men and women, torturing Bolshevists, Socialists, Liberals and Jews in concentration
camps and shooting many of them "while attempting
to escape." Public offices and the universities were
purged of Jews, and the newspapers owned by Jews
were forced to do homage to the anti-Semitic régime.

With Italian aid Hungary began to arm secretly and
she also set up a conscripted army in violation of the
Treaty of Trianon. Irredentism became the key-note
of the government's national policy and its countless
blunders were responsible for the setting up of the
powerful bloc of Little Entente States.

The new régime promised a New Deal to the peasant
and to the factory worker. The landless proletariat
was to share in the land of the real estate barons, and
the socialism of the factory was to be introduced on a
national basis. These ambitions have come to grief
and despite her rich soil Hungary is a poverty-stricken
country, isolated from the world and inefficiently managed. Apart from exceptional cases, the peasants have
not received their piece of land and the factory workers are worse off than ever.

After such a tragic experience with National Socialism, Hungary's population wants to have nothing to
do with it. Prime Minister General Julius Gömbös, once
an ally of the German Nazis, has made several anti-
Nazi speeches in parliament and has put all kinds of
restrictions upon the Hitlerite organization. The Nazi
agitation is strong at the universities, where it is directed exclusively against the Jews. At certain universities Jewish students were forced to occupy "ghetto
benches." Until the beginning of 1934 there were two
principal Nazi factions, the one headed by Count Alex-

ander Festetich, and the other one by Zoltán Meskó, who was subsequently entrusted with the command of the united Hitlerite party. Archduke Albrecht, once a candidate for the Hungarian throne, has imported a few German Nazis to refresh Budapest's memory about the meaning of Hitlerism.

Such movements as National Socialism have a way of bursting into flame unexpectedly. Who could have foreseen in the autumn of 1929 that in a year Hitler would shed his rôle as the funny man of German politics and become the leader of the most powerful party in the Reich? After having exposed himself to ridicule during the Munich Beer Hall *putsch*, he would have seemed to be out of the running forever. Even though the Nazi parties of the European continent do not represent vast popular movements, they should be given all the attention to which such outbursts of fanaticism and cruelty are entitled.

THE WAR UPON WORLD JEWRY

BY STEPHEN S. WISE

I T is not to be thought that the tragedy of the Jew is a
new or unknown thing in Jewish history. The tragedy
of the Jew is become the commonplace of common-
places. The tragedy of the Jew is none other than
the paradox of the servant despised and rejected of
men. The Jew has been a bringer of blessings to the
world, yet is he accursed. The Jew has been a light
to the nations, yet is he doomed to darkness. The Jew
has not dared to be himself and yet has not been free
to be other than himself. The Jew has a genius for
at-homeness, yet always and everywhere is regarded
and treated as if he were an alien. The Jew is a victim in every generation, yet is he victor through the
ages.

No need of further indictment of Hitler and the
Nazis. The case has been stated not by his victims, but
by impartial and objective witnesses from many lands,
of many races and tongues, and the statement of the
case has been made with such fullness and accuracy,
that it were masochistic again to recite the horrors bound
up with the program and purposes of the Third Reich.

Truth and honor and integrity have been banished
from the Third Reich. Men of distinction and learning and public record disappear on the barest suspicion
of dissent. Espionage or *Spitzelei* has become the chief
science of the Reich, and the basest of the nation are

202

its high-priests.   Only semi-occasionally is a leader frank, as in the case of Göring, who declared the policy of extermination in the noble terms: "No Jews shall be left in Germany but Jewish beggars.   An Aryan prostitute is dearer to me than a chaste Jewish woman."

The modern Haman, who has set out to destroy the Jewish race, is a world-menace, forasmuch as he has enslaved and degraded Germany.   A mighty nation is in chains and who dares to dissent or protest? England recently celebrated the centenary of Wilberforce, the liberator of a slave-race.   Hitler, a century later, enslaves a free race.   A world menace Hitler is become, for, despite a thousand Reichstag speeches, he is broadening the Empire of war and all unreason.   To the age-old horrors of international war, he is adding the crime of *intra-national* and *inter-racial* war.

In only one respect has Nazism been fair, in that ample notice was served in advance of what was to come.   The earlier notice was as of the date, February 25, 1920.   Germany has never said, "We are warring upon the Jews of the world," but merely "The Jews, not being Aryans, shall not be citizens of the German Reich."   In one word everything was cancelled that had been won over a period of a hundred years, the results of '48, the special emancipation acts and the gains of the Weimar Republic.   We deal not with quasi-private utterances of leaders of the Hitler régime according to which the Hitler assault upon the Jews was to serve as an example to all other countries with a view to the complete elimination of the Jews everywhere, for these do not enter into the totality of the case.   We must judge Hitlerism not by what some men, however high placed, say, but by its deeds and its laws or decrees. What are its acts? What are its laws?

Difficult, too, to determine what the acts of Germany are or have been, grievous and unspeakable though they have been, because it may never be known what Hitlerism really planned to do on the "Night of the Long Knife." The question is rather, what was it that Nazism was restrained from doing? What would Nazism have done if a note of warning had not been sounded in England, and the subsequent protests had not come from America and other lands of civilization?

Let it not be imagined that Hitlerism is, as is often claimed, Germany's business alone, with which the world need not, indeed, dare not, concern itself. The truth is that Hitlerism is the business of all humanity. The truth is inevitably borne in upon us who have come to see certain things: (1) what we have cherished as the values and standards of civilization are being broken down; (2) the nations surrounding the Hitler Reich are being compelled to pay the price and to bear the burden of that inevitable emigration from Germany which is become another Exodus; (3) the racial fanaticism of the Hitler Reich may be a most immediate and deadly peril to us Jews, but it is no less truly a threat and a danger to all races and to all nations. For a time the Jewish people has been singled out as the most inferior division of the human race.

Once the Hitler Government succeeds in getting that dictum accepted by public opinion, the query is, which will be the next race to be proclaimed inferior, debased and debasing? It may be Czechoslovakia, or Poland, or France. Only one thing is certain, namely, that the most vulnerable of the neighbors of the Reich will be singled out for doom. Not only are the Slavic neighbors of Germany liable to be held up to something like the contempt which is now being visited upon the Jewish people, but it may even be the Latin race, already graciously alluded to as a negroid or semi-negroid race. That way not only madness lies, but the utter destruction of all the hard-won human values. Who knows whether even Britain is safe, for some new Hitler pundit may find that the British represent an inferior and imperilling sub-division of the Aryan races, and are therefore to be dealt with as Germanic Austria may be dealt with on the morrow, or the still more Nordic Danes may fare on the day thereafter. The answer to all the empty and mendacious boasting by the Hitler Government about Germany having saved Europe from Communism is that Hitlerism is exposing all of Europe to this danger—graver than Communism or aught else.

Hitlerism offers yet another strange phenomenon, as far as Jews are concerned. In the past, difficult, rebellious, and intransigent racial and religious minorities have at times been brutally suppressed by dominant majorities. As for the Jews of Germany, these have been a loyal and faithful minority (or group) of the German people, a minority who still love Germany, and would remain Germans, who loved and served Germany in every way, who fought and died for Germany for a thousand years. And the true reason, the chief reason, is that Jews are not Aryans, whoever Aryans may be; are of a race other than and different from the Germanic or Aryan race. Other pretexts are added —the Jewish race is poisonous, too liberal, too democratic, too pacific, but the basic accusation and indict-

ment is bound up with difference of race, twenty-five
per cent, even twelve and one-half per cent of Jewish
blood sufficing to constitute an inexpiable stigma.

It is not without significance to note that Jesus, whatever else he was, was fifty per cent Jewish, and his
Mother one hundred per cent Jewish, and every one
of the Apostles was one hundred per cent Jewish. Under the régime of Hitler, no one of them could have
taught as did Peter, or practiced medicine as did Luke,
or have been a public official as was Matthew. Only one
man would have been safe, and his name Pontius
Pilate!

When a nation attacks the Jews on the ground of
difference of religion or on the ground of irregularity
of some acts, at least they who are attacked are free,
as not a few Jews have been through the ages, to change
their faith or to alter their mode of life. In other words,
the Jews in the past have, for the most part, been attacked touching things which do not leave them helpless under attack and utterly without freedom. Jews
might in the most tragic days mend their ways or end
their creed.

Hitlerism has devised a new thing, a frankly brutal
attack upon race, which means that, whatever the Jew
is, whether good or evil, whatever he thinks, whatever
he believes, whatever he does, he must be destroyed
because of something over which he has no control.
That is the heart of this evil thing. A man may have
some measure of control over his faith and over his
conduct but he has no power of choosing the blood
stream which is his. That stream, his race, after all,
is determined for him and not by him.

In saying that Jews may not be Germans because

they are non-Aryans, Hitlerism has done something more and worse against the Jews. Namely it has shown the way of destroying the life of the Jews in other countries. If Jews may not be citizens of Germany because they are non-Aryan, then it may yet be urged that they shall not be citizens of Italy because they are non-Latin, or they may not be citizens of Soviet Russia because the are non-Slavic, and may not be citizens of England because they are non-Saxons. Nazism sets a most dangerous precedent and incidentally sets up an arbitrary standard of racial values which is fraught with infinite hurt.

Hitlerism is a new phenomenon in world-history. The tendency of mankind had been to accept the fact of human differences and different viewpoints, and concepts, and to base existence upon the tolerant and friendly understanding of such inevitable human differences and racial and religious variations, and ideological disagreements. Hitlerism declares that toleration of every difference, even racial, must forever cease and that the business of the state is to enforce identity and uniformity by every means human and inhuman.

Religious uniformity can mean only one thing, the reduction of all religious groups to the lowest common denominator and the Aryanism that begins with the attempt to cancel the pages of the Old Testament will not rest until after it shall have destroyed the pages of the New. Hitlerism challenges civilization insofar as it is in truth the substitution of a new paganism, the paganism over which Christianity once triumphed, for Christianity itself. The Jew may be hurt first. It is the very heart and fabric of Christianity that will ultimately, has indeed already, come under attack.

Wherein lies the tragedy of the Jew in this hour in Germany? In this—that the German Jews were unprepared in every sense, unprepared inwardly and outwardly, though some of us foresaw and foretold what would happen. The Jew is doubly unprepared, insofar as he was unprepared for the worst that the world could inflict upon him because he was unrooted and unanchored in the best of his own tradition. The Jew who had so long denied the reality and the authenticity of the people Israel finds himself at last denied a place in Germany. If it be true that all things are ready if our minds be so, then were the German Jews tragically unready for the awful hour that came upon them. The tragedy of the Jew cannot be stated nor yet summarized in mere facts. And still the truth is that German Jewry presents the picture of a people on the rack. I have seen torture chambers in the course of the summer in European castles very near to Germany. Germany is a torture chamber for the Jewish people.

The tragedy of the Jew lies in the two-fold purpose of the new rulers of the German Reich—to exterminate on the one hand and, in the meantime, to degrade on the other. As if economic, industrial extermination were not enough, degradation, humiliation are ceaselessly inflicted. They of the intelligentsia who ought to stand apart from the band of Jewish torturers identify themselves with the unfaith and the misdeeds of their people. The tragedy of the Jew lies in the Nazi threat to Jewish children. Not only are the children wounded in their souls from day to day, but Germany is preparing for a future of hatred, of reprisal, of unrelieved shame.

Over and above all, the Jewish tragedy for us lies in

the danger of Jews forswearing their ideals, ideals by which and for which they have lived, not the ideal of religious loyalty for, happily, religious disloyalty and infidelity do not avail to save the faithless. The real danger is that under the pressure of the Nazi movement, Jews may be moved consciously and deliberately to surrender their ideals, such high and abiding ideals as the ideals of democracy, of the forward-looking human collectivity, of war-resistance. In a word, the tragedy is being enacted before our eyes of the current and urgent Jewish need for an hour leading us to surrender ideals which are eternal. We are not fighting for ourselves alone in all the great battlefield to which the Third Reich has summoned us. We are battling for the world's ideals, for the ideals of democracy and liberalism, human peace and co-operation. To battle and even to die for these things is not to make a vain sacrifice. No vain sacrifice is made by them that battle for eternal causes as we have done throughout the generations. Let not Nazism achieve the triumph over us of moving us to forswear the things by which and for which our fathers lived. Whatever may be the suffering which Jews must endure in Germany, whatever tortures may be visited upon them, Jews may not, dare not, forswear their highest faith and their loftiest ideals. Israel disloyal to itself is Hitlerism triumphant; Israel unimpairably and indeflectibly loyal to its faith in and its power of sacrifice for its divine and eternal ideals is the doom of a thousand Hitlerisms.

How then shall Jews meet the onslaught of Hitler and his cohorts? For one thing Jews must unite. The failure of the Jewish people in this and other lands to reach complete and effective unity in the field of

self-defence in the sight of the Hitler war is treasonable not only to Jewish interests but to those interests
of civilization, which it is become the lot of the Jew
to defend and to preserve. In this hour which finds
neo-paganism under the name and title of Hitlerism
attacking the most precious possessions of humanity,
the possessions of human liberty and human toleration,
of political democracy and of spiritual brotherhood
and their hope of peace, we Jews are as we have always been, privileged to serve as shock-troops.

But if we are the shock-troops in this battle of
paganism against the supreme ethical and spiritual
values of mankind, it behooves Christendom to see to
it that Jews are not needlessly sacrificed in their post
of infinite difficulty. I thank God that in America and
England above all and in other lands as well, the voices
of Christians have been heard in protest against the
unutterable wrongs of Hitlerism against the Jewish
people.

Recently, the American Federation of Labor under
the leadership of William Green, found its voice and
spoke in the name of human solidarity and human
brotherhood as have many leaders of Christian thought
and life against the immeasurable woe inflicted upon the
Jewish people by Hitlerism and its minions. Oh, that
Jews might feel that, whatever else befall us, the understanding and the sympathy of the American people are
our own, even though up to this hour our government
has in every sense been strangely and lamentably
silent.

When the President of the United States appealed
to the nations of the world for peace, Hitler, in order
to save the Reich, found it needful to respond to the

President's magnificent appeal to the nations of the world in fitting terms. Whenever the governments of the world, led by our own, decree that the barbarity of the Hitler treatment of the Jews shall end, there will be an inevitable response of compliance.

No truer word on the whole matter has been spoken than that of Wickham Steed: "One Dreyfus case convulsed France. Germany has six hundred thousand Dreyfus cases but is unconvulsed. Hitlerism is a Nordic myth based on the question of negation of Christ and the affirmation of Odin. The governments of America, France and England which stand for liberty must concertedly declare that those who trample liberty underfoot cannot expect our good-will."

Once again the Jewish people seems called upon to play a great rôle, perhaps the greatest rôle in all its tragic history. Once again the Jewish people seems to be called upon not only to suffer that humanity and civilization may survive and endure, but to make clear to the whole human race the peril which inheres in the Hitler theory which begins with the insistence upon uniformity, and the claim of superiority, and will end, unless challenged and checked, by the enslavement of all mankind.

THE DANGER TO

WORLD PEACE

BY PIERRE VAN PAASSEN

SINCE August, 1933, a marked change has come in the tone of the utterances of the Nazi chiefs, especially when these utterances were destined for foreign consumption. The régime, tried more than anything else, from that time onward to create the impression abroad that the terroristic period of the Nazi "revolution" has definitely been terminated and that the Reich, once and for all, has settled down, under the aegis of the National-Socialist party, to seek the reward of those ten years of peace and hard work which Hitler has prescribed in order that, as he says, Germany might again find her soul. The "Jewish traitors" and the "Marxist scoundrels" having been rendered impotent, the brown régime wants it understood abroad that it has liquidated party strife, silenced demo-liberal discussion, finished with all internal opposition and in the short space of one year has welded the German people together into one single-willed, determined and regenerated unit whose only desire is to reconstruct and set into motion once more the economic structure of Germany which was almost irreparably damaged as they say by democratic incompetence and Jewish sabotage. The Hitler régime is out to win the good graces of the world. It wants commendation instead of condemnation. We actually encountered Nazi agents after October, 1933, who apologized in a half-hearted sort of way for that "campaign of stern repression" which was "regretfully" but "necessarily" launched against Jews, pacifists, liberals, and the revolutionary bodies right after Hitler was called to the chancellorship by President Hindenburg. Secretly alarmed by the growing hostility abroad, the Hitler chiefs could think of nothing better to calm an outraged world-opinion than that attempt to convince the world that they had acted with the full and unanimous approval of the German people. This was the plebiscite of November, 1933. By that referendum, the *Führer* hoped to kill two birds with the one stone. He sought to disarm the demo-liberal critics of his régime by proving to them that he would be upheld even in applying a test which is part and parcel of democratic procedure, but he also sought, and this is far more significant, to render the German people in its entirety co-responsible with his own murder-régime for the crimes he had committed in the immediate past and for the great crime he is to perpetrate in the future. As was inevitable, some naive souls here and there were taken in by the cynical fraud of that referendum. From the debates in the House of Commons on the subject of the disarmament conference it became clear that men like Sir John Simon and Mr. Ramsay MacDonald had been deeply impressed with what they chose to regard as "an expression of the sovereign will of the German people." How remarkable, was it not, that ninety per cent of the prisoners in the concentration camps had voted for Hitler? But wasn't this remarkable, too, that ten per cent of those human beings chained up like wild beasts voluntarily took upon themselves further martyrdom—and possibly death—by flinging a courageous "No" in the face of their torturers? Yet, after all, it did not require a great deal of political perception to see, as Heinrich Mann remarked, that if the question posed in that plebiscite had been whether Goebbels is a blond, yes or no, or whether the sun is a German colony, yes or no, the forty million voters, most of them, as they say now in Germany *"Nazis aus Angst,"* would have responded with an equally fervent: *"Ja!"*

Politically the plebiscite was a retreat. Dictatorships do not ask for ratification. Revolutions require no substantiation by popular vote. But then, of course, the Nazi raid on the state-apparatus of Germany lacks every scientific qualification of a revolution. It brought about no change in the ownership of the means of production, but merely consolidated the system that prevailed prior to 1933 by giving it the protection of a praetorian guard, in this instance the *Sturm-Abteilungen.* Fascist régimes do not come into the world by conquering power. Power is handed to the Fascist chiefs by the real masters of a country, the owners of the means of production, at a moment in the historical process when the lower middle-classes, uprooted and declassed by destitution and misery, begin to seek a solution in a leftward direction and ally themselves with the revolutionary working-class.

The plebiscite did show, however, that the brown régime sought justification in the eyes of the world and that it had abandoned the attitude of challenge and provocation which it assumed at the outset *vis-à-vis* France, Poland, Czechoslovakia, and other lands con-

taining German minorities. The Nazi régime henceforth desires to be known as the force which raised a
barrier against "the waves of Asiatic barbarism." Hitler seeks recognition for the check he has administered
to communism. He poses as the savior of Europe, who,
as such should not receive condemnation, but unstint-
ed praise and approval for the eminent services rendered the cause of "civilization."

But in reality the sadistic Fehme-murderers, the am-
nestied assassins, the frustrated half-intellectuals and
criminally insane morphinomaniacs who were entrusted with power by German big business and who
function as cabinet-ministers in Berlin, will it so. They
are thirsting for blood. They are intoxicated with a
lust for world-power. "We are prepared to plunge
back into the Middle Ages and wade through rivers of
blood," declared Dr. Alfred Rosenberg, "rather than
see the spirit of internationalism gain further headway
among the peoples."

In these words is summed up the ideology of German Fascism. Its real meaning is *war*. The object of
the Hitler régime is world power through armed conquest. The ten years of peace demanded by Hitler
is the period required for the physical and spiritual
mobilization of the German people. And the inevitable fate of mankind for having permitted the accession to power of Fascism in Germany is a catastrophe
of such magnitude that it may well eclipse European
civilization.

Ten years for Germany to find her soul! If it were
only ten years! Hitler will be compelled to strike out
much sooner. Much sooner will he stake all on the
desperate gamble of a European war, because he must

take that course as the obedient servant, the puppet of
the armament manufacturers, the oil-kings and the
dye-trust magnates, whose creature he is, whose man
of all jobs he is, he the glorified and deified *Führer* of
National-Socialism. The men who financed his movement during the years of incubation expect to be re-im-
bursed for their services. Or is there anyone who
imagines that the Deterdings and the Kreugers, the
Froweins and Cotys, the Schneider-Creuzots and the
Skodas, the Russian White-Guard organizations in Europe, the Junkers and the militarist clique of Germany,
financed and nursed the Hitler movement in order that
the hard-pressed middle-classes in the Reich be relieved
from their economic burdens and regain something of
the well-being and influence they enjoyed in the period
which closed with the great war?

Since the signing of the peace treaty, Germany has
built up and has perfected an industrial apparatus without equal on the European continent. Originally de-
signed to effect the payment of reparations in kind,
this huge machinery gradually slowed up and finally
came to a complete standstill when the statesmen
reached the belated conclusion that the plundering of
Germany was wrecking industry and commerce in the
former allied countries. Too late a halt was called
to this insane method of paying reparations which had
the effect of closing down British shipyards, Belgian
coal-mines, French steel-ovens, and the Polish textile
industry. The war had also intensified the idea of economic self-sufficiency in the different countries and
tariff walls were built up everywhere to protect the
infant home industries. These walls went up higher
and higher in the measure that the home-market be-

came saturated and the export market declined. The
inevitable result was a world-wide economic depression
from which there is no issue so long as the mode of
production remains unchanged. Hitler has promised
that he is able to set the stalled machinery in motion
and bring back prosperity without changing the mode
of production. It will be a *tour de force* but he is
willing to try and, if he fails, to stand discredited before all the world. Today there is little doubt that the
Führer has launched out upon this gigantic undertaking.

General von Hammerstein remarked shortly after
the institution of the Fascist régime in Germany that
a large army is a country's best customer. The trouble
with Germany is that under the stipulations of the Versailles Treaty she is not permitted the equipment of a
complete modern fighting force. The immediate task
for Nazi diplomacy is therefore to persuade the signa-
tory powers to that treaty to modify it in such a way
that Germany might usher in an era of economic re-
cuperation by allowing her as first customer a new
military establishment. Nazi diplomacy could make
no headway in this direction so long as the chiefs of
the Hitler Government persisted in that cocky attitude
of defiance and challenge, filling the air with threats
to left and right about recovering lost provinces and
irridenta. Difficult as it must have been to abandon this
initial stand in foreign affairs, the "national" interests
demanded a retreat once more. Hitler announced himself a friend of peace. In view of the fact that the
German people had been given to understand that the
Nazi way of rattling the sabre was a surer method of
gaining the ear and the respect of the world than the

conciliatory attitude assumed by Stresemann and Bruening, the change from militant chauvinism to pacifism was not without hazard. This difficulty was overcome, however, by keeping the German masses in perfect ignorance of the about face in foreign policy. At home the martial clangor goes on unabated, while knowledge of what is destined for foreign consumption does not come within the ken of the German people, or at best in a very garbled form.

Edouard Herriot, who remains the "grand patron" of the radical-socialist governments in France, has revealed in the Parisian weekly *Marianne* that on two occasions, once in the course of the Papen administration and once since the Nazis attained power, the German Government has sent secret emissaries to Paris to make definite and detailed proposals for a Franco-German military alliance against the Soviet Union. "The Germans proposed," writes M. Herriot, "a joint campaign for the conquest of White Russia and the whole of the Ukraine as far south as Odessa and a division of that huge territory into spheres of influence for exploitation by the Reich, France and Poland. We rejected this proposal," he continues, "for we have no intention of playing the game of the Prussian Junkers against the heroic peoples of the Soviet Union." M. Herriot then points out the danger of the possible existence of a victorious German army to French security. "We know our neighbors," says Herriot. "We know that they would never be content with conquering Russia alone, but that their eyes and their armies would almost certainly turn in the direction of the people of whom they still speak as the heriditary foe."

The double rebuff received in Paris has by no means disheartened the rulers in Berlin. Although two successive French Governments have rejected the infamous deal, Hitler and his associates figure that the radical-socialist control of the French parliament is not eternal. The Nazis are therefore biding their time. Ten years of peace if needs be! And we must admit that time, seconded by the deepening economic crisis, is indubitably working in their favor. The composition of the French Government is bound to change. The inability of the radicals to work out a financial program that will satisfy the Socialists, will ultimately compel them to go to the right for the personnel of their cabinet. Crypto-Fascist movements in the meantime are deploying a feverish activity in France. The tumult over the Stavisky scandal is a welcome occasion for royalists, *"Croix de feu," Jeunesses Patriotiques,* national-socialists, neo-socialists and kindred organizations to persuade the lower middle-classes of the wastefulness, the incompetence and the impotence of democratic institutions. All these bodies are unanimous in demanding that there shall be an end to the ever-shifting cabinet compositions and the parliamentary jockeying, and that France be given a régime that will know how to enforce: *"autorité et continuité."* The course set by Mussolini and by Hitler, at a moment when the lower middle-classes under the impact of the deepening economic crisis turn more and more in a leftward direction, is now openly advocated by the reaction in France as a solution for the country's ills. Yet the unconcealed admiration for Fascist methods does not prevent the right in France from exploiting to the full the military menace of a "regenerated Germany." In the face of that danger, the radical governments are denounced as weaklings and traitors because they have not immediately replied to the challenge of a resurgent German chauvinism with a substantial increase in French military equipment. Tens of thousands of posters in the capital and in the provincial cities, renewed at short intervals, condemn the pacifism of the radicals in the most bitter and violent terms. And as we saw it happen in Germany in the Weimar days, the democratic government of France, does nothing to curb the wild attacks of the neo-Fascists outside parliament. The republicans, as in Germany, retain their naive faith in legality and in the unassailability of democratic institutions. They seem to be blind to the lessons offered by Italy and Germany where legality for left-wing elements was suspended, the moment the Fascists obtained control of the state-apparatus.

At the time of writing (February 1934) it is merely a question of months before France will have a government of national concentration. The tendency at present is to the right. This throws into relief the figure of Tardieu, the coming "strong man," who is to "restore authority" by curbing "the evil of party-despotism" and make an end to the "vitiation of national energy through outworn parliamentary methods." Now Tardieu is by no means averse to a Franco-German discussion on the subject of Soviet Russia. An editorial writer on the staff of *Le Temps*, a regular contributor to *Liberté*, the *Journal des Debats* and other periodicals of the extreme right, no reader of the French press entertains the slightest doubt as to M. Tardieu's attitude toward the Soviet Union. He is, moreover, a member of the board of directors of the *Comité des Forges* the most powerful international steel-trust in Europe. This organization owns the *Journal des Debats* and subsidizes *Le Temps* and several other influential periodicals in the capital. Then again, the *Comité des Forges* and the French armament trust of Schneider-Creuzot have interlocking directorates and Schneider-Creuzot figured among the financial contributors to the Hitler movement in Germany during its formative days. These financial contributions to Hitler by Creuzot were made via the firm's subsidiary, Skoda, in Czechoslovakia, as was revealed by M. Paul Faure, the deputy for the town of Creuzot in a full session of the French Chamber of Deputies.

While French armament firms are represented on the *Comté des Forges* by Tardieu, German steel-concerns are represented there by Herr Franz von Papen, one of the most sinister figures in the *coulisses* of the contemporary European scene, and by Herr Arnold Rechtberg, who was one of the secret emissaries who come to Paris to propose a Franco-German military alliance against Russia. The argument of these men is that it is downright folly for France and Germany to fight one another when they have one mighty common enemy: Communism. Hitler, so they say, has brought Bolshevism to a standstill in Central Europe and has therewith, incidentally, saved France from having the "red imperialists" of Moscow as neighbors on the Rhine. Why does France not permit the *Führer* to finish the job he has started by crushing out of existence the "breeding nest of Asiatic barbarism" in Moscow? Does not France see, asks Dr. Alfred Rosenberg, that her enemy is ours, that we have a common task: to liberate Europe from the menace of Communism and bring back prosperity to our hard-tried peoples?

Bringing back prosperity by means of a fresh and
joyous war against Russia! This is the enticing prospect which is being dangled before the eyes of French
big business. An irresistible appeal, the more since
Germany is willing to do the major share of the fighting.

The Soviet Union, however, cannot be invaded without Poland opening up a passage-way for an expedi-
tionary force, whether it be German or Franco-German
in composition. Now relations between Germany and
Poland have not been of the best since the *Führer* began to insist that the Corridor must be restored to
the Reich. In the beginning of the Hitler régime there
were several occasions when the strained relations assumed the character of grave tension. But as we have
seen, German diplomacy has enforced a change in the
outward attitude of the *Führer* and his associates toward Poland. The flamboyant declarations about German eyes being turned longingly and affectionately in
the direction of their brethren under the barbarous
Polish yoke have ceased to be forthcoming of late. The
German press has apparently received its orders: no
more infringements on Polish national sensibilities. Poland must be wooed. Poland may yet become an ally
instead of an opponent. For cannot Poland be persuaded to join an anti-Soviet campaign and share the
fruit of conquest in the Ukraine? Does not Poland
need an outlet on the Black Sea? Would Odessa and
a share in the exploitation of White Russia as well
as a Baltic and Ukrainian market not compensate Warsaw for the loss of the Polish Corridor? A tempting
offer indeed. The more since the Polish economic situation is utterly precarious. Here also war would set
the wheels a-humming again. From bitter hostility

Polish-German relations have changed so much in the last few months that a non-aggressive pact between the two States has been concluded. German diplomacy is making headway. Then there is the League for Ukrainian Independence, of which Hetman Skoropadski, the successor of Simon Petlura, is the chief, Alfred Rosenberg, Hitler's chief of intrigue the patron, and Messrs. Coty, Deterding and Rothermere the financiers. The League's branches in Germany have been granted permission to form para-military units and its newspapers openly proclaim the imminence of the day of Ukrainia's liberation, by which is meant of course the detachment of that country from the Soviet Union. The League's subterranean activity brought about so serious a situation in Soviet Ukrainia in the summer of 1933 that a nationalist uprising was but narrowly averted.

Is there any question today that Japan is turning Manchukuo into a base for attack on Russia? The operations in China, we can now see, have been merely a preliminary to what is to follow. By the occupation of Manchuria and the persistent penetration of Mongolia, Japan has driven a wedge between the Union of Soviet Republics and its potential allies the Chinese Soviets. Documentary evidence that Japan is working hand in glove with the Nazi régime has come to light through the French Counter-Espionage Service. Japan will most likely lead off with an attack at an early date on the Pacific Maritime Provinces, later to be joined by Germany as the head of a Holy Alliance in Europe. And Britain? It is scarcely credible that Britain will support the Soviet Union in the event of a conflict. It seems much more likely that the British,

who always had an eye for business, will want a share
in the vast markets of Russia, which cover a sixth part
of the habitable globe and which have been closed to
foreign exploitation since the Bolsheviks seized power.
That in itself has been the unforgivable offense of Russia in the eyes of British business men. Will they then
not look with sympathy on the man and the movement
which hold out a promise of re-opening those markets?

Wherever we look we find that Hitler's plan for an
armed intervention in Russia is the most tempting prospect that has been dangled before the eyes of the decaying capitalist system.

The fight against Bolshevism is his trump card, the
conquest of new markets appears as a God-send. Much
can be forgiven him, the attack on the Jews, the crushing of the liberal elements, the suspension of democratic institutions, so long as he brings back the Baku
oil fields within range of exploitation by the desperate
capitalists, so long as he opens up the vast closed market
of Europe and Asia. In his opening speech at the
Sèvres Russian Orphanage Sir Henry Deterding told
the boys: "A new leader has come in Europe. . . . The
day is not far distant when you will be marching home
to Kieff and Moscow and Petrograd. . . . The rule of
the Bolshevik bandits is drawing to a close." And
General Miller, chief of the anti-Soviet concentration
in Paris, told me personally: "We are ready. . . . We
have 200,000 men to put at the disposal of Hitler or
any other leader the moment he declares war on the
Bolsheviks. . . . The moment we arrive at the Russian borders we will sweep the peasants with us. . . .
Since Hitler came to power in Germany our hope has

turned to certainty: our beloved motherland will be freed from the murderous grip of Judea and Marxism."

But even if Hitler succeeds in getting his war, the huge stocks of armament and chemical poisons which he is now piling up will not guarantee victory. In order to assure victory in the coming struggle Hitler requires a gigantic army of docile servants. This is at present still lacking in spite of appearances. To go to war now would mean placing arms in the hands of his political opponents, the millions of young communists and socialists.

Yet he needs millions of men who will not reason why, but who will only do and die. In order to win Hitler needs a completely subjugated popular mind, a wholly debased, servile, degenerate national spirit. *The Manchester Guardian* remarked on one occasion, in the beginning of the Hitler terror, that the German working class knew nothing of anti-Semitism and that they could only with difficulty be roused to anything resembling militant racial hatred. With difficulty!

Nevertheless, Hitler believed that it could be done. He is straining every ounce of energy to implant a furious brand of xenophobia in the German masses. Anti-Semitism served as the thin end of the wedge. To be sure, anti-Semitism existed before Hitler. But he sharpened it to serve as an instrument for the spiritual mobilization of the German people. The spiritual preparedness campaign pursued by the Nazi régime to stimulate industry is as indispensable as the material re-arming of Germany in Hitler's program. The spiritual preparation campaign for war is in full swing in the Reich. He is bringing up a youth which instead of truth hears nothing but lies. History is being re-

written to conform to the theories of men like Frick.
The lie has a clear right of way in Germany today.
"Lies, distortion and falsehood are the guiding principles in the Reich, even in the highest quarters since
Hitler came to power," said Dr. Schweyer, the Bavarian
Minister of the Interior, a day before he was arrested.
Hitler's friends in America, who are attracted by his
resounding declarations about law and order, respect
for religion, sacredness of the family and the identity
of interests of capital and labor will have a rude awakening.　The journalists who have begun to hold up
Hitler in our papers as another brilliant example of
a self-made man, as an essentially decent fellow, as an
authoritative politician who has read the signs of the
times in breaking frankly with the demo-liberal ideals
which Europe inherited from the French Revolution,
as a man of will-power and determination who rose
from the humble position of house-painter to the chancellorship of the German Reich, are either consciously
or unconsciously misleading American public opinion.

The aim of the Hitlerite ideology, its preliminary
task, is to numb the critical faculties of the German
masses, to becloud and muddle their judgment, to steer
them off on side tangents, to teach them hatred, to
drive them into tantrums of fury against other nations.
The Jews were but the victims of an experimental test
in hatred and xenophobia, preliminary practise for
more and bigger hatreds to come, for in the Nazi plan
hatred must be kept at the boiling point.　The Germans
must be whipped up into a frenzy of mass hatred. And
they will be, if Hitler succeeds in having his ten years
of peace—ten years of Nazi peace!—which means of
a certainty, the bloodiest war that mankind ever saw.

PART THREE

THE CHALLENGE TO AMERICA

THE INVASION OF AMERICA

BY ALBERT BRANDT

THE question, "Is Germany spreading propaganda in the United States?" is by this time rhetorical. One might as well ask, "Is Germany persecuting Jews, pacifists, and Marxists?" or, "Does Germany nourish imperialistic ambitions?"

To all these queries, the Nazi régime, for the benefit of the outside world, vehemently protests in the negative. But for home-consumption there is no attempt to conceal the hostility to pacifism as well as to pacifists, to Jews and to Marxists, to anti-expansionists.

The history of Nazi propaganda in the United States is no more than another instance of the brazen opportunism of the Nazis. Propaganda here has been overt whenever conditions made it possible. When American opinion seemed to be turning hostile, when a congressional inquiry and other investigations indicated a link between Nazi groups here and the German Government, those links were ostensibly dissolved. But the work of propaganda went on, more subtly, and, therefore, more dangerously than ever.

The childish slyness of Hitler's words in "My Battle," "The masses must be misled in order to be led," would be ludicrous if history had not demonstrated their tragic efficiency. In the same way, Hitler's naive denial of the existence of Nazi propaganda in the United States would be ridiculous if events had not proved him a master of the art of propaganda. The *Voelkische Beobachter*, official Nazi organ, on November 2, 1933, published the following:

Chancellor Adolf Hitler recently received Mr. Karl von Weigand, one of the outstanding figures in the American newspaper world. The newspapers of the Hearst chain which Mr. Weigand represents everywhere, featured this interview on the first page and were unanimous in their approval of the *Führer's* assurance that National Socialists in other countries are being strictly enjoined from carrying on their party propaganda there. This, they declared, would react favorably not only on official relations between Germany and the United States, but on public opinion in America as well, a consideration of paramount importance to Germany in the present situation. Such propaganda, the *Führer* stated, must inevitably endanger friendly relations between Germany and other nations. He, at any rate, would not hesitate for a moment to call those who acted in contradiction to this command strictly to account, and to expel them from party membership. This interview, according to the American press, is gratifying particularly for its timeliness, Congressman Dickstein having just an-

nounced that he is about to present proof of National
Socialist propaganda in the United States to a Congressional Investigation Commission. The interview
should prove once and for all that such propaganda,
if and where it exists, is being carried on by unin-
structed and irresponsible persons, and against the
expressed wish and desire of the *Führer*.

Five days later, on November 7, the press section
of the Nazi party announced that Colonel Edwin Emerson of New York had been named representative of
the party's interests in the United States. The same
day there arrived in New York, Georg Schmitt, with
plenary authority from the Berlin headquarters of the
Stahlhelm. He displayed a document recording the
co-ordination of the *Stahlhelm* with the Nazi party and
urging *die Kameraden* to pledge their efforts without
reservation to the New Germany and to the Nazi party.
This document was signed in October in Hamburg by
Ernest Wilhelm Bohle, as head of the Foreign Office
of the Nazi party, although some months previously
it had been officially announced that the foreign division of the Nazi party had ceased to exist. Mr. Schmitt
was asked how he was going to co-ordinate the *Stahlhelm* and the American division of the Nazi party, which
has no official existence, unless by it is meant the
"Friends of New Germany," organized after the official
"dissolution" of the American division of the Nazis.
Schmitt smiled and said, "We will effect such co-ordination as the situation seems to require." "But suppose
some of these organizations are not willing to accept
your directions?" he was asked. "They will," he replied.

Schmitt's frankness was finally too much even for
the Nazis and he dropped out of sight. But the work

of propaganda went forward with unabated vigor. It
will go on as long as the Nazis continue in power, for
it is the very breath of their existence.

The American Nazi units, like all other organizations
propagating Nazi ideas the world over, are controlled
through the *Fichtebund* of Hamburg. Dr. H. Nieland,
until a short time ago director of the central body, was
recently congratulated upon his efficiency. "You must
not forget," he replied modestly, "that our organization
is most experienced in propaganda." Dr. Nieland knew
whereof he spoke. The *Fichtebund* was founded in
January, 1914, to defend the justice of Germany's cause
throughout the world. Millions of propaganda letters
were sent out, at first to neutral countries and later to
the enemy camp. Since the war, the letterhead of this
organization reads, "League for the Fight against the
Treaty of Versailles." This organization today is still
using its vast fund of experience to spread Hitlerism
throughout the world. Much attention is paid to America where the ideas of democracy, freedom, and tolerance, so despised by the Nazis, still maintain a strong
hold on a backward people not sufficiently apprised of
the celebrated Hitler's revelations in politics and race-
ology!

As early as 1925 the inner circle of the Nazi party
was considering ways and means of winning over the
United German Societies of America, especially their
most powerful constituent, the Steuben Society. But
propaganda in that era was furtive and comparatively
feeble. The energies of the Nazis were directed mainly
toward building up power in the Fatherland, and the
matter of winning sympathy in America was left to

thousands of volunteer workers. At that time the movement in America was—in a manner of speaking —almost idealistic. It was inspired largely by a sincere, if misguided, patriotism. The day when this work was to become an extremely well-paid racket had not yet dawned. Thus, when the National Socialist party, in 1929, became a real power in Germany, when it decided to expand its activities and to found Nazi cells in other lands, the seeds of its propaganda in America did not fall on virgin soil. Already thousands of copies of the Nazi Bible—Hitler's "My Battle"— had been distributed, copies of the so-called "Protocols of the Elders of Zion," and the "Myth of the Twentieth Century" by the super-Nazi, Alfred Rosenberg. The free and paid distribution of such propaganda material has since reached enormous proportions.

Georg Stolzenfels, an automobile mechanic, and an enthusiastic Nazi, was one of the pioneer leaders of the party's propaganda in this country. However, his efficiency did not keep pace with his zeal, and Paul Manger succeeded him as director of American activities. It was Manger who undertook to organize not only parallel Nazi cells but also Storm Troops and Brown Shirts, patterned after the illustrious example of his German commanders. But funds were still meagre, the cells were not closely knit and the propaganda lagged.

In the fall of 1930 new impetus was given the work on this side of the Atlantic when the Nazi party sent well-paid propagandists to the United States. Ernest Luedecke, registered representative of the *Voelkische Beobachter* in Washington, took active charge of the work. He was regarded as the unofficial ambassador of Hitler in this country. With untiring effort he sought the company of Congressmen and other officials, losing no opportunity to spread the gospel. When Congressmen McFadden of Pennsylvania and Banton of Texas rose in the chamber dedicated to freedom and tolerance to mouth vituperative attacks on the Jews, Herr Luedecke and the Nazi party had good cause to congratulate themselves. Here was indisputable evidence of the value of the propaganda work of that period.

But Herr Luedecke in some way offended his superiors. Despite his good record here he was recalled and imprisoned in Germany. On September 30, 1932, Dr. Nieland issued a decree establishing an auxiliary of the party in the United States. Heinz Spanknoebel of Detroit, Michigan, who had made a trip to Germany to convince the Nazi leaders of his qualifications as a master of propaganda, was named chief of activities. Leaders were designated in New York, Chicago, Cincinnati, Detroit, Los Angeles, San Francisco, St. Louis, Boston, and Jersey City.

When Hitler acceded to power on January 30, 1933, there was an immediate influx of more money, more literature, and more man-power into American propaganda channels. The Nazi zealots in America, who up to that time had been fighting among themselves, were now given extensive instruction in the party's principle of leadership. A well-knit active organization with iron discipline replaced the rather slipshod body which had preceded Hitler's rise to dictatorship. The work of this group did not pass unnoticed in the liberal press, however. There were protests against this dissemination of ideas inimical to American institutions and tradition.

The brazenness of the German party in openly carrying on activities here was a particular point of attack. The German leaders, even the opportunists, on April 30, 1933, ostensibly dissolved their American branch and recalled Manger. The very next day, May 1, the Nazis established in America the "Friends of New Germany." Under the cloak of this amiable title, the Nazis have from that day to this carried on active pro-Hitler propaganda, including all its ramifications of anti-Semitism, and the like. In Detroit, Herr Spanknoebel carried on his work under the new organization. Every member became automatically a member of the German Nazi party. By this time, the group had grown more ambitious; it sought to spread Nazi ideas to Americans of non-German origin. For this purpose another group was formed which calls itself "The Friends of Germany." The omission of the word "New" in this second title is a typical example of what the Nazis no doubt felt to be a master stroke of intrigue. They seemed to think that it would be easier to enlist Americans as friends merely of Germany than as friends of the *new* Germany.

The Nazi talking point of "racial purity" was emphasized and Aryans of non-German origin were invited to join as contributing members. However, only non-naturalized Germans were allowed to be active party members. These had to swear allegiance to Hitler, and, as a necessary corollary, to repudiate any intention of becoming American citizens. Officially this new organization had no status as far as the National Socialist Party is concerned. Actually, however, the group has, since its inception, taken no step without the knowledge and approval of Nazi headquarters in

Germany, and its leaders have been subjected to the
strictest party discipline.

Later on, when Spanknoebel had disappeared, following his indictment for having failed to register as
a diplomatic agent for the German Government, Ambassador Luther insisted that neither he nor his embassy had ever been connected with him in any way.
It is, however, a fact that Spanknoebel visited the legation in Washington and that Dr. Rudolf Leitner, coun-
sellor of the embassy, came at least twice to New York
from Washington to confer with Spanknoebel behind
closed doors. At regular intervals Spanknoebel con-
ferred with Consul General Kiep and his successor, Dr.
Hans Borchers.

Dr. Nieland's decree, previously referred to, was reproduced in the January, 1933, number of the Nazi organ, *America's Deutsche Post*: "In order to consolidate
all local German groups in America," the decree reads,
"and to pave the way for the establishment of units to
comprise an American section of the National Socialist
party, I hereby appoint Camerade Heinz Spanknoebel,
of Detroit, national confidential agent for the United
States of North America. . . . The confidential agent
shall be responsible only to the chief of the foreign
division (Nieland). It shall be his task to build up
the national movement. . . ." The *Voelkischer Beobachter* on August 5, 1933, hailed the organization of
Nazi cells in America and referred to Heinz Spanknoebel as their leader. The paper stated that one of
the objects of the American group was to raise a fund
of $5,000,000 to spread Nazi ideas.

The German Government itself repudiated Spanknoebel and his activities. Its repudiation was appar-

ently based on an extremely technical distinction between the government itself and the Nazi party. Actually, of course, the two were identical.

Before his flight, Spanknoebel's propaganda had made such inroads into the United German Societies that four component groups of the Federation of German Jewish Societies were forced to withdraw. The Ridder brothers, publishers of the *New Yorker Staats-Zeitung*, who had the temerity to refuse Spanknoebel's demand that they publish only what he directed, were also compelled to resign. At a meeting of delegates of the United German Society, ninety per cent of those present voted to have Spanknoebel speak for the projected German Day celebration, October 29, 1933, at a New York armory. They planned also to fly the Swastika on that occasion. The opposition, crushed at this meeting, made charges through the New York press that fake delegates had packed the meeting and that intimidation had been used. Mayor O'Brien prohibited the celebration on the ground that it would be dangerous to the peace of the city. However, on December 10, the meeting was held under the auspices of the Steuben Society. It turned out to be a Nazi mass meeting.

The fact that members of these societies, ordinarily non-political and intensely loyal to America, could be stampeded into following Spanknoebel, into becoming hysterically pro-Hitler, and anti-Semitic, is the best possible illustration of the power and the danger of Nazi propaganda in this country.

Members of the "Friends of New Germany" have organized an extensive espionage system. Every German refugee is carefully watched. Passports are scrupulously checked. If refugees overstay their permits they are denounced to the immigration authorities. Lists of writers are compiled, and important articles dealing with the Nazis are cabled to Germany.

On several occasions Germans were arrested on their return to their homeland because of uncomplimentary remarks about the Hitler régime to which they gave vent in New York; in New York restaurants. Hundreds of servant-girls are acting as spies in Jewish families in New York; German Americans who have expressed opinions unfriendly to Hitler have been warned that they may ben endangering the welfare of their relatives in Germany. To detail the activities of the "Friends of New Germany" alone would require volumes. But there are numerous other channels of propaganda in this country which merit description.

The North German and Hamburg-American lines' offices in New York are hotbeds of Nazi propaganda in America. The North German Lloyd Director, H. Mensing, is the official representative of the Nazi Labor Front in America, working under the direction of Dr. Robert Ley, his direct superior in Germany. Employees of these lines, in accordance with the German laws, have been forced to join the Nazi shop organizations. Mensing has forced thousands of German employees of American firms to join the labor front on the threat that if they should ever return to Germany they would be refused jobs and persecuted. The steamship lines have brought tons of propaganda to this country. As recently as on February 7, 1934, *The New York Times* informed its readers that United States officials had discovered six burlap sacks containing three hun-

dred pounds of Nazi propaganda on the German freight-
er *Este*. All this material was addressed to the chief
propagandists in New York and other cities. A share
was consigned to "The Friends of the New Germany."
Naturally this propaganda dealt with the Jewish question, though the anti-pacifistic and cultural phases of
Nazi ideology were duly stressed. Spanknoebel is reported to have fled to Germany on the S.S. Deutschland
without registering as a passenger. According to the
New York World-Telegram, Colonel Emerson did the
same thing on the S.S. Europa late in January, 1934.
Propagandists are smuggled into this country after coming across ostensibly as members of the crew. Nazi
conspirators have complete privacy for their conferences aboard these ships in port. Employees of the
lines have taken part in Nazi meetings in New York.

Thus far the Nazis in America have not been able
to secure a daily newspaper. Their efforts to take over
the *New Yorker Staats-Zeitung* failed. At present they
have two weekly papers in New York—*America's
Deutsche Post* and *Deutsche Zeitung*, as well as papers
in other cities. These newspapers for the most part
are replicas of the Nazi papers in Germany. The
America's Deutsche Post recently declared: "Fight each
Jewish boycott! Fight every store, every business house,
every commercial firm that takes part in the anti-German boycott. Support Christian business. A large
part of the American people who have also sensed the
Jewish peril in this country stand by our side." And
during the last election it advised its readers to vote
for McKee as Mayor LaGuardia would sell out the city
to the Jews.

American children have not been overlooked by the

Nazi propagandists. In New York a group called the Hitler Youth has been formed, on the surface a kind of boy scout movement, but actually a recruiting movement for the Storm Troops. The literature distributed to the children included such statements as "If the world at large bares it teeth at Germany we will smash it." Clearly the main objective of this group is to breed soldiers for a war in which Nazidom will conquer the world.

Colonel Emerson, whom we have mentioned before, maintained a "translation and advisory bureau" in the Whitehall Building, 17 Battery Place, New York, which is also the address of the German Consul General. Colonel Emerson has denied that he was paid by the Nazis for defending Hitler—both as speaker and writer. The Colonel insisted that his zeal for Nazism and his love of Germany were inspired by the kindly treatment he received while interned in Germany during the war. This phase of his history is rather obscure, but it is known that from 1914-1917 he edited the Continental News, published in English by the German government to carry on pro-German propaganda among English-speaking soldiers. When the United States became a combatant he officially resigned from this paper, but to the end of the war he remained friendly with the German authorities.

Emerson had gathered around him for his pro-Nazi work here a group which included T. St. John Gaffney, former American Consul General in Munich, whose pro-German activity during the war led to his retirement from the diplomatic service; Frederick Franklin Schrader, who carried on the pro-German propaganda in this country during the war and who had also been employed by the German embassy; Ferdinand Hansen, Joseph J. O'Donohue, Rev. Francis Gross, Arthur Fleming Waring and others.

All these gentlemen have written extensively for the English sections of the Nazi press in America. In fact, the columns of these publications are kept well filled by these men with indignant letters in which they deny any Nazi affiliations. This group has been active in political and military circles in Washington. In May, 1933, a letter attacking the Jewish people was sent to every congressman and senator over Gaffney's signature.

But these are the more obvious propagandists. Far more dangerous are those who pose as unbiased. They include professional lecturers, college professors, "goodwill" lecturers and exchange students. Their name is literally legion, but there is space here to mention but a few.

Ellery Walter, who specializes in travel talks, always finds occasion to tell his audiences that Hitler's storm troopers have committed no atrocities; that he himself never saw a single Jew mistreated. John G. Bucher has been telling Rotary and Kiwanis clubs of the merits of Hitlerism; that good Jews were never molested; that the Nazi anti-Semitism was justified because the majority of Jews were Communists. Naturally it was better strategy to use Bucher, an American, than avowed Germans.

Dr. Frederick Schoenemann, head of the American division of English seminars at the University of Berlin has been telling cultured American groups about the ideals of Germany today. Dr. Schoenemann is too clever to deny all the charges against Hitlerism. He

avoids the question of anti-Semitism, but when pressed
to discuss this point recently in Baltimore he said "We
know we have sinned. Radical instincts are stirred up
in revolutions. But in time there will be moderation.
We do not defend everything that has taken place during the revolution, but at the same time one cannot
generalize and condemn the National Socialist policy
on just one item. Hitler did not go to power on anti-
Semitism."

Douglas Brinkley, former N.B.C. announcer and
news commentator, was one of the numerous American
publicists who were invited to Germany ostensibly to
study conditions there. None of this group, which included such men as George Sylvester Viereck, paid his
own expenses. These visits have already begun to
show results in a wave of propaganda. Brinkley, for
instance, had no sooner returned to this country than
he told a New York Nazi audience at the Central Opera
House that Hitlerland is a veritable paradise, that the
concentration camps are models of humane comfort,
and that stories of atrocities are all untrue. Brinkley
was the only man who addressed this meeting in English. He informed the audience that he intended to
travel throughout the United States to carry this message. Mr. Brinkley, as far back as July, 1933, knew
what he wanted. On July 11, he declared from a German shortwave radio station: "I came to Germany to
become acquainted with actual conditions—to establish
the naked facts, and to enlighten the American people
about the new Germany. Nowhere have I been able
to find even the slightest sign of unrest or mistreatment.
I am a witness that all disquieting reports about Germany are mere fabrication."

Brinkley is regarded today as the most important Nazi propagandist in America. The Nazis hope he will eventually secure time on the national radio networks here. In the meantime he is preparing to syndicate a series of articles. The *Deutsche Zeitung* on January 20 said of him: "We know Germany has a very good friend in Douglas Brinkley and we hope in the interest of our Fatherland and of the whole world that his important voice will be heard so that the world will know better the blessings of National Socialist Germany."

But it is Viereck who is the real brain-trust of Nazi propaganda in America. It is Viereck who sends an indignant letter of protest to the editor whenever an American publication exposes the machinations of Nazidom here. It is Viereck who censors all the Nazi publicity material in this country. Viereck's trip to Germany was made with Carl D. Dickey of the firm of Carl Byoir and Associates of New York, the publicity outfit which formerly represented the infamous Machado. Apparently the theory of the Nazis was that if this firm could sell Machado to the American public it could sell even Hitler and Göring. The, no doubt, disinterested opinions of Messrs. Viereck and Dickey on Germany will soon be fed to Americans through a series of syndicated articles. One may expect that these gentlemen will be more circumspect than the crude, outspoken Georg Schmitt.

German exchange students are seeking in this country to duplicate the success of the Nazis in Germany in winning the support in universities. If anti-Semitism appeals so readily to European students, the Nazis reason, why not to American? Before the exchange stu-

dents leave Germany they must sign a pledge to speak
only good of the Hitler régime.

A demand that the activities of German exchange
students at American universities be investigated to
disclose whether they are engaged in Nazi propaganda
work was made in October, 1933, by Dr. Franz Boas,
Professor of Anthropology at Columbia University. In
a letter to Representative Samuel Dickstein, Chairman
of the House Immigration Committee, Boas cited the
official order of the German Government requiring all
exchange students in foreign countries to spread Nazi
propaganda.

Detlef Sahm, son of the Lord Mayor of Berlin, who
attends Columbia University, is a typical member of
this group. He has spoken at numerous meetings in
defense of Nazism. This bright young man disposes
of the entire matter of Jewish persecutions by pointing
out that after all the Jews comprise only one per cent
of the population of Germany and that, therefore, they
warrant only one per cent of his discussion.

Sahm resides at the International House at 500 Riv-
erside Drive, New York. More than five hundred students of about thirty different nationalities reside there.
The institution has always been dedicated to the highest ideals of racial tolerance, but this has not prevented
German students there from creating a Nazi cell. Similar cells have been organized in Harvard, Dartmouth,
and other universities, at the Rockefeller Institute, and
in many hospitals, among them the Medical Centre
of New York City.

German Language departments of American universities in some cases become centers of Nazi propaganda.
The extremely helpful *America's Deutsche Post* in its

issue of January 20, 1934, declares: "We are very happy
about the announcement that Professor John A. Walz
of Harvard University has been chosen as President of
the American Association of German teachers, succeed-
ing Professor A. R. Hochfeld of the University of
Wisconsin. Professor Walz is known in true German
circles as a staunch fighter for German culture, literature, and music. Our happiness glows. Professor
Frederick Betz of Washington Irving High School of
New York was unanimously elected Vice-President of
the same association. His election also we heartily welcome for our cause."

The equally informative *Deutsche Zeitung* pleads
with its readers to supply at least five hundred new
students for the German language courses given through
the C.W.A. by the University of the State of New
York. This newspaper hails with glee the appointment
of Martin Hartman and Frederick Scheibe as instructors. Both of these gentlemen are active propagandists.
The happy plan of spreading Nazism through these
courses is credited to Fritz Gissibl, present leader of
the Nazis in New York.

The Nazi press in America is urging its readers to
buy good receivers for short wave radio broadcasts from
Germany. "German stations on the air every night
for North and South America," headlines the *German
Outlook*, English edition of the *Deutsche Zeitung*. There
are three broadcasts on shortwave stations every day,
spreading propaganda from Germany to the United
States.

The German Consul General's office in New York
has been the center of most of the propaganda in this
country. Here much of the funds were distributed.

Bills for propaganda activities were frequently paid by
Herr Loeper, treasurer of the German General Con-
sulate, and the receipts sent to Berlin along with diplomatic correspondence. Ambassador Luther, formerly
of the moderate and republican People's Party, with
the accession of Hitler became an ardent Nazi sup-
porter. Propaganda bills have also been paid by Dr.
Degener of the German American Commercial League,
which, with the German American Board of Trade and
the German Legion, has carried on active anti-Semitic
and pro-Hitler propaganda.

The drain on the German Government's funds was
such that in June, 1933, Dr. Luther and Dr. Kiep, acting on orders from Berlin, summoned German big
business men in this country to a meeting at the Con-
sulate and told them it was their duty to finance Nazi
propaganda in America. Adolph Scheurer, director
of the American office of the Hamburg-American line;
Willi von Meister, American representative of the Dor-
nier Motor Works, Friedrichshaven; General A. Metz
and Von Rath of the I. G. Chemical Corporation, were
given leading rôles in organizing big business as a factor
in Nazi propaganda.

Only a hint of the manifold workings of the Nazi
propaganda machine in America has been given. Much
of what is here set down centers in New York, but
everywhere in America the same story of the manufacture of synthetic hatred is being written. Not the Jews
alone, but France is vilified, as is every potential enemy of the Fatherland. In Union City, New Jersey, a
storm troop detachment drills, dressed in blue trousers,
white shirts, black ties and swastika caps, the official
uniform adopted wherever it might be dangerous to

wear the authentic brown uniforms of their prototype rowdies. Gangsters, bouncers, boxers have been enlisted by Nazi groups. The *Stahlhelm* has a branch in America, with a permanent resident here, as its head.

But the Nazis do not work alone in the cause of reaction and hatred in this country. Allies have not been found lacking among native groups. There has been so much cordiality between these groups and the Hitlerites, so much active co-operation, so much similarity of "ideas" and tactics, that a study of the native Fascist organizations must be included in any consideration of the Nazi invasion of America.

Chief of these groups in America are the Silver Shirts and their imitation *Führer,* William Dudley Pelley, who operates from Asheville, North Carolina, on the more gullible citizens of the South and West. The barest outline of Pelley's "ideas" and tactics, not the characterization of his critics, but his own words as recorded in his magazine, *Liberation,* must inspire more amusement and incredulity than disgust, such is their absurdity. But when one remembers how laughable Hitler and his ideas were once held by intelligent Germans, when one considers Pelley's boast that the membership of his group now runs into the millions, one must pause a moment, even in the midst of laughter, to take stock of this man who, today a clown, may yet change his rôle in this modern world where the impossible has already happened.

Pelley frankly acknowledges his debt to Hitler as the man whose ideas and program furnished him with inspiration. In a pamphlet distributed by the thousands in New York and other cities, Pelley's early career as

a newspaperman and hater of Bolshevism is outlined.
In 1929, we are informed, Pelley nobly cast aside the
writing of popular fiction stories which "had netted
him $25,000 a year" to start the League for the Lib-
eration:

"Its surface purpose was metaphysical research.
Under cover it perfected a great national organization, drawing people of importance from the highest walks, people whose names have never been published and may never become known. Some of them
are now high in our Government.

"Steadily, inexorably, during 1930, 1931 and
1932, Pelley drew his organization tighter, calked
and stabilized it, weeded out the 'curiosity seekers'
and the 'chicken hearts,' appointed his keymen in
all the states of the Union, made his contacts with
influential Protestant Christians in Washington.

"On January 31, 1933, the day Hitler came into
power in Germany, Pelley came out from under
cover with his Silver Shirt National Organization.

"Having planted depots of his facts through the
entire United States, enlightened police and vigilante
groups, secured the co-operation of outraged Christian citizens to carry on regardless of what happens
to him personally, his organization of Silver Shirts
is now snowballing exactly as Hitler's Nazis snow-
balled in Germany when the German people were
at last persuaded to the truth."

Major Luther I. Powell, Pelley's chief of staff, a
former Ku Klux Klanner, speaking of the Shirts, declared frankly:

"Our order maintains the depression is the result of
predatory minds. We are anti-Semitic because the

Jews are a predatory people. Of course, we are in sympathy with the Hitler movement, and constantly in touch with his representatives in America."

Hitler's anti-Semitism, his Red phobia, his Aryan appeal, his denunciations of the powers-that-were of his pre-victory days, are all aped by Pelley.

To Pelley, as to Hitler, all, or practically all, communists are Jews. Practically all the rulers of Soviet Russia are also Jews. The real rulers of our country, he opines, are such "anti-Christs" as Baruch, Morgenthau and other Jewish bankers. As nearly as one can understand the language of Pelley, the spiritualist turned politician, these Jewish communists and bankers are in a conspiracy to rob the country and then turn it over to the Bolshevists! Pelley professes a great deal of reverence for Americanism, but he warns that the present administration is being duped by Jews and includes in his platform of significant words, "to preserve our representative form of government, *if possible . . .*"

If Pelley's boasts of the size of his organization are anywhere near the truth, he has small cause to rue the "$25,000 a year" which he nobly sacrificed. Each of the alleged 2,000,000 members must pay an initiation fee of $10 into the "National War Chest," and thereafter $1.00 a month. *Liberation* is ever on the lookout for more funds.

Many of Pelley's articles in *Liberation* are mystically worded in a jargon which seems to be a bad attempt at poetic prose. These are ideas, "psychically received." For Pelley—you have his own word for it—gets his ideas from "voices," or "clairaudient contacts" from mystic beings whom he calls "mentors."

"It was from these mentors," *Liberation* explained in April, 1933, "that the chief of the Silver Shirts in America first heard of Adolf Hitler." "Writing clair-audiently one day in a New York apartment at their dictation, he was told of Hitler's existence in Austria as a house painter who was shortly to come to power in Germany . . . Much of Hitler's pre-natal history was also received in this clairaudient communication . . . Hitler has a destiny to fulfill . . . He has already set his hand against the so-called 'Lord's Chosen' in Germany, and disturbed the status thereby of Israel all over the world. That disturbance is only in its beginning. But Hitler is not going to finish this work. The finish of it comes here in America."

It cannot be said that Pelley does not know where he stands. "To be grouped in the class and company of the Klan and the Nazis," he writes, "is unwittingly to be complimented . . ." In imitation of Hitler's Storm Troop, Pelley has organized a "Protestant Christian Militia" which wears silver shirts. In addition to *Liberation*, this group also publishes *The Silver Ranger* at Oklahoma City.

There are many imitations of the Silver Shirts and of the Brown Shirts, for that matter; the pattern of hatred propaganda is in every case strikingly similar. The Khaki Shirts of America, organized in Philadelphia by Arthur J. Smith, tried unsuccessfully to march on Washington and then fell into temporary eclipse after their leader's exposure and arrest. In Seattle, a faction of the American Legion organized the fascist White Shirts. In New York the Order of '76 is busy distributing Representative MacFadden's strictures against the Jews. From Boston the Industrial Defence Association, a "Gentile group," spreads anti-Semitic propaganda and aids and abets Hitlerism in this country. The association publishes calumnies against Jews in their organ, *What's What*. The frank name of the "Swastika League of America" is taken by another Massachusetts group, which publishes the *American Guard* in Brookline. In Huston, Texas, appears the *Nationalist*, whose avowed purpose is to "put the Jews in their place." Should all these Nazi groups ever pool their energies—a consummation not impossible, but devoutly to be avoided—not merely Jews, but the entire structure of the American republic will be imperilled.

Thus hatred rears its ugly head here, as it did in republican Germany. The campaign of venom is not important merely as an unjust attack upon the Jews. It is important because, as Germany's experience has so eloquently demonstrated, the practise of raising up a scapegoat in times of stress simply enables the ruthless and the dishonest to seize power, while evading the real issues. But once the objective of power has been reached, those who have played upon the hatred of the masses are powerless to control it even if they wish to, and the horrible tragedy of persecution must be played out to its bloody conclusion. Hence, those Americans—whether Jews or Gentiles who would preserve their hard won rights of freedom and justice, must lead the battle if the Nazi invasion of America is to be repulsed.

THE AMERICAN REACTION

BY CHARLES H. TUTTLE

In America there is a widespread fear that Hitlerism menaces all that has been gained for tolerance, for democracy and for peace since the Dark Ages.

We fully recognize that the German people have a right to choose such rulers and such form of government as they may wish; and, however naturally we in America may regret the destruction of the republican system, it is our duty to leave that political issue to the German people themselves, hopeful that in the long run their ultimate decision will be worthy of their great contributions to human progress in literature, science and art.

But America sees Hitlerism as more than a political issue. It sees Hitlerism as the antithesis of the American system, tradition and aspiration. It sees it as the old theory of an enlightened despotism, furbished with new plausibilities derived from chaos within and without; maintaining itself by a systemized intolerance and by appeal to racial egoism; and merging the rights of the individual in the totality of a state held in iron discipline from above.

On the other hand, the American system of government and political and social philosophy is founded on an invincible Faith in Man,—in the extraordinary capabilities in ordinary people if only the door of opportunity be opened wide enough. The American Constitution is second only to the Scriptures as the expression of a great optimism concerning human nature irrespective of race or creed. The American secular religion is a moral conviction of the innate fitness of the ordinary individual to be the foundation of government itself, and a militant belief that there is a national and individual character which only freedom can know how to make.

Hence, according to the American way, successful democracy must be and is the accomplishment of the many. It is they who make the conscience of the nation, strengthen the voice of public opinion and preach and demonstrate the gospel of human potentialities. It is they—the nameless many—who give a glory to obscurity while fame is busy with her proclamations about the conspicuous few.

In consequence, when the American creed speaks of individual liberty, it speaks also of individual enlightenment. There can be no independence without universal education, no freedom without equal mental and spiritual opportunity for all. Those who won American independence esteemed liberty both as an end and as a means. They believed that freedom to think, to write and speak, freedom to have equal participation in public affairs, to enjoy the equal protection of the laws, and to possess an equal right in matters of conscience, were conditions essential to the development of the self-governing man and, therefore, of the self-governing state. They believed that the lesson of history was that man progressed in proportion as he replaced control from without by control from within, and substituted for ruthless individualism or regimented compulsion a voluntary and enlightened cooperation regulated and encouraged by law and invigorated by a lively private and public conscience. Hence, the rise of that Eighth Wonder of the World, —the American system of education. The vast multitude of our schools and colleges, by their freedom from centralized control, preserve liberty of thought and research, and prevent that worst of all possible arguments,—silence coerced by law. They throw open to all the equal fellowship of the mind, and hence leave no room for that most unsuccessful of all efforts to control men from without,—intolerance of the sincere beliefs and opinions of others.

Economic disaster and widespread unemployment may in America make some centralization of power, as in time of war, a temporary expedient born of a temporary emergency; but the original principles of equal opportunity and popular government have not thereby lost their spring or elasticity and remain indispensable in the habits of the people and impregnable in their affections.

This American gospel of toleration and liberty ennobled by cooperation is rooted in the origins of the American people and is kept alive by necessity. Into our land have come the emigrants from many nations bringing with them their imports of glory, in art, letters, handicraft and religion; and all this variant material, with its diverse textures and elements must be transmuted into one citizenry pursuing an order by progress under one constitution and one flag. Of necessity, we must seek unity through the cooperation of diversities, and out of this need has come the American creed that to realize in its immanence the dynamic doctrine that "all men are born free and equal," is a major goal of mankind.

The antithesis of this American gospel is Hitlerism. The latter's unity is in uniformity and not in harmonized multiformity. It exalts singularity and denounces plurality of culture. The result is a new type of particularity that can well prove dangerous to the peace of the world and to the solidarity of mankind. By transferring the doctrine of Divine Right from king to race, it convinces itself of an anointed superiority which seems to outsiders to be a pathological exaggeration and which apparently seeks to convince itself of the validity of its own assumption by obliterating all minorities and by silencing even self-criticism. The results are a planned intolerance; a fanatical national worship of racial blood and tradition; a regimentation of thought, expression and education; a dictatorship which has crushed both the form and the spirit of democracy and the predominance of a single will—leadership in the narrowest sense.

The persecution of the Jews, which followed the ascendancy of Hitler to power, produced universal protest in America.

In the first place, we were quick to perceive that if the challenge of intolerance sounded across the ocean went uncondemned among us, we inevitably would face a similar challenge issuing from our own midst. Indeed, we were aware that we ourselves had not been above reproach; and, in a spirit of humiliation, we were prepared to remember our own shortcomings in the matter of racial and religious prejudice and of capitulation before the successful grafter, the racketeer and the bootlegger. But these internal evils convinced us the more of the necessity of developing a strong and pulsating national consciousness of justice and brotherly love, and of fighting prejudice and persecution wherever they might entrench themselves. The very diversities of our national, racial and religious antecedents, which normally make for richness and power in our country's life, are always exposed to the dangers of social disruption through propaganda from without. America, therefore, rose in protest lest prejudice and hate should overrun the world and our nation with it, and lest civilization at home and abroad should lose all that has been gained for tolerance and understanding through ages of painful experience.

In the second place, the religious instincts of America were deeply revolted. The idea of deliberately persecuting, through decree or instigation of government, any group of people because of blood or conscientious convictions, was an offense against the laws of humanity and of God, and, in American opinion, placed upon the whole commonwealth of mankind the instant right and duty to speak aloud. Hence, the leaders of the Christian Faith, clergy and laity alike, united in appealing to the German people not to permit within their borders continuance of acts of aggression against the Jews. They deplored that the age-old cry of Jewish sorrow should arise again from a Christian land. They declared that the Jews are the spiritual fore-fathers of the great peoples professing Christianity; and that all Christians are bound by the noble spirit of their Faith to see to it, wherever persecution of the Jewish race occurs, that it meets stern and instant opposition. For the sake of Germany, for the sake of the world, and for the sake of Christianity, those who professed the Christian Faith in America could not stand passive, and without protest watch the forcible conversion of Jews into citizens of low caste, into Jewish "untouchables," into prisoners of a ghetto.

One result of this religious reaction in America has been a heightening of the effort of men of good will, Gentile and Jew alike, to promote as between Catholic, Protestant and Jew the national ideals of amity, justice and co-operation. In this task the National Conference of Jews and Christians has taken the foremost part. The purposes of this national organization are to promote, as between these three Faiths, that spirit of toleration and sympathetic understanding which is their common treasure, and to stand on guard against tendencies in this country which make for religious and racial prejudice and discrimination. The Conference is not interested in finding the lowest common denominator but in working out in unison through the religious ideals of each group the universal obligations of social justice and fraternal charity.

Moreover, there is a deep conviction in America that the new political order in Germany once more justifies the fear of war. If it be true, as Hitlerism insists, that world power is to be with the disciplined state whose people are racially the purest and physically the strongest and most prolific, the time cannot be far distant when the disciples of this doctrine must put it to the test. On the other hand, the American tradition is by no means convinced that in the long run God is on the side of the strongest battalions, and it

instinctively believes that peace goes out when the
Caesars come in.

Notwithstanding all these considerations, however,
there is in America no ill-will for the German people.
We gladly recognize the great contributions which they
have made in the past to civilization and to liberty
of conscience; and we acclaim the brave and persistent
stand of those German pastors who are struggling to
maintain liberty of conscience, the universality of fellowship and the government of religion by reasonable-
ness and charity and not by force. We also recognize
that the German people have suffered grievously from
unrevised international treaties; that their present militant nationalism is due in large part to their deep
conviction that the spirit and letter of the peace conditions laid down in 1918 have not been kept; and
that they too have the right to demand of us and of
the world justice and co-operation. But those who
seek justice must themselves extend justice. Those who
seek freedom for themselves must preserve the freedom of others. Those who complain of international
discrimination should not allow racial and religious
discrimination within their own borders.

HITLER UNEXPURGATED:

DELETIONS FROM "MEIN KAMPF"

BY MIRIAM BEARD

SINCE the translation of his autobiography into English is not a pirated edition, Hitler must have authorized it. Whether or not he is the real editor, as was assumed by leading newspapers in London when the work appeared there, the ultimate responsibility for presenting it in so shrunken and garbled a shape to the Anglo-American publics must rest upon him. These then are the crumbs, the stale fragments of his original thought and feelings which he has considered safe to offer abroad.

The version is opened by a frontispiece depicting the Leader shaking hands with a humble cottager, and a mere woman at that, an act of graciousness twice distilled which earns the caption, "the human side of Germany's chancellor." This is most appropriate, for the other sides of Hitler's nature, the vengeful, the slippery, the coldly-calculating, for instance, which he with such astounding frankness reveals in the original German, have been discreetly veiled from our gaze. Before we take the hand the Leader offers us humble cottagers of England and America, let us find out from the original editions what he is concealing in the other hand. And let us not be shy about it, either, for on

page 109 of the original (Munich, 1930), in words
wiped with care from the translation, he indulges in
a hearty laugh at readers "unable or unwilling to verify what they read" and therefore susceptible to his
propaganda—a category into which, it is to be feared,
most of his foreign public which cannot easily verify
the texts, is likely to fall.

The first page offers us a foretaste of what is to come.
A long description of how the child Hitler learned to
hate France with a fury that has never waned is cut
out, together with a touching picture of the young
Adolf poring over his "favorite reading-matter," a
tome on the Franco-Prussian conflict, the "hero-battle"
which "became my greatest inner experience. From
now on I was more and more enthusiastic over everything that had to do with war or soldiery. . . . Why
did not Austria fight in this war, why not my father
and the rest? Are we not the same as all the other
Germans?" Only this very last question, absurd without its context, has found its way into English.

But the translation that has suppressed the juvenile
Hitler's wish to attack France has concealed also his
more adult determination to assume the government of
the globe. The very last words on the very last page
of Hitler's autobiography in the original German contain this challenge to humanity: "A State which . . .
devotedly fosters its best racial elements is bound one
day to became Master of the Earth" (*Herr der Erde*).
With a final exhortation to his followers to count no
sacrifice too great in view of an ultimate prospect so
pleasing, the present German dictator had brought to
a grand climax his bellicose behemoth of a book. But
this supreme message, this final bloom of his medita-

tions, is missing from the English "translation"; and indeed the entire closing page of which it is the crown has been *spurlos versenkt.*

Between the garbled opening and the amputated finale, the present bowdlerized version is one amazing piece of *Lochstickerei,* eyelet-embroidery—more hole than stuff. Less than a third of the original material remains and this, to form the semblance of a fabric, is held together by skillful stitches which span enormous gaps. The result is admitted by the preface to be "somewhat abridged," a term surely "somewhat" mild to employ about a translation which omits, at the very least, 158,400 words of the original.

It may be urged, and is in fact maintained by the preface, that the abridgement contains "all of the sentiments and ideals of government" of Hitler, and omits only "matter not of general or international interest." Is then the violently derogatory passage on America from page 723 of the original entirely cut away because it is lacking in general interest? Are the decapitated passages voicing a dream of German world-dominion then so wholly devoid of international interest?

Some defenders of the present version have pointed to the fact that, whatever has been done, it still is not a pretty book. This is true; it would have been impossible, by any sort of juggling, to get together two dozen pacific pages from an original which breathes hatred over almost every aspect of modern culture and expresses admiration for hardly anything or anybody save the pure Aryan, the Prussian Army, and Hitler's master of propaganda, Lloyd George. But all that is beside the point; the mere toning down of Hit-

ler's sound and fury is inconsequential and so is the prun-
ing away of epithets until not a single "pimp," "dung,"
or "maggot" is left to bring a blush to the cheek of
any gentlewoman or render the work unsuitable for
classroom use. What is serious is the concealment of
the method behind this madness; the erasion of whole
pages in which Hitler revealed the strategy behind his
moves, the calculation that leads him to moderate his
tone for foreign consumption and assume hysteria for
domestic effect—pages which in short uncover him as
he really is—not mad but "Machiavellian."

The translation which so blurs our view of the man
also hides his supreme aims, which form an immediate
threat to world stability. It obliterates his references
to Germans as the "best of humanity" and therefore
its God-appointed rulers; it removes the admonition,
for example, to Germany to prepare herself for her
"holy mission"—to govern us all—by first cleansing
herself of democratic taint (page 493 of the original):
"A *Weltanschauung* rejecting the democratic mass-idea,
which aims to turn the earth over to the best people,
the highest of mankind, must also logically carry out
this aristocratic principle within that people and assure
to its best brains the leadership and influence." Even
more remarkable is the elimination of Hitler's ring-
ing definition of a desirable millenium (page 438 of
the original): "A peace, supported not by the palm-
leaves of lacrimonious hired female-mourners, but
founded by the victorious sword of a Master-People
which brings the world into the service of a higher
Kultur" and leaves Germany *"Herrin des Erdballs"*—
mistress of the globe.

A neat sample of the type of elision which has taken

place may be found on page 271 of the English version which reads: "We will be armed once more!
Every opportunity has been missed." Opportunity for
what? What does Germany intend to do with her
weapons? Surely this is a practical question in view
of her approaching rearmament. But we simple Anglo-
Saxons are not to be told, at least not yet. Only in
the original German, on page 715, may one discover
the stirring trumpet-call to war which belongs between
the two sentences: "*Jawohl,* that is how a peace treaty
may be used . . . the greatest propaganda-weapon for
the shaking-awake of a nation's slumbering life-forces.
Then indeed everything, from the baby's first story-
book to the last newspaper, theater, and cinema, every
placard-pillar and every vacant wall-space, must be
put to the service of this one great mission, until the
nervous prayer of our modern verein-patriots, 'Lord,
make us free!' has been changed in the brain of the
tiniest urchin to the glowing plea: 'Almighty God, bless
our weapons again; be as just as ever Thou wast; judge
now if we deserve freedom; *Lord, bless our battle!*'"

An abridgement of Hitler's *"Mein Kampf"* which
consistently hushes over the author's determination to
prepare for and precipitate a clash of arms with France,
and which furthermore conceals his intention to win
over the English-speaking peoples to his side by subtle
propaganda and smooth promises, cannot claim to represent fairly his aims. Yet of all this, the English
version is guilty. It comes dangerously near to being
that ultimate absurdity: Hitler's "My Battle"—minus
the battle.

In a long exordium, for example, which was printed
on pages 704-5 of the original in type so extra large

that even a hasty translator could hardly have avoided seeing it, Hitler said: "France remains by far the most frightful enemy. This folk, sinking steadily into a negroid condition, means, through its relation to the goals of Jewish world-domination, a constant danger to the survival of the White Race of Europe. For the pest-spreading through Negro blood on the Rhine in the heart of Europe corresponds quite as much to the sadistic-perverse thirst for revenge in this chauvinistic arch-enemy of our folk, as to the icily cold calculation of the Jew, who plans in this way to begin the bastardization of the European Continent in its middle point and by infection with lower types of humanity to rob the White Race of its gloriously independent existence. What France, spurred on by her own craze for revenge, and systematically led by Jews, is contriving in Europe is a sin against the safety of white humanity and one day will bring on that folk all the vengeful spectres of a coming generation that has learned to recognize in race-poisoning the supreme human sin."

The determination to loose the whirlwinds of Aryan revenge against France is again and again concealed by the translation. Thus page 288 of the English edition is neatly shorn of emphasis in the following manner (we have put in italics all words missing in the translation, while those to be found in both translation and original are left in ordinary type):

"Since we need strength, and the deadly enemy of our people, France, is mercilessly throttling us and robs us of our power, we must take every sacrifice upon ourselves, that in its results is apt to contribute to an annihilation of French hegemonial tendencies in Europe. Every Power is nowadays our natural ally that

like ourselves finds France's lust for domination on the Continent unbearable. No pilgrimage to such a Power should be too hard for us and no renunciation should appear too unpronounceable if the final result only offers a chance of crushing our grimmest hater. Let us then simply leave to the mild working of Time the healing of our lesser wounds, if we are able to cauterize and close the biggest one. We shall of course come up against the spiteful yappings of the enemies of our race at home. . . . *It is therefore necessary that the National Socialist movement in the eyes of the rest of the world be recognized and known as the bearer of a definite political intention. Whatever Heaven has in store for us, we shall be recognized by our visors."*

This is the sort of "translation" that has been done; a few inconsequential sentences have been detached from a long threat to world stability and a promise that, to gain allies for his attack on France, Hitler is willing to make any sacrifice—even to the extent of eating two-thirds of his words. He is still to be recognized by his visor, which continues to conceal his true face, but he would appear to have grown more shy about being known as "the bearer of a definite political intention."

On page 161 of the English version, for another example, there has been left only the harmless assertion that "Germans are without the herd instinct," but there has been omitted the whole flood of passionate verbiage which follows: "If the German people . . . had possessed that herdlike unity . . . then the German Reich would probably be today Mistress of the Globe. World history would have taken another course" and Germany would then "have reached what so many blinded pacifists hope today to get by begging with whimpering and whining." And this goal would not be merely a victory over France; it would be the remapping of Europe.

On page 291 of the translation Hitler appears to be saying with sweet reason that he seeks "a final settlement with France." The original word, "*Auseinandersetzung*," implies more heat than argument, and the whole of the following passage, which has been deleted, bears that out; on pages 766-7 of the original it reads: "under the precondition, however, that Germany sees in the annihilation of France merely a means to give thereafter to our people finally and in another place the possible extension. Today we number eighty million Germans in Europe! Only then, however, will that foreign policy be recognized as right when, after scarce a century, two hundred and fifty million Germans shall live on this Continent, and not indeed compressed together as the factory-coolies of the rest of the world, but as peasants and workers who accord one another life by their creative activities." This means, if it means anything, that Hitler wants to expand Germany to three times its present size.

That Hitler seeks territorial expansion, and will by no means be satisfied with a mere conquest of France, is hidden from English readers. On page 277 of the English version, is omitted this declaration: "the National Socialist movement must then without regard to 'tradition' and prejudices, find the courage to gather our people and its force for an advance on that road which leads out of the present narrowness of the life force of this people, out to new ground and soil, and therefore save it forever from the danger of dwindling

away from this earth or of doing the chores of other
nations as a slave-people."

And how much more land will this take? Only the
German original permits us to guess. The English version on page 275 quotes but a vague plea that "nothing
but sufficient space on the earth ensures freedom of
existence to a nation." But has Germany enough? No,
says the suppressed original, not enough for nourish-
ment or security. Page 276 of the English version
merely reads: "From a purely territorial view, the area
of the German Reich is insignificant compared with
those of the so-called world powers." This is not merely
a case of bad selection, it is a direct mis-translation,
obviously purposeful. What Hitler had said was that
in an age when other nations "almost cover whole con-
tinents it is not possible to speak of a world power in
reference...to the ridiculous extent of hardly 500,000
square kilometers."

But this is not all. For schemes so Bonapartian he
needs help. In the English version, Hitler mentions
his need of the English (and Italians) as "comrades."
Only the original German text explains that what he
wants is *"Waffengenossen,"* allies in arms. There—in
omitted words—he says that Germany's duty is, "re-
pressing all natural emotions, to reach the hand" to
potential allies for a fight which will be carried on,
he elsewhere declares—also in omitted words—with
total disregard for "religious, humane, and absolutely
all other considerations," which are to be "dropped
without exception."

Only in the original German may one discover by
what subtle means Hitler proposes to win over us sus-
picious foreigners. There he says he will get around

us by treading gently and bespeaking us softly. He advises his followers to breathe low until their swords are whetted. He caps this advice on page 712 with the omitted cry of warning: "Woe, if our movement should vent itself in protests instead of preparing for the combat!"

He reveals, in short, in the original that he has learned a supreme trick—to deliver violence to the home population, and dulcet messages to the foreigner. In a striking passage on page 650 of the original wholly wanting in the English version, he defines the Ideal Organizer in terms strangely paralleling those employed by Machiavelli to describe his Ideal Ruler. Where Machiavelli had said that the Ruler must be a centaur—half man, half beast—Hitler says that the Organizer of a folk-upheaval "must first of all be a psychologist. He must take men as they are and know them. He must neither overestimate man as an individual nor underestimate men in the mass. He must, on the contrary, attempt to give *equal weight to weakness and to bestiality* (*Bestialität*) in order to form an organization that includes all factors . . . and is fitted to carry an idea through to success."

For the German masses whose "slight power of abstraction thrusts them into the sphere of emotions" and are "only open to expressions of force," he has developed all the technique of frenzy. Though the stormiest of orators, he is never swept away by his own tempests. He has calculated every roar; he is in a state of premeditated froth when, as an observer describes it, "after two hours of fiery speech his collar is a wilted string about his neck, the hair sticks to his temples, his sleeves are hitched up and his buttons burst." At that time he may strike some persons as hysterical, but he explains to the initiate in an interesting passage on page 371, omitted from the translation, that hysteria is handy: "Hate is more lasting than dislike, and the thrusting power for the mightiest upheavals on this earth has at all times come less from scientific recognition than from a fanaticism that fills the souls of the masses and in a *forward-driving hysteria*" (*vorwärtsjagenden Hysterie*).

He sees through everybody, and, while making use of all, indulges in a blunt jocosity at the expense of his dupes; not a trace of this robust and cynical merriment touches the pages of the cleansed English version. He roars on page 296 of the original (wholly deleted for us), over those who are today his foremost followers, those "fellows who wave their old Germanic tin-swords, wearing an artificial bearskin with ox-horns over their heads" and "get excited about old Germanic hero-dom, the grey dawn of history, stone axes, and shields." He tells us, "I have got to know these fellows too well not to be filled with the deepest nausea before their pitiful play-acting . . . the Jews had every right to spare these popular comedians" who "are the biggest cowards that anybody can imagine." They are dirt in his eyes compared to the only men he really admires, the Prussian soldiers, and he does not suppose they can be used in his battalions, but they will serve to drum up recruits.

He will promise anything, he tells us. In many interesting pages which are entirely missing from the translation he explains how he felt that to fulfill his holy mission—the annihilation of France—he knew he must rouse the masses, and that could only be done with a vital *Weltanschauung;* then, he tells us, he picked up a bit of a notion here and there to form it. From the translation, one might suppose his ideals, his *Weltanschauung,* to be his motivating force; but he tells us in the original that these are but tools for his revenge. One might suppose from the translation that his course was dictated by pure inspiration; from the original one sees that every move is calculated in cold blood and with an eye to strategy. He says, for example, in deleted words, that he adopted Feder's anti-usury cry for its drawing-power, with no intention of keeping his promise, since a great politician "has to bother himself less with means than with the goal."

Words so coldly chosen may be discarded equally callously. And this Hitler has done for the English reading audiences. Determined, as he tells us, to use the genuine weapons of foreigners, which will be more useful than the tin-swords of the bearded Germanic professors, he has set about the work with characteristic premeditation. He will not be squeamish about his methods: "Whenever people fight for their existence all questions of humanity or esthetics fall away to nothing." Mercy is a vain illusion, he informs us on page 267 of the original, cut from the translation, "in a world . . . in which Force is forever mistress over the weak" and in which "Nature does not know" it.

He is going to avoid the mistakes of his predecessors. These lay partly in old-fashioned republican honesty which, in a deleted sentence of the original, he designates as an *"unbegrenzte Dummheit,"* an unbounded stupidity. The flavor of regret which belongs to that passage is missing from the translation which notes only

the harmless assertion that the Germans are "very much
more honest—being free from that specifically British
perfidie." The sigh with which he said that is gone.

He has learned the arts of propaganda from the Allies, who, says he, in an expunged sentence, were op-
erating (though not speaking) correctly when they accused the Germans of "hunnish" practices. From them
he has learned, he says on page 200 in words absent
in English: "Propaganda . . . does not have to seek ob-
jectively for the truth so far as it favors an opponent
. . . but exclusively has to serve our interests." It must
adopt every device of slander that ingenuity can suggest: "whenever our propaganda permits for a single
moment the shimmer of an appearance of right on the
other side, it has laid a foundation for doubt in the
right of our cause . . . especially among a people that
so suffers from objectivity-mania as the German!"

So he wrote; but perhaps he has since then grown
less confident. Perhaps he will be willing to listen
to the good advice of some American public relations
counselor, some man of a genius akin to that of Mr.
Ivy Lee, for example, who may inform him of our
latest technical advances in the art of selling a personality made since the War.

He has done his best with the reduction of his book
to a kindergarten version. With a systematic thoroughness that might, of course, be the result of acci-
dent, but seems more likely to be German, passages
have everywhere been lopped away or toned down that
might have annoyed capitalists, church-men, liberals,
lovers of peace and the arts, trade unionists, Freema-
sons or the bourgeois who might be ruffled were he to

suspect that Hitler thinks him "happy-drivelling," or the "man-in-the-street" who might be pained by Hitler's derision of his mental capacity.

Since the conciliation of the Anglo-American publics is a first step in his preparation program for war, there was deleted his original shriek that England reaches "out to the Yellow fist of Japan" for an "alliance which . . . offers the only chance for a consolidation of British world position in the face of the rising American Continent." He goes on (page 723) to cry, in words also missing in English, that America is ensnared through her democratic institutions by the Jews: "Jews are the regents of the Stock Exchange forces of the American Union. Every year permits them to rise further to control over a labor power of a folk of 120 millions," while but a few stubborn men "to their exasperation, stand independent today." In later editions, that is, since 1930, independence is conceded to a few Americans, but in early ones the sentence reads: "a single great man, Ford, stands yet independent there, to their exasperation."

To refashion for two great liberal countries like England and America a book which attacks almost every institution sacred to them was a task requiring tact. That the translator, Mr. E. T. S. Dugdale, is acquainted with the arts of diplomacy follows from the fact that he translated documents from the German Foreign Office for "Bismarck's Relations with England" (London, 1928.) But the real credit should all go to Hitler, who has been whittling away at his words ever since they first appeared in 1925-26.

Tact was exercised, first of all, by leaving out passages likely to alarm capitalists. Such passages have,

it is true, been modified in editions of the German
original, as Hitler approached power, and began to
shift the accent away from the socialism in national
socialism and throw away the bait. Little of a revolutionary hang-over remained, but that little is removed,
such as the information (page 676ff.) that the business
man must take his orders from on high like the workers,
and the claim (page 256) that capitalism was a chief
cause of the downfall of Imperial Germany: "A serious
symptom of decay was the . . . passing over of the
whole of economy into the possession of shareholding
companies . . . speculation of conscienceless usurers
. . . The Exchange began to triumph and . . . gather the
life of the nation into its control."

The feelings of churchmen have been spared. They
are not to guess that Hitler is a foe of Christian poison
as of Jewish race; the claim that Christian churches
"sin against the image of the Lord" by preaching the
sinister doctrine of the "brotherhood of man" has been
dropped, as Hitler has been persuaded to a more moderate attitude by Catholic lieutenants like Goering and
von Papen. So, too, is the reflection that "the pious
missionary wanders to Central Africa and founds Negro
missions, until our 'higher culture' shall have made
there a foul brood of bastards." No syllable of this
escapes into English.

Attacks on our international and democratic ideals
and institutions have been blurred by the omission of
such key passages as that on page 741 of the original
in which Hitler rejects the spirit of fair play: "We
are not the guardian police of the well-known 'poor,
little peoples' but soldiers of our own." Omitted is his
taunt that the old Imperial Government tolerated a

"bandit-gang" of liberals, out of sheer delicacy "about
the freedom of the press and the freedom of public
opinion," a mere "scream" before which, forsooth, "the
strongest men grow weak."

The real sting is taken from his remarks on labor.
His intention to "free economic life from the influences
of the mass" is omitted. An admission that strikes
are necessary in capitalist states is translated; the following statement that none will be tolerated under
Fascism is cut out. Gone is most of page 498 in which
he explains that Jews, wishing to ruin the Anglo-Saxons
by hampering the initiative of their rulers, have de-
coyed Aryan workers "into the trade union movement,
which does not serve the real interest of the employees,
but exclusively the destructive purpose of international
Jewry." And the picturesque words have vanished in
which he told on page 679 that the only reason he did
not attack trade unions openly and early was lack of
money and "one single brain to whom I could have
entrusted" the task; "Whoever in that time could really
have smashed the Marxist trade unions . . . would
have belonged to the truly greatest men of our folk
and his bust should have been dedicated to posterity
in the Valhalla at Regensburg. But I do not know
of any skull that would have looked well on such a
pedestal."

Bitter outbursts against any form of representative
government are gone. We are deprived of his vow
on page 501 that "There are no majority decisions" in
the Ideal State, and of his conception of that State as
purely military: "The guiding principle which made
the Prussian Army in its time the most wonderful instrument of the German People must be carried over

to form the guiding principle of our entire state constitution." This is omitted from a translation that purports to include *all* of Hitler's "ideals of government."

Naturally, his Ideal State will not resemble the fallen Republic, but the English version does not fully explain why he hates it. It omits his denunciation (page 605) of its worst crime: "having through a pacifistic-democratic mode of education robbed young men of their natural instincts . . . and gradually turned them into a patient herd of sheep."

Gone is his flat statement on page 584 that no honest German could support a Republic, particularly a peaceful Republic. The Austrian Hitler declared: "Since the first and only support of their state authority—their popularity—was rooted solely in a society of pimps, thieves, housebreakers, deserters, slackers, and so on, that is, in that part of the folk which we must designate as the Extreme of the Bad, it was necessarily in vain that they looked among such circles for men ready to sacrifice their lives in the service of new ideals." This statement was wisely omitted from the English version; it might have had a queer ring, coming as it does from the leader of a movement in which the chief popularized hero, Horst Wessel, upon whom as a pattern all German youths are told to look, was an underworld character supported by the earnings of a sometime-Communist prostitute.

But Hitler's ragings at democracy are not more watered down than his enthusiastic glorification of the proper substitute—militarism. The most striking tribute to the old Prussian Army is omitted from page 118 where it belongs: "The most powerful school of the German nation . . . It was the school which yet taught the individual German to look for the salvation of the nation, not in the lying phraseology of an international fraternization between Negroes, Germans, Chinese, French, English, and so on, but in the strength and uniformity of his own folkhood." Upon this Prussian Army, the only pillar of virtue he can find in the past, Hitler proposes to remodel future Germany.

How he intends to operate is hushed over in the translation which omits his proud assertion on page 510 that his Brown legions are, not "intelligent and independent" but "the most disciplined, blindly-obedient, best-drilled troops. That is a fundamental principle . . ." It omits his lengthy cogitations upon the best ways of re-arming in secret, which can only be done "when the army of inner spies is decimated." And first of all comes the proper martial fervor, he says on page 265 in deleted words: "The question of regaining German might does not run: how shall we make weapons? But: how shall we produce the spirit that enables a folk to bear weapons? When this spirit rules a folk, the will finds a thousand ways, of which every one ends in a weapon!"

The new State will infinitely surpass in bellicosity the old Imperial Germany, which he derides, in words neatly expurgated from the English, for its weak-kneed sentimentality, its drivelling democracy, its lukewarmness toward martial exploits and its poor state of preparedness. This point of view, though novel enough to merit our attention, is erased from the translation which excludes such remarks as these: "Everything would have been bearable if to the general half-heartedness had not fallen victim the power on whose existence the preservation of the Empire ultimately depended: the Army. . . . If on land too few recruits were drilled, so on the sea the same half-heartedness was at work. . . . The tendency to make ships . . . always a little bit smaller than those laid down at the same time in England, was scarcely far-seeing. . . . It should have been a duty to go over to the 30.5 centimeter gun, since the goal was the reaching not of equal but superior fighting force."

It was no wonder, thinks Hitler—though the thought is concealed from English readers—that so supinely pacifistic a country as Imperial Germany should have been defeated. He claims that it failed to strain *every* nerve toward preparedness; and this was because it was eaten by the canker of democracy. The "original starting point of this plague lay largely in the institution of parliament . . . unhappily this illness was carried over and infected the whole of life." Therefore, he says on page 690, in deleted words, "the absolute regimentation of a folk for the preparation of an approaching clash of arms" was not achieved, since this "cannot be entrusted to the power of decision of a majority of block-heads and good-for-nothings. Preparation for combat could be accomplished by the father of Frederick the Great, but not by the fathers of our democratic nonsense."

In expurgated passages he explains that he will not be half-hearted about his war-preparations like Imperial Germany. It will be time, he says, for the amenities of culture after Germany has won her rightful place, when, he believes, these will arise like those of ancient Greece after the Peloponnesian Wars. In the meantime, all advocates of peace must go, and chief of these is the Jew. Not because he is commercial or

even an alien, dóes Hitler shout for his blood, but
chiefly because the wretch persists in upholding peace
and democracy and thus hindering Hitler's return to
primordial ruthlessness and the Nazi back-to-Nature
movement.

This is scarcely apparent from the English version,
which merely suggests that Hitler hates the Jewish liberal press, but entirely fails to tell why. The original
explains that the crime for which Jewry must now
suffer danger and disgrace was the support of peace
and democracy: "What fare has the German pre-war
press served to the people? Was it not the worst poison
that one can imagine? Was not the worst pacifism
injected into the hearts of our people? Was it not the
German press which understood how to make palatable
to our people the nonsense of a 'Western democracy'
until this people at last . . . believed it could trust its
future to a League of Nations?. . . . Has it not degraded
the Army by perpetual criticism, sabotaging general
conscription, demanding the withholding of military
budgets and so forth?"

The translation covers up Hitler's real reason for
opposing the Jews, the chief claim that they have committed high treason in advocating a democracy for a
pure-blooded Aryan race which would never of itself
have stooped to such superstitions. But the translation
also glosses over his real rôle as agitator, who lashed
the frenzies of the mob by outbursts against Jews as
"true devils" with "the brain of a monster—not of a
man," whose hideous organization "must finally lead
to the breakdown of human culture and thus to the
devastation of the world." It omits his comparison of
Jews to maggots in a decaying body, or to a "sling-ma-

chine, dashing its filth into the faces of other people,"
or his pictures, vivid to the point of insanity, of some
"black haired youth with satanic joy on his face" lying
in wait for an innocent Aryan girl, and the—to our
minds most fantastic—suggestion that the scheming
Jews had systematically married into the Prussian nobility with the sole purpose of depriving the poor German folk of pure-blooded aristocratic rulers.

The translation suppresses the fact that Hitler advocated violence. In words sponged from page 24 of the
translation he gives point to his theories: "There was
left as the last salvation, fight; fight with every weapon
that human spirit, reason and will could grasp." And
this fight was not to be with spiritual weapons. No one
could guess from the white spaces of page 279 of
the English version that Hitler told his followers: "No
folk can remove this fist from its gullet except by the
sword. Only the gathered, concentrated strength of a
powerfully rising national passion is able to oppose
the international enslavement of peoples. Such a procedure is, however, and remains, a bloody one."

Throughout the English edition, therefore, we are
given a misleading picture of Hitler's enormous ambitions and unscrupulous character, of his thirst for destruction and of his ultimate purpose, which is to be-
stride the world. And this was not for lack of space,
for a dozen pages or so more would have sufficed to indicate all these aspects. It is the more unfortunate
because, aside from this prime source-book, so little
reliable information is available from the Nazi side
about Hitler, who was not even in the German "Who's
Who" until his victory, and about the almost equally
obscure men around him. With so little to counter-act

this decoy-version, we are in danger of falling into a trap: we might believe that, in so modifying his book, he has perhaps changed his views.

The pressure is growing upon us to believe that; a prominent American lady pacifist recently assured us that Hitler is "developing into a statesman," and she seems cheerful about the prospects for his learning moderation. Are we to suppose that Hitler, because he has dropped his biting words on "lacrimonious female hired-mourners," waving palms and whimpering for peace, has really been converted to dove-fancying?

If so, it will be an exception. Though in the English version he softened his attack upon the Churches, he has smashed the Churches in the months following the appearance of the book. Though he pruned away his denunciation of trade unions, he has since eradicated them from German soil. Though he weeded out his threats against the Jews, he has gone on destroying them. Though he hid his scorn for a free press, he has since annihilated it. Though he obliterated his picture of a nation properly aroused by propaganda penetrating "the brain of the tiniest urchin" to the burning cry, "Lord, bless our battle!"—he has gone right ahead with the execution of that plan, putting it into effect to the last detail and including the tiniest urchin.

To be sure, we have a speech pledging peace to put up against this book—a few hundred soothing phrases to set against 250,000 words of exhortation to combat. But how much does a solemn pledge mean to Hitler? As Konrad Heiden, author of one of the best informed books on the movement, *"Die Geschichte des National-sozialismus"* (Berlin, 1933), has recently shown, the path of Hitler to power has been strewn with broken promises and forgotten assurances. With his right hand on his heart, he swore before a Bavarian Minister in 1922: "Herr Minister, I give you my word of honor, I will never make a *putsch* in my life, Herr Minister, I will never in my life make a *putsch*"—but a few months later he had the pleasure of making a *putsch* and lodging the Bavarian Ministers temporarily in jail. He broke similarly solemn promises to General von Lossow and Police President von Seisser, to von Papen and the head of the Stahlhelm, Duesterberg, and to the German churchmen; he was publicly accused by both General von Epp and Hindenburg himself, of irresponsibility. He has paid many a visit in sheep's clothing before this, but never was known to have pulled any of the wool over his own eyes.

If Hitler really holds to his latest pledge, to keep peace, it will mean trampling upon all those principles to which, in *"Mein Kampf,"* he has sworn as constituting the guiding-lines of his life. But, of course, by thus discarding outworn principles, he will automatically rise to the status of "a statesman." He has, however, another alternative: sticking to his principles. Then, of course, he cannot be considered a statesman, but perhaps it will be a consolation to him to become, instead, *"Herr der Erde."*

Hitler is confronted with the necessity of rejecting his pledge or his principles. Upon his choice, in these coming months and years, hangs the peace of Europe and the world.

THE ATTACK

ON LABOR

BY WILLIAM GREEN

THOSE who believe in the principles of democracy were greatly encouraged when some fifteen years ago the German people established a republican, representative form of government. Such action was hailed as a great step forward, and Labor in America was proud indeed of the part which the German Trade Unions had played in bringing it about. Unfortunately, the distressing economic situation in Germany was seized upon for the dissemination of false propaganda by those who plotted against the Republic; propaganda which resulted in the establishment of a dictatorship cruel, oppressive, and shocking to those with faith in democratic institutions and in a democratic form of government.

The American people have been deeply touched by the tragic stories regarding persecution of the Jews in Germany. This is particularly true of Organized Labor, for there is a broad and fundamental sympathy between the Trade Unions of the United States and those of Germany, and the solution of their common economic and social problems has been our fixed purpose. Moreover, needless to say, there are included in our membership both in the United States and in Germany many men and women of the Jewish race.

Wherever any nation has attempted to deny to its citizens the exercise of the fundamental rights of freedom of speech, freedom of the press, and freedom of religion, Organized Labor has been aroused to a challenging and fighting spirit, and it has likewise steadfastly subscribed to the great American doctrine that there shall be no discrimination because of race, creed, color, or nationality. Our Trade Unions have of necessity practised this doctrine as a living principle. By their very existence they have become welded into a common brotherhood, formed for the purpose of promoting the economic, social, and industrial welfare of the masses of the people; men and women who may speak different languages, whose creeds and customs may be alien, but whose basic human needs are the same.

In voicing our protest against the outrages perpetrated upon the Jewish people in Germany, we disavow any intention of interfering in the political affairs of that great country. But when any nation violates the laws of humanity, shocks international conscience, engages in persecution of minorities, and follows a primitive barbarian course toward helpless men and women whose only crime is to have become the victims of racial hatred, then the voice of the American Federation of Labor must be heard in solemn protest. We cannot remain passive and unconcerned when the families and friends of the Jewish members of our own great economic organization are being persecuted and oppressed. We must raise our voice in their defense, because the bonds of brotherhood which bind us so closely make their problems in part our own.

Organized Labor also feels that the betrayal of one

human right leads inevitably to further betrayals. The
publication of the so-called German Code recently promulgated by Chancellor Hitler reflects the amazing extent to which his government has gone in the destruction of the hard-won but by now well-established rights
of the workers in all enlightened countries. The new
decree abolishes all the rights and privileges upon
which the organized labor movement in Germany
rested. It completely annihilates labor unions, pro-
hibits strikes, and does away with collective bargaining
and the right to organize. This is Chancellor Hitler's
finishing blow in the destruction of German trade
unions; it spells a return to the primitive relationship
between master and servant.

The working people of the United States cannot understand how it has been possible for the German
working people to submit to such enslavement and such
autocratic control. The American Federation of Labor
believes that only force of the most cruel and repre-
hensible kind could have brought about these distressing conditions. It cannot believe that the German
workers will either willingly or permanently submit to
such injustice. Meanwhile, the working people of
America share with the German workers their feeling
of resentment against those who are responsible for
this destruction of their hard-won rights.

The boycott of German manufactured goods and
German service subscribed to by the American Federation of Labor as a protest against the persecution of
the Jews in Germany has been bulwarked by this recently promulgated German Code infringing upon the
basic human rights of all German workers. Therefore,
in addition to its earlier outcry against the shocking

and inhuman treatment of the Jews, Organized Labor voices its solemn protest against the cruel injustices which have recently been imposed upon all German workers.

SOUTH AMERICA REACTS

TO HITLERISM

BY SAMUEL GUY INMAN

WE were sitting in the lobby of the Parque Hotel at Montevideo, with the delegates to the Seventh Pan American Conference passing back and forth, discussing political and social currents in South America. Several of us journalists from North America were picking the brains of South American confreres concerning various questions—why President Terra of Uruguay had revolted against his own socialist government, which has done such remarkable things for the people, and turned himself into a dictator—how far Argentine land interests and North American oil interests were behind the Chaco war—what is the chance of the growing Socialist party in Argentina—why university students are the leaders of radical movements in these countries—the explanation of the extreme dislike of the Monroe Doctrine—and other interesting questions which are stirring these young growing lands. The discussion turned to Hitlerism and race prejudice.

In our group was a brilliant young Spaniard who has been living in Buenos Aires for several years as the secretary of the great publishing house "Atlantida" owned by Señor Constancio Vigil, which goes beyond the great Curtis house in Philadelphia by publishing nine different weekly and monthly journals, with millions of circulation in Argentina and neighboring countries. "The Hitler movement, with its theory of race superiority," said this publisher, "is completely opposed to the fundamental psychology of the Latin American people. It has not, nor will it, find any popular appeal in South America. Nowhere does one find such a cosmopolitan spirit, such a welcome to and mixture of all races as in these countries. It would be going completely against their most fundamental conceptions of life for South Americans to accept any theory of superior or inferior races." To the opinion of this informed journalist have been added countless others confirming the belief that no movement against race equality will there find favorable soil.

A notable illustration of the resentment against the introduction of race persecutions in South America is the way the intellectuals of Brazil have recently protested against Hitler's persecution of the Jews, which has a tendency to be introduced by Germans in Brazil recently. One of these protests is in the shape of a book called *Por que Ser Anti-Semita?"* "Why Be Anti-Semitic?") published last year by Civilãzacio Brasileira. The dedication is to the many Israelites who have been killed in an inglorious campaign. The preface states that the German campaign against the Jews has reached Brazil, whose traditions are hostile to race prejudice. The book consists of essays written by thirty-five Brazilian authors, the ablest contemporary writers of that country, who present their opposition to anti-Semitism in vigorous language from various points of view. Some of the chapters in this notable book are: "South America and German anti-Semitism" by Baptista Pereira, "What Kind of Civilization is This?" by Plenio Barreto, "A Small Great People" by Alfranio Peixoto, "Martyrdom and Force" by Origenes Lessa, "Jewish Prodigies" by Galeão Coutinho, "Jewish Contribution to Brazilian Civilization" by Solidonio Leite Filho, "Democracies and the Jews" by Hermes Lima. Raul de Polillo wrote:

In America anti-Semitism is understood as religious hatred, as strife between two or more creeds, and as such a thing it belongs to the past. The anti-Semite who is able to live in America today is not an American, he is European. He must disappear, if for no other reason because he cannot find here the pasture for feeding his stupidity. He is like a warrior who would arm himself in modern days as though he were going to the Thirty Years War . . .

Considered as a race, the Jew interests us as would any other individual of any other race . . . As a religion, Judaism also interests us as the religious attitude of any other man facing the phenomenon of nature; he may contribute to our wisdom, he may satisfy our curiosity. But he is not a special part of our spirituality because the spiritual integrity of America reposes as much in Buddhism as it does in Christianity or any other "ism" which the religious spirit and the tendency to worship may have developed for use in any other part of the world.

Brazil is making probably the most interesting experiment in race mixture of any nation in the world. She is deliberately setting out to absorb all peoples within her borders, which include a large number of

Negroes who came as slaves from Africa, and an increasing group of Japanese who number at the present time about 150,000. A leading Brazilian scientist predicts that within fifty years all of the African population will have been absorbed. The Negroes now number about 5,000,000, living in the northern part of Brazil. That population is getting whiter with each decade. In Southern Brazil 700,000 Germans are more and more becoming lost in the Brazilian population itself, as are a million and a half of Italians in the State of Sao Paulo. The Consul General of Brazil said to me not long ago, when I inquired of him about the difference between treatment of Japanese in California and in Brazil, "In California they seem to be afraid that Japanese will intermarry with the nationals; in Brazil we are afraid they will not."

José Vasconcelos of Mexico speaks along these lines of a "cosmic race" which he believes is developing in Latin America. He says: "The civilization of North America is a one-race civilization, a white-race civilization as you insist on calling yourselves, sometimes even to the exclusion of other whites such as for instance the Spaniard. A white civilization that may contain, and does contain, millions of other racial stocks such as the Negro, but does not consider such dissimilar stock as a part of itself and does not as a rule intermarry with it . . .

"On the other hand we have, in the south, a civilization that from the beginning accepts a mixed standard of social arrangement not only as a matter of fact but through law, since the Indian after being baptized became the equal of the Spaniard and was able to intermarry with the conqueror . . .

"If we compare the results of the English policy in India with the results of the Spanish policy in America, even at a time when the British policy is not yet ripe, not having had the centuries of the Spanish colonization's experience, I believe that we shall be justified in declaring that the cultural results of the Spanish method are superior . . .

"The Spaniards did not obey this rule of abstention even with the Negro, the population of many of our tropical sections is largely mulatto, a mixture of the Spanish and the Negro; the Portuguese have also created a mulatto population in Brazil; so here again, we find the Latin system of assimilation and intermarriage and mixture opposed to the Anglo-Saxon method of matrimonial taboos and pure-race standards."

The Nazi movement which challenges this Latin American conception of race amalgamation, is entering South America through the embassies, legations, and consulates of Germany in those countries. Literature concerning the movement is received by an American educator, so he told me, practically every week from the German Legation in Asunción, Paraguay. Specially established press agencies are now appearing to furnish cables and mail articles for dailies and weeklies, the service being gratis or nearly so. Newspaper men in Brazil say that cables from Germany, flattering to Hitler, have become prominent in papers of Rio, Sao Paulo, and other cities in the last three months. "*Associacão Brasileira*," a Brazilian news agency, is used by most of the papers in Brazil because its services are secured at a small cost and it is through this agency that much of the news is received from Germany.

Clubs, schools, commercial and cultural organizations conducted by German colonies or influenced by them are being rent in twain by the struggle between Hitlerites and anti-Hitlerites for control of these organizations. An illustration of this struggle is seen in Bahia, Brazil, where English-speaking people report having been forced to withdraw their children from the German school because it has been turned into a place for Nazi propaganda, the Jewish head has been removed, and the children were commanded to learn Hitler salutes. The same report was given the author by residents of Asunción, Paraguay, where the German school, which has so long enjoyed an excellent reputation for its educational facilities, is now seeing its students enroll in other schools. The Swastika flag flies above the German School in Montevideo, as it does on many similar German institutions, clubs, and cultural societies. German ships recently seen in South American harbors by the author all displayed the Nazi emblem.

Most of the diplomatic representatives of Germany in South America have been changed recently, the new incumbents immediately beginning to advertise the Hitler program. In Montevideo recently the German Minister protested officially to the Uruguay Government because a Jewish theatrical company was announced to give a series of performances in a local theatre. The government refused flatly to heed the protest and the company had a most successful run of several weeks. The protest caused considerable resentment among the public, since Uruguay has, at least until the recent reactionary movement of 1933, been especially liberal in its treatment of foreigners and of radicals. The Consti-

tution provides that a foreigner may, under comparatively easy conditions, become a citizen of Uruguay
and retain at the same time his citizenship in his native
land. So sure have the people of this progressive land
been of the security of their socialized democracy that
they have until 1933, allowed the Communist Party to
conduct openly in Montevideo its general offices for
South America. In spite of the coup d'etat of March
31, 1933, since when a number of foreigners have been
expelled as radical agitators, the public has resisted all
efforts at anti-Semitism. The Jewish colony in the capital has grown considerably and prominent Uruguayans
spoke to the author with pride of the commercial and
residential districts where Jews lived their lives with
all the liberties and social privileges which Uruguay
has been accustomed to offer all residents of that
country.

A good illustration of the penetration of the Hitler
movement is found in the recent experience of "Pro
Arte," a cultural society of Rio de Janiero. Some reported it to be entirely under German influence, having Germans as leaders, and others alleged it was a
Jewish society and one to be boycotted by all true Germans. However, a Jewish member of the society recently said to a North American in Rio, "The last stronghold has fallen, and 'Pro Arte' has had to go down
before the Nazi onslaught. For months it has been
holding out, but now the German Ambassador has given
absolute orders that all Jews are to be removed from
offices in the society. These officers are told they are
'second-rate' men, an inferior kind of beings, and are
not real Germans."

A business meeting of "Pro Arte" was held on December 12, 1933, at which a Roman Catholic priest, by the name of Sinzig, and a distinguished Brazilian historian, named Max Fleius, took turns at presiding. Compliments to the retiring officers were effusive. During the course of the meeting it was brought out that the Jewish members had decided to demand a place on the council to protect their interests. It was agreed that a place be given them, but it must not be for German Jews—it must be for Brazilian Jews.

This society has a membership of between 500 and 600. At times it has had as many as 250 Brazilian members; now perhaps it has 150. The Brazilians take little part in the business, but confine their interest to the cultural side. The Jews number about forty or forty-five, and have always taken an active part in all phases of the society's life. Even the German leaders of "Pro Arte" are in personal sentiment anti-Hitler, and have most reluctantly accepted discrimination against Jewish members, but they seem willing to sacrifice the Jews for the sake of other influences. The Jews themselves do not make any protest publicly. They feel they must not speak or act in their own behalf. Following the meeting in December, the German Nationalists are reported to have complained to the German Ambassador that the priest who presided had paid too many compliments to the retiring officers, including the Jews. The Ambassador replied that as long as they kept their agreement not to elect Jews, the Nationalists should be satisfied. The priest seemed simply to be attempting to conciliate the old crowd.

A German Jew now living in Brazil, who was baptized into the Protestant Church, was one of the officials who had to give up office in "Pro Arte." He is sales manager for Brazil in a large German corporation. Recently the local company received orders from Germany to drop from the roll certain names, either because they were too liberal or not of Aryan blood, the name of the sales manager being on the list. The local house refused to comply, explaining that in Brazil those questions were not an issue. Later a representative of the corporation from Berlin told the sales manager that if he were in Germany they would have to let him go, but in Brazil it was different. However, if orders of dismissal were again received from the German Government it was declared that they would have to be followed. This same sales manager has Jews in his employ and as they are good workers he continues to retain them.

There are about 40,000 Jews in Brazil, some 30,000 of them having arrived since the World War. They are mostly in the cities of Rio de Janiero and Sao Paulo, with the colonies established in Rio Grande do Sul by the Jewish Colonization Society. The central office of this society in Paris has appointed the distinguished Rabbi, Dr. Isaias Raffalovich, as its agent for the purpose of inspiring the religious life of Jews in Brazil. Dr. Raffalovich is emphatic in saying that German-Jewish doctors and lawyers are not coming to Brazil in large numbers, and he is doing everything he can to discourage them. The trouble is that they have no money and no prospect of employment, and that the Brazilian Government puts such difficulties in the way of foreigners' practicising these professions.

Brazil is the only country in Latin America that has an avowedly Fascist organization, although it claims to be purely national with no connections between German or Italian Fascists. This organization is called "Integralismo" and is described in a little book of that same name. The author is Dr. Gustavo Barroso, who was president of the Brazilian Academy of Letters before he was compelled to resign recently. He was visiting another State in the interest of this movement and is alleged to have given out an interview in which he said that the younger members of the Academy were lazy, while the old men did not know how to die. Later he denied the interview, which was re-affirmed by the paper, and he was forced to resign from the presidency of the Academy. He speaks in his Brazilian-Nazi uniform with great force and claims to have strong organizations in eight states, and rapidly spreading all over Brazil. The movement insists that Fascism in Brazil has no connection with other countries, and does not share the prejudice against the Jews. Dr. Barroso, nevertheless, displayed to an inquirer Henry Ford's "International Jew" in Portuguese, manifesting his enthusiastic approval. Dr. Isaias Raffalovich cabled Henry Ford that as he had repudiated the book he ought not to agree to its circulation in Brazil, thereby disseminating misinformation and stirring up hatred here. No reply had been received by January 1, 1934.

In some of the South American countries political conditions give a certain amount of encouragement to Fascism. Brazil's chief executive at the present time, Dr. Getulio Vargas frankly calls himself a dictator. He took office in October, 1930, after a revolution in which he led the forces against the predatory interests who had controlled the elections. Since then there has been a serious but unsuccessful revolution against his government in Sao Paulo. A constitutional convention is now in session, considering a very radical reorganization of Brazil's government with more liberal tendencies. At present, however, there is considerable restriction of liberty of movement in Brazil.

In Chile, President Arturo Alessandri was granted at the close of 1933 extra constitutional powers which practically suspended the constitution and the Chilean Government seems to be ruling with the aid of the most conservative forces. A voluntary group called the "Guardia Republicana" has been organized recently under the patronage of the government. It is an armed group that is pledged to support any legal government. The group was organized as a reaction against the revolutions led by various military groups during the last years, but has not become a protector of the status quo. At the present writing restrictions on all kinds of movements in and out of Chile are severe.

In Argentina the strong-willed and personalistic President Irigoyen was replaced during a revolutionary movement in 1931 by General Jose Uriburu who in turn was succeeded by President Augustin Justo, who as a minority leader declared in December, 1933, that the country was facing revolution and, therefore, initiated a state of siege. In a fine study of these recent revolutions in South America and especially the one in Argentina, Dr. Alfredo Colmo* describes the reactionary influence of the *Legion Civica* which is symptomatic of the dictatorial attitude of the present Argentine Government. He says: "This is a conglomeration of citizens sympathizing with the revolution and the situation created by it, particularly its government and

---

* *"Le Revolución en la América Latina,"* p. 179.

its chief of military education and spirit. It is amply
aided by the government and, like a pretorian guard
celebrated the glories of the revolution and exalts the
President and his work, preparing at the same time
against any possible revolution and declaring itself
ready to pass judgment on causes and persons of the
opposition. The 'Legion' is a threat to any government which does not accept its principles and a liberal leader has recently taken action before the courts
against the 'Legion' as a seditious organization. The
'Legion', however, continues, as it declares, to combat
by all means the forces who conspire against the state."

Even Uruguay, famed for its extra liberal asylum to
radicals as already indicated, has recently witnessed a
revolution led by President Terra against his own government, he having taken unto himself complete power
and the only right to criticize his government.

The Hitler movement is now appearing in Peru,
where a weekly paper is published in Lima called
Signo (Swastika) which contains pictures of Hitler and
his activities, especially of his youth movement. This
is a particular challenge to the strong reform movement
known as "Apra," led by university students, which
is working for a new social and economic order in
Peru. That country had been under a reactionary dic-
atorship for many years until President Benavides came
to power in 1933. At present it is an open question
whether the government will give the Apra party a
chance for an open educational campaign or will support the reactionaries. The Hitler propaganda will,
of course, oppose the Apra program.

Just as this manuscript is finished, February, 1934,
word comes of the organization of the *Camisas Rayades*

(striped shirts) in Mexico, led by ex-Senator Lauro G.
Caloca.   This group has as one of its objects the stop-
ping of "continuity"; that is, the elimination of the
present revolutionary party which has been dictating
the politics of Mexico for a number of years.   The
"striped shirts" claim that they are a doctrinaire party
with no connection with any outside group and at present are not interested in public office.   The party now
in power in Mexico will no doubt elect its new President in June, 1934, and with that Mexico will swing
still further to the left, giving an opportunity, of course,
for a sharp division created by those who want to return to the old days of Porfirio Diaz.

It is not surprising then to find in several Latin
American countries political movements along Fascist
lines with the dictatorial government often encouraging
them for its own protection.

There are three small reactionary dailies now published in Buenos Aires for sale on news-stands which
defend the Conservative Government now in power and
point out the dangers of liberalism, preaching hatred
to the Jews as dangerous radicals and commercial com-
petitors.   One of these, *Crisol*, dated December 10,
1933, has a long article, with a three-column display
headline, entitled "The Jewish question not a literary
problem but a grave political, social, economic, and
spiritual problem."   The article begins by stating that
now that the Jewish problem is becoming recognized
as universally important the paper desires to present
data showing that this problem profoundly affects not
simply Germany but the whole world.   It goes on to
take the usual position that the Jews are responsible

for the radical movements in Russia, Hungary, Germany, and other parts of the world, referring to the defense by Sholom Asch of the Jews in Germany. The article says that Mr. Asch does not mention the three million Aryans sacrificed in Russia by the Jews nor the many millions who have died recently in that same country because of hunger, nor does he speak of the victims assassinated in Germany during the revolution of 1918-1919 nor of the uncounted number of men, women, and children who were assassinated by Bela Kun in Hungary during his short tyranny for all of which, the author intimates, the Jews are responsible. The article goes on to show the predominance of Jews in the more important professions in Germany and justifies the attack on the Jews because they were capturing the best positions in that country. A long list of names is given of Jews occupying important positions and statistics to prove these contentions.

Crisol, on Christmas eve, 1933, had an article telling of the expulsion from the National College Rivadavia of two Jewish students, one having falsely represented the other during examinations. This fact has no particular importance in itself, says the article, but is an index to the immorality which the sons of Lenin are accustomed to practice. If the career of these most noble Hebrews had not been cut off their simulation would have been repeated in the University, and later these students, having graduated as physicians, would have sold their names for the price of a cheap overcoat to any of the quacks who pester the City; graduated as pharmacists their names would have been displayed on fake boticas, as lawyers their firms would have united in the most repugnant defense of questionable cases. "This expulsion," declared the article, "has therefore stopped two brilliant careers but these ex-students will not be content; they have still open to them illegitimate commerce, the questionable press and, in a democratic society, a wide opportunity to carry out Jewish simulations in which they failed as students."

The *Bandera Argentina* (December 22, 1933) has an article on the "Nationalistic Front" divided into three sections—"The Vanity of a Triumph," speaking of the supposed triumph as prophesied of the Jews in Soviet Russia in 1919; second, "How a Prophecy is Fulfilled," referring to the prophecy of Nietzche that either Christianity or Judaism must eliminate the other and the way Hitler is now carrying out this prophecy. In the third section, "The Struggle Has Begun," the author declares, "In our country, Argentina, where the Jews have not shown the same weakness up to the present which caused their failure in Germany, we need a fire as strong as that which raised the Swastika as a guide to the future of the country of Frederick the Great. The same situation that existed there prevails here. Argentinians who in their administrative positions in the government are examined and controlled by Jews have understood their duty, which I pointed out clearly in these columns some months ago. We will see that public Christian officials act energetically very soon. If the state itself does not expel the Jews from its midst, the Argentine people will do so on their own account."

Criterio, a weekly journal, published by the Roman Catholic Church in Buenos Aires, has as its leading article in the issue of December 7, 1933, a study of anti-Semitism by the editor, Bishop Gustavo J. Fran-

ceschi. The Bishop says that when he was ordained
twenty-nine years ago, anti-Semitism did not exist in
Argentina. That was a day when, if a man had shown
opposition to the incoming of Jews, he would have been
designated as incapable of understanding the human-
itarian epoch in which he lived. In the tragic week
of 1919 during serious labor troubles there appeared
the first manifestations of anti-Semitism, when the Russian, as a Jew who was more and more populating our
cities, appeared as a usurer, but the violences of the
Russian hunt did not last more than three or four days
and following that time, Jews by the thousands from
Poland, Rumania, Hungary, and other countries entered Argentina. Thus Buenos Aires became one of
the Jewish capitals of the world. The Bishop thinks
that Argentina now contains more Israelites than
France and Italy together, the amount being excessive,
as the famous Argentine novelist Manuel Galvez pointed out in a former article in *Criterio*.

After discussing the biological and racial problems
and considering the question of the Jew in Germany
and in Russia, the Bishop comes to the question in
Argentina. The situation in other lands, he says, explains somewhat the feeling in Argentina, which might
be translated some day into as lamentable explosions
as have taken place in Germany. There is no doubt
that there are Hebrews in Argentina who have sincere
love for the Republic but it is certain that many are
like the Turks who have lived five centuries in the
Balkan Peninsula without losing their ethnic individuality. The Jews here constitute their ghetto, found
their associations, maintain their schools and periodicals—in a word, maintain themselves in a separate

colony although they may have been born in the Argentine Republic. The colony is now invading the professions, such as medicine and law. While one knows Israelites of absolute honor one also sees that in Argentina the list is growing larger of those who, in commerce, in industry, in exporting, in banking, remind one of Shakespeare's "Merchant of Venice." The Jews are among the extremists of Argentina. Last week the police arrested a group of supposedly unemployed that were robbing public places; the list shows us that the predominant number were Jews. The celebrated Yuyamtorg, representative of Russian Bolshevism, recently destroyed by the Government, was dominated by Hebrews, showing that they are the leaders in red propaganda. It is natural that Argentines who do not admire this materialism react against such leaders. Continuing, the Bishop declares: "My impression is that no immigrants have provoked such reaction in Argentina as have the Hebrews. If the sons of Israel continue this attitude of a colony the hour will arrive when the Argentine people will expel them from their midst."

This article is answered in a well edited magazine of Buenos Aires entitled *Judaica*. The Editor, Solomon Resnick, is a writer of considerable force and dignity. The article which appeared in the December, 1933, number, speaks in the first place of a previous article which Bishop Franceschi had published in favor of the Jews in Germany. Now it is pointed out that while the Bishop does not admit that he is anti-Semitic, he does much harm by raising questions. The author asks if the Germans are really so innocent as to have the Jews completely fool them, guide them without any

thought. He shows that Jews as Jews are not responsible for much of what they are charged with. As for
the situation in Argentina he calls attention to the fact
that this country is young and naturally looks for immigration. Jewish immigration dates from the period
1888-1890. No one can justify the charge that the
Jews have not become good Argentines. Certainly the
Bishop would not desire the Jews to abandon their
religion. English, Germans, Italians, and other foreigners maintain their schools and their clubs without
being accused of working against Argentina. Therefore the Bishop's ultimatum to the Jews, that if they
do not change their attitude they will be expelled from
the country, is unjust: "Do not demand that we be more
perfect than you. There may be a Jewish scoundrel
but generally we are honest men, we combat social and
moral injustices, we have before us one great object
—to construct the Argentine nation, to better conditions of life in order that this country may be an excellent patria for all of its citizens."

The Seventh Pan-American Conference, held at
Montevideo December 3-26, 1933, offered a splendid
opportunity to feel the pulse of the Continent in this
as in other matters. Ten Ministers of Foreign Affairs
of the twenty countries represented, were present as
delegates. A comparison of the results of two most
recent international conferences, with the failure of
the London gathering and the success at Montevideo,
leads one to inquire why these differing results? The
answer seems to lie in the fundamentally different attitude toward life as found in these two cities, representative of two different parts of the world. Pessimism

might dominate Europe, facing the failure of the Disarmament Conference, the threatened breakup of the League, the weakening of parliamentary government and the waning of internationalism. But not so in South America. Here no advocate of a plan began by pointing out the ruin facing the world or the need of returning to nationalism, or the uselessness of peace machinery. Such dire analyses of present chaos and predictions of future failure as are the style among orators in the older countries, seldom found an echo in that conference.

Statesmen of the American Continent, as demonstrated in the Montevideo Conference, are anxious that this continent maintain its historic place as refuge for all who are persecuted because of political or religious beliefs. At a time when the other parts of the world seem to be moving toward extreme nationalism and the elimination of all who differ from the party in power, leaders in the Pan-American movement seem to be more than ever in favor of respect for every race and creed. In personal conversations that the author had with many of the delegates at Montevideo they expressed this opinion.

As to the place for refugees from Germany, expelled because of the Aryan complex of the present German Government, these Latin American gentlemen were sure their countries generally would open their doors to such immigrants. At the same time these delegates were careful to point out that all of the countries were facing grave economic problems and the question of unemployment, so that it would be impossible to open their doors without restrictions to new immigrants. The largest opportunities would be given to colonies who

could be transplanted on the land. Almost every Latin
American country would seem to welcome agricultural
colonies, providing there is an organization with sufficient capital back of such colonization to insure the
furnishing of land, equipment and means of living until these colonies could be thoroughly established.

The experiences of the Jewish Colonization Society
in Argentina and Brazil would be, of course, very helpful since these colonies are looked upon as highly successful. A group of Hebrews in Argentina have raised
100,000 pesos to help in such work. The Jews as well
as others agree that Latin America is already over-
staffed with physicians, lawyers, and other professional
classes. The representatives of some of the countries
at Montevideo suggested that there would be room for
a few technical people who could better the technique,
for example, of small factories now beginning in these
countries, improve agriculture, railroad management
and other businesses.

There are, of course, individual instances where spe-
cialists might be used in university positions and where
individual physicians and lawyers might find a place
in offices already established. It would seem to be
advisable to organize commissions in various countries
composed of such people as the Brazilian intellectuals
already referred to, who have taken upon themselves,
of their own initiative, to see that the American Continent continues its historic position as a land of freedom. Such a group could also study with the League
of Nations Commission and other organizations the number of refugees which might be received in various
American countries. Purely as individuals and in no
way committing their governments, which, of course,

would be the only authority to speak definitely on the subject, various delegates at Montevideo gave their opinions. A representative from Venezuela said that his country had particular interest in immigration of technical workers and agriculturalists, there being ample opportunity for industrialists. A Mexican delegate, referred to Mexico's sympathy toward Israelites and other political immigrants from Germany, and said that General Calles takes a special interest in this matter. A Cuban delegate felt that Cuba needed immigration of a certain kind of technical people to build up their general industries. Paraguay has had good experiences with German immigrants; there is a great deal of agricultural land open there and some commercial and industrial opportunities. Land can be bought very cheaply and there is a homestead law by which immigrants may secure small tracts of fifty to seventy-five acres on promising to cultivate the same and construct a home there. Guatemala, according to one of its delegates to Montevideo, is open to immigration and there are no limitations to white people. They would have special interest in the immigration of technical and industrial people. Panama requires that each immigrant entering the country deposit the price of a third class return ticket to his native country to be used in case he returns within a year. No restrictions on immigration seem to exist in Nicaragua.

Beginning at the Rio Grande and stretching on down through Mexico, over Central America, beyond Panama, through Colombia and Venezuela, the Andean countries, Brazil, Chile, down through the abounding plains of the Argentine to the Straits of Magellan, is the largest expanse of undeveloped, fertile land in the

whole world.   There is more undiscovered territory
in Brazil than there is in the whole continent of Africa.
One state in that mighty republic equals the area of
Great Britain, France, Germany, Austria, and Switzerland.   If Argentina were as densely populated as is the
State of New York, and it is far more capable of caring
for a dense population, it would have three hundred
million people instead of its present population of
twelve and a half millions.   Venezuela is not considered one of the largest republics but it has almost twice
as much territory as Japan, while Japan has a population approximating that of all South America.   Arguments might have been made in the old days against the
dense population of these lands because they were
tropical, but modern science has overcome the difficulties of the tropics for men.   The over-crowded populations of the Orient and of Europe will without question seek the great fertile fields and friendly climates
of these Latin American countries.   Latin America is
adrift today as is the rest of the world.   Most of its
countries, after experiencing revolutions, have recently
undergone major upheavals. They are all going through
fundamental reorganizations.   Will they be swamped
by nationalism or will they lead the world into a new
internationalism?   The fundamental psychology of
Latin America lacks race prejudice, favoring rather the
idea of a cosmic race.   Such a conception is worth
fighting for in the present day of overwhelming
nationalism.

THE CHALLENGE TO AMERICA

BY ALFRED E. SMITH

THERE is no better way of measuring the benefits of constitutional, democratic government as exemplified in our experience, than by analyzing recent events in the late German Republic. The German Constitution showed numerous evidences of a study of our own fundamental law. It was assumed that what had, on the whole, worked so well here could be transplanted and made to flourish in Berlin, but the people of Germany were unable to live up to, or under it. They began by suspending important provisions, and ended recently by scrapping the entire document. The spirit and letter of every provision of our bill of rights has been violated by the Hitler Government. Freedom of religion, of speech and of the press have been destroyed overnight. The right of people to be secure in their persons, houses, papers and effects against unreasonable search and seizure, has been wantonly violated. Civil rights and impartial judicial processes have been abolished. The home rule powers of the several independent and ancient states which united to make up the German Republic, and of their people, have been ruthlessly sacrificed to an arbitrary central authority. Government, business, the professions, the arts, the sciences and even religion itself must goose-step under the orders of the brown shirts. Democratic government, in the sense that we know it, has died with the German Constitution.

The greatest indictment which can be brought against the German people is that to date they have proved themselves incapable of living under a democratic government and that there is so little of the tradition of a free people among them, that order can be maintained only through the dictatorship of a Hitler. It is clear that the world has not yet been made safe for democracy.

If the present order is the kind of government the German people desire, well and good. Thomas Jefferson said that every people gets the government it deserves; he might well have added "and desires." It certainly is nobody else's business what sort of government a nation seeks to set up within its own territory provided, however, it does not menace the peace and actual existence of other peoples and provided that such a government does not seek, by propaganda, to bring all other countries into conformity with its own ideas.

Those of us who believe in democracy and who love liberty find it difficult to remain silent for not only are the Jews proscribed; not only are the Catholics attacked, but all men and women, including Protestants who seek to think for themselves, who seek to find happiness by living their own lives in a quiet and orderly manner, are either forced into exile or molded in an iron form that permits of no deviation.

The fight for political and religious freedom and for racial tolerance has been the biggest part of the development of our American democracy. The fight has been, perhaps, the most distinguishing characteristic that marks the difference between the American democracy and the social and political structures of other countries. We have not yet won that battle, as too frequently there are revivals of religious and racial prejudices arising in America—survivals of conditions more actively existing elsewhere and heritages from lands where such prejudices are fanned, as is the case in Germany today.

Whatever may be the shortcomings of the American scene, it is undeniably true that we have never by law recognized these private hates. It is equally true that in every community the underlying and leading opinion has frowned upon—although sometimes without complete success—all manifestations of persecution and forced inferiorities.

Speaking before the German Reichstag, Bismarck once said: "The German people fear God and nobody else." He undoubtedly meant by that that they feared to offend Him because of His supreme love for all of His children. In the day of Bismarck the young people of Germany were taught to love their neighbor as they loved themselves in order that they might inherit the Kingdom of the world to come. Today, the young folks of Germany are being taught to hate some of their neighbors because of their race and religious beliefs.

Hates, fears, prejudices and all the other emotions set free by Hitler and his followers in the Nazi campaign cannot continue unless the rank and file of the German people approve it. It is considered weak and childish according to the Nazi tenets to recognize the divine qualities of love, of understanding, of faith, of charity, of sympathy and of tolerance. What has come over the German people who at one time held these attributes to be necessary to right living in this world and preparation for the next? How can these people who are prouder of being Nazis than they are of being Germans, expect justice from others when they do not give it to their own? How can they ask a place in the great family of nations unless they come in prepared to discharge their human obligations. Surely they cannot expect fair treatment from the nations of the world when they refuse that same treatment to their own people. They must come into court with clean hands. They cannot hope for help if they decline to give it.

There was slowly growing up in this country, prior to the Hitler régime, a widespread belief that probably some of the terms of the Versailles Treaty put too much of a burden on the German children yet to be born, and when this sentiment found expression the French people said: "You do not know Germany." Maybe the French people are right. Maybe we do not know Germany if the rank and file of her people persist in sustaining a régime such as now seems to be in full control of that great country.

Hitler, in his autobiography declares it is a fundamental that men are not equal before the law. To make good the principle that they were equal before the law as declared in the Declaration of Independence this country went through four years of strife and bloodshed and we cannot subscribe to the Hitler theory that it is not an individual's sense of justice and his orderly behavior that determines his value to the community nor can we agree to his precept that there is one sort of justice for one set of men and no justice at all for the others.

For thousands of years the relations of the white races of the world have been governed by fundamental laws and customs which the Nazis denounce and sneer at. The basic Roman laws on which the present European and American civilization rests are over with and done they say. Liberalism is an empty word, they declare and from now on the mission of the Aryan Nazi is to make the world over according to his formula. Of course this can never be done. No system can live that depends for its maintenance on violence and falsehood; no system can live that extinguishes liberty of thought, because of the danger that thought is to pretence.

A great many years of my life have been given over to fighting against the very things Hitler exalts. If his teachings prevail, than I and the millions, who, like me, have fought for spiritual and political freedom, have fought in vain. The things I have tried to stand for, I stand for now, more than ever, in the face of this desperate challenge, which is not merely a Jewish question, a Catholic question, a Protestant question, a political question, or a labor question, but which goes to the very foundation on which we have erected America and on which we have stood all during our political life to preserve civilization.

A WHO'S WHO

OF CONTRIBUTORS

ROBERT F. WAGNER was born in Germany and came to the United States as a youth. A graduate of the College of the City of New York, he has served in the New York State Assembly, the New York State Senate, and as Justice of the New York Supreme Court. Since 1927 he has been United States Senator from New York.

JAMES WATERMAN WISE, editor of *OPINION—A Journal of Jewish Life and Letters*, and author of "Swastika: The Nazi Terror," recently represented the American Jewish Congress at the London Conference for the Relief of German Jewry.

DOROTHY THOMPSON (*Mrs. Sinclair Lewis*) has served in Central Europe as correspondent for the *Philadelphia Public Ledger*, the *New York Evening Post*, etc. She made an intensive study of conditions in Germany and Austria in the summer of 1933 and is the author of "The New Russia" and "I Saw Hitler."

STANLEY HIGH is a contributing editor of *The Literary Digest* and author of a number of books including "Europe Turns the Corner" and "The Revolt of Youth." Until 1933 he served as correspondent of the *Christian Science Monitor* in Germany, Russia, and other European countries.

BERNARD S. DEUTSCH who is president of the American Jewish Congress, has served as president of the Board of Directors of the Bronx County Bar Association for three terms, and was a member of the Committee on Character and Fitness of the First Judicial Department of New York City. He is at present President of the Board of Aldermen of New York City.

WERNER HEGEMANN is an economist and historian, and is an expert in city planning. Since the advent of the Nazi régime in Germany he has come to the United States where he is a member of the faculty of the New School for Social Research.

ALICE HAMILTON who is a physician and a member of the faculty of the Harvard Medical School, served on President Hoover's Committee on Social Trends. During the summer of 1933 she made a study of conditions in Germany which was published in a series of articles in the *Survey-Graphic*.

I. A. HIRSCHMANN who founded and directed the Bamberger Musical Scholarships in Newark, has been active in the introduction of educational and musical programs in national radio broadcasting, and has written on musical subjects for various periodicals. In the summer of 1932 he spent considerable time in Germany and was in Berlin in the summer of 1933.

LUDWIG LORE, a writer on political and economic subjects, was active in the German labor movement until he came to this country. He is the author of a forthcoming volume, "Drums Over Europe," and a contributor to leading American periodicals.

JOHN HAYNES HOLMES is pastor of the Community Church of New York City and chairman of the City Affairs Committee. He is the author of "New Wars for Old," "Patriotism is not Enough," etc., and the editor of *Unity*.

LUDWIG LEWISOHN is at present living in France and has had intimate and extensive contact with the refugees from Nazi Germany. Among his books are included "Upstream," "The Island Within," and "Expression in America."

MAX WINKLER is Associate Professor of Economics at the College of the City of New York and was formerly economic adviser to the United States Sub-Committee on Banking and Currency. He is the author of "Foreign Bonds—An Autopsy," "Investment of United States Capital in Latin America," etc.

EMIL LENGYEL who was born in Hungary, has served as European correspondent of numerous newspapers, and is the author of a number of books including "Hitler," "The Cauldron Boils," and a forthcoming volume, "The New Deal in Europe."

STEPHEN S. WISE is Rabbi of the Free Synagogue in New York and honorary president of the American Jewish Congress. During the summer of 1933 he met with great numbers of exiles and refugees from Germany at the World Zionist Congress at Prague and at the World Jewish Conference at Geneva over which he presided.

PIERRE VAN PAASSEN has acted as European correspondent of the *New York World* and the *Toronto Star*. In March 1933 he was arrested by

Storm Troopers in Munich on the charge of spreading "atrocity propaganda" abroad. After having been subjected to punitive treatment, he was finally expelled from Germany.

MIRIAM BEARD (Vagts) is the author of a book on Japan and of numerous articles on Germany where she has resided for most of the last six years before and after the advent of the Nazi régime. She is the daughter of Professor Charles A. and Mary R. Beard, the American historians.

CHARLES H. TUTTLE was formerly United States District Attorney from New York. He is at present chairman of the Greater New York Interfaith Council and a member of the Laymen's Advisory Council for the National Conference of Jews and Christians.

ALBERT BRANDT has been for many years a close student of European affairs and was active in opposing the rise of the Nazi party in Germany. Since coming to this country in 1933 he has contributed articles on the German situation to leading American periodicals.

WILLIAM GREEN has been President of the American Federation of Labor since 1924. At the last convention of that organization he introduced a resolution for the boycott of German goods and services which was unanimously adopted.

SAMUEL GUY INMAN who has spent at least half of his time during the past twenty-seven years in South and Latin America, is Executive Secretary of the Committee on Co-operation in Latin America, and Director of the Spanish magazine *La Nueva Democracia*.

ALFRED E. SMITH was four times Governor of New York State and presidential candidate of the Democratic party in 1928. His activities at present include the presidency of the Empire State Building and the editorship of *The New Outlook*.

Printed at the Herald-Nathan Press, Inc., 460 West 34th St., N. Y. C.